New Casebooks

WILKIE COLLINS

New Casebooks

Further titles are in preparation

New Casebooks Series
Series Standing Order ISBN 0–333–69345–0
(outside North America only)

You can receive future titles in this series as they are published by placing a standing order. Please contact your bookseller or, in case of difficulty, write to us at the address below with your name and address, the title of the series and the ISBN quoted above.

Customer Services Department, Macmillan Distribution Ltd
Houndmills, Basingstoke, Hampshire RG21 6XS, England

New Casebooks

WILKIE COLLINS

EDITED BY LYN PYKETT

First published 1998 by
MACMILLAN PRESS LTD
Houndmills, Basingstoke, Hampshire RG21 6XS
and London
Companies and representatives throughout the world

ISBN 0–333–65770–5 hardcover
ISBN 0–333–65771–3 paperback

A catalogue record for this book is available from the British Library.

This book is printed on paper suitable for recycling and made from
fully managed and sustained forest sources.

10   9   8   7   6   5   4   3   2   1
07   06   05   04   03   02   01   00   99   98

Printed in Hong Kong

 Published in the United States of America 1998 by
ST. MARTIN'S PRESS, INC.,
Scholarly and Reference Division,
175 Fifth Avenue, New York, N.Y. 10010

ISBN 0–312–21269–0 clothbound
ISBN 0–312–21270–4 paperback

Contents

Acknowledgements

The editor and publishers wish to thank the following for permission to use copyright material:

Partick Brantlinger, for 'What is "Sensational" about the "Sensation Novel"?', *Nineteenth Century-Fiction*, 37 (1982). Copyright © 1982 by the Regents of the University of California, by permission of the University of California Press; Ann Cvetkovich, for 'Ghostlier Determinations: The Economy of Sensation and *The Woman in White*', *Novel*, 23 (1989), by permission of the author; Deirdre David, for 'Rewriting the Male Plot in Wilkie Collins's *No Name*: Captain Wragge Orders an Omelette and Mrs Wragge goes into Custody' from *Out of Bounds: Male Writers and Gender(ed) Criticism*, ed. Laura Claridge and Elizabeth Langland (1990). Copyright © 1990 by the University of Massachusetts Press, by permission of the University of Massachusetts Press; Elisabeth Rose Gruner, for 'Family Secrets and the Mysteries of *The Moonstone*', *Victorian Literature and Culture*, 21 (1991), by permission of AMS Press, Inc; Mark M. Henelly, Jr, for 'Reading Detection in *The Woman in White*', *Texas Studies in Literature and Language*, 22:4 (1980), by permission of the author and the University of Texas Press; Tamar Heller, for 'Blank Spaces: Ideological Tensions and the Detective Work of *The Moonstone*' from *Dead Secrets: Wilkie Collins and the Female Gothic* (1992), by permission of Yale University Press; A. D. Hutter, for 'Dreams, Transformations and Literature: The Implications of Detective Fiction', *Victorian Studies*, 19 (1975), by permission of the Trustees of Indiana University; U. C. Knoepflmacher, for 'The Counterworld of Victorian Fiction and *The Woman in White*' from *The Worlds of Victorian Fiction*, ed. J. H. Buckley (1975). Copyright © 1975 by the President and

Fellows of Harvard College, by permission of Harvard University Press; Walter M. Kendrick, for 'The Sensationalism of *The Woman in White*', *Nineteenth-Century Fiction*, 32 (1977–8). Copyright © 1977 by the Regents of the University of California, by permission of the University of California Press; D. A. Miller, for 'From *roman-policier* to *roman-police*: Wilkie Collins's *The Moonstone*', *Novel*, 13 (1979–80), by permission of the author; Jenny Bourne Taylor, for '*Armadale*: The Sensitive Subject as Palimpsest' from *In the Secret Theatre of Home: Wilkie Collins, Sensation Narrative and Nineteenth-Century Psychology* (1988), by permission of Routledge.

Every effort has been made to trace the copyright holders but if any have been inadvertently overlooked the publishers will be pleased to make the necessary arrangement at the first opportunity.

General Editors' Preface

The purpose of this new series of Casebooks is to reveal some of the ways in which contemporary criticism has changed our understanding of commonly studied texts and writers and, indeed, of the nature of criticism itself. Central to the series is a concern with modern critical theory and its effect on current approaches to the study of literature. Each New Casebook editor has been asked to select a sequence of essays which will introduce the reader to the new critical approaches to the text or texts being discussed in the volume and also illuminate the rich interchange between critical theory and critical practice that characterises so much current writing about literature.

The series itself, of course, grows out of the original Casebook series edited by A. E. Dyson. The original volumes provide readers with a range of critical opinions extending from the first reception of a work through to the criticism of the twentieth century. By contrast, the focus of the New Casebooks is on modern critical thinking and practice, with the volumes seeking to reflect both the controversy and the excitement of current criticism. Because much of this criticism is difficult and often employs an unfamiliar critical language, editors have been asked to give the reader as much help as they feel is appropriate, but without simplifying the essays or the issues they raise.

The project of the New Casebooks, then, is to bring together in an illuminating way those critics who best illustrate the ways in which contemporary criticism has established new methods of analysing texts and who have reinvigorated the important debate about how we 'read' literature. The hope is, of course, that New Casebooks will not only open up this debate to a wider audience, but will also encourage students to extend their own ideas, and think afresh about their responses to the texts they are studying.

John Peck and Martin Cyle
University of Wales, Cardiff

Introduction

LYN PYKETT

Wilkie Collins was one of the most popular and widely reviewed novelists of the nineteenth century. He was closely involved with Dickens's success in extending the market for reading in general and fiction in particular from the late 1850s; as Dickens's collaborator in a number of essays and stories and as a named (rather than anonymous) author of serials for Dickens's weekly magazine *Household Words* and its successor *All the Year Round*. He made a distinctive contribution to the sensation novel, which dominated the fiction market (and debates about fiction) in the 1860s; Collins's bestseller, *The Woman in White*, was widely regarded as the inaugurator of the sensation phenomenon. Collins also played a significant part in shaping the modern English detective story; *The Moonstone*, another of his bestsellers, is one of the classics of the genre.

As many of his self-justificatory Prefaces to his novels indicate, Collins was a writer who took his art seriously and who wished to be taken seriously by others. From the outset, however, his artistic status was compromised for reviewers because his chief successes were in popular genres such as the detective novel and the sensation novel, the latter of which was particularly associated with women writers. From the mid-nineteenth century to the present day critical debate about Collins's fiction has been shaped by questions of categorisation and definition, and by contests about boundaries, not least that most disputed of nineteenth-century border territories, the boundary between high art and popular culture, literature and light reading. Indeed, some of his recent defenders have retained a suspicion of Collins's association with popular culture and his interest in the common reader, as can be seen in Sue Lonoff's somewhat dismissive comment in her authoritative study of Collins and 'the rhetoric of authorship' (a book which has played an important part in restoring his fiction to critical view):

> If he had been less obsessed with pleasing the common reader, he might have given more thought to the development of the intellectual side of his talent. Reading the best of his novels today, one is aware of exceptional powers of analysis insufficiently developed, of psychological perceptions rarely worked through, of a writer, in short, who might have had the genius to be more than a masterful story-teller.[1]

If Collins's association with women writers and the feminised domain of popular culture was responsible for undermining his critical status in the nineteenth century (and beyond) as several recent studies have suggested,[2] his renewed critical prominence in the latter part of the twentieth century may be attributed in large measure to the same cause. Writers such as Collins have received greater critical attention as a result of a new (often feminist or feminist-influenced) interest in popular literary forms such as 'genre fiction'. Sensation fiction and the detective novel are among the many cultural fields which have been recovered and reassessed by the new cultural history of the nineteenth century, which has been constructed in the last twenty years or so by feminist, and also Marxist, cultural materialist, and Foucauldian literary and cultural historians who have rethought dominant definitions of the literary and traditional conceptions of genre as well as the relations between text and context, and between literary production and reproduction. Exponents of the new cultural history have engaged in a radical rethinking of the relationships between high art and popular culture; they have challenged traditional views of cultural centrality and cultural marginality, of what is major and what is minor, and have called into question the status and usefulness of these categories. Although the renewed critical interest in Collins's work pre-dates the rise of feminist literary history and a more politicised and historicised literary and cultural criticism in the late 1970s, the 'Collins revival' clearly owes a great deal to these developments as will be evident in the discussion of his work reprinted in this volume.

In a recent (1992) brief review of critical work on Collins in the last twenty years, Peter Thoms suggested that much of it 'locates Collins's merit as a novelist' not in 'the very conspicuous and thrilling surfaces of his stories', but 'in his subtexts'.[3] It is undoubtedly the case that many of the most interesting explorations of Collins's novels have focused on their social, political and psychological subtexts, although (as Thoms's own study demonstrates) there has also been a great deal of interest in the structure of those novels, as well as in their contexts (variously defined). As will be evident in the essays reprinted here, many writers on Collins have been concerned to claim him as a social critic who engages in a critique of the hypocrisies involved in constructing and sustaining Victorian bourgeois respectability, and of the aggressive individualism of Samuel Smiles's doctrine of self-help.[4] Others have seen Collins's social critique as that of a proto-feminist. For example, in a study of Dickens, Thackeray, Trollope and Collins published in 1982, Richard Barickman, Susan MacDonald and Myra Stark describe Collins as 'the most directly concerned with issues of women's rights and the most openly irreverent towards Victorian sexual conventions', and they read his 'bizarre' plots as 'parodies of conventional sexual alignments',[5] and a critique of Victorian gender ideologies. Collins's bizarre plots have also been re-examined by critics interested in the Victorian novel's preoccupation with providential plotting, a form of plot structure which reveals or suggests a divinely ordained pattern.[6] Thus, on the one hand, Jerome Meckier has argued that Collins's plots – like Dickens's – emphasised the 'paramountcy of providence as an abiding supernatural superintendence in an era daily becoming more profane', while, on the other, Winifred Hughes has described the plots of Collins's novels of the 1860s as evidence of his search for a new design to replace the traditional providential morality of stage melodrama.[7]

In the following selection of essays and extracts published between 1975 and 1992, I have been concerned to demonstrate a range of different theoretical and methodological approaches to Collins's fiction, and, at the same time, to demonstrate points of convergence in the kinds of questions that have been asked about his work, and about nineteenth-century fiction and the culture in which it was produced. In selecting essays for this book I have included a number of 'landmark' essays which have been (or are now becoming) widely cited, and which have thus helped to establish the terms on which Collins's work is now being discussed. I have also included some more recent essays, usually by younger critics, in order to indicate the ways in which Collins studies are developing. I have followed conventional wisdom in focusing on Collins's novels of the 1860s and in allocating most space to *The Woman in White* and

The Moonstone, his two most popular novels, and those which are generally regarded to be his most significant achievements. However, I have also included an essay on *No Name* and an extract on *Armadale*, in recognition of the fact that these two fascinating novels have received a great deal of very interesting critical attention in recent years. It is worth pointing out to the reader who may only be familiar with *The Woman in White* and *The Moonstone*, that quite a high proportion of Collins's large output of fiction will repay further reading in the light of some of the questions raised in this volume, and that many of his lesser-known works are now available in relatively inexpensive paperback editions.

I begin my selection with an essay which is not exclusively (or even primarily) concerned with Collins, but which has been widely cited by subsequent writers on Collins because it locates his fiction in one of its generic contexts, the sensation novel. Patrick Brantlinger's 1982 essay addresses the question of 'What is "Sensational" about the "Sensation novel"?', and concludes that the term 'sensational' partly designates a specific kind of fictional content (murder, adultery, bigamy, blackmail and fraud), and partly a range of special structural qualities (among others, the subordination of character to plot, the mixing of domestic realism with Gothic romance, and the development of particular forms of narrative secrecy). This opening essay synthesises, adds to, and in several significant respects diverges from, several accounts of the sensation genre which appeared between 1969 and 1980. The first of these was Kathleen Tillotson's attempt to provide an historicised cultural context for Collins's fiction in the 'lighter reading' of the 1860s in an introductory essay to *The Woman in White* in 1969, in which she situated Collins's novel in relation to a range of contemporary sensation writing, much of it by women, which had long since disappeared from critical view. P. D. Edwards provided a similar sort of account of the sensation decade in his 1971 pamphlet, *Some Mid-Victorian Thrillers: the Sensation Novel, Its Friends and Foes*, and Winfred Hughes developed this work further in her important and wide-ranging monograph, *The Maniac in the Cellar* (1980) which reads Collins's fiction alongside the fiction of Mary Elizabeth Braddon and Mrs Henry Wood (among others) in the context of mid-Victorian fictional practices and critical debates about the novel and its readers. Like these, and many other later accounts of the sensation novel (including the books by Jenny Taylor, Ann Cvetkovich, Tamar Heller and Lyn Pykett noted in the Further Reading section) Brantlinger does not focus on the genre (which he describes as an ephemeral and 'minor subgenre') in order to restore it to a place in a literary canon from which it has been unjustly excluded by critical misprision. His concern is rather to sketch in the history and offer an evaluation of a particular cultural phenomenon or symptom.

Brantlinger examines the sensation novel from three 'different but complementary perspectives': historical, structural and psychological. These perspectives, singly or in various combinations, are those which are adopted in each of the essays which is reproduced here. Brantlinger traces the sensation novel's genealogy in the Gothic romance, the Newgate novel of criminal 'low life' and the 'silver fork' novel of fashionable (and sometimes criminal) high life, and reads this generic hybridity through Derrida's 'law of genre', which is a 'law of impurity or a principle of contamination' (p. 31), according to which the defining characteristic of any genre never belongs exclusively to that genre.[8] Brantlinger also explores the various manifestations and significances of the sensation novel's preoccupation with mystery and secrecy, and focuses on the ways in which Collins, in his novels of the 1860s, develops a range of narrative methods for producing and prolonging secrecy. Collins's handling of the 'mystery element', so that the sensation genre modulates into the genre of detective fiction, is seen as a particular exemplification of the Derridean theory of generic impurity or hybridity.

Unlike many other commentators on the sensation and detection novels and/or on Collins's contributions to those genres (including most of the contributors to this volume), Brantlinger concludes that their mysteries 'do not connect with anything outside of themselves' (p. 47).[9] Brantlinger takes issue with Albert D. Hutter's contention (in essay 8) that detective fiction is akin to the process of psychoanalysis, arguing that the genre is both 'diversionary' and 'reductive', and only 'mimics' the pattern of psychoanalysis, just as it simply 'mimics aspects of serious fiction' (p. 50). In the end this particular scrutinising of genre fiction results in the reinforcing of cultural barricades, with the 'minor subgenre' clearly on the wrong side of the great divide.

Among the many issues explored in this opening essay which recur (in some form or other) in virtually all of the essays reprinted here, is the issue of the sensation novel's relationship to the tradition of realism which dominated the nineteenth-century novel. Brantlinger's version of this relationship is that it is an interrogative one: the sensation novel is seen as interrupting, or 'punctuating' with question marks, some of the conventions of realism. Brantlinger argues against the view (advanced by Hughes, and later by Jenny Taylor and Tamar Heller, among others) that sensation fiction offers a *subversive* challenge to the hegemony of mid-nineteenth-century realism, arguing instead that it is merely symptomatic of a crisis within literary realism. Sensation fiction, Brantlinger argues, is not productively subversive, but rather its subversion is 'regressive'; sensation novelists were constantly 'backing away from the deepest truths in their stories' (p. 53). As we shall see, the question of Collins's subversiveness (or retreat from, and/or containment of, subversive impulses) is one of the central issues raised by his work for most recent critics.

I

U. C. Knoepflmacher's 1975 essay on the 'counterworld' of Victorian fiction (essay 2) has come to be regarded as making an authoritative case for the 'subversive' Collins. Knoepflmacher includes a substantial section on *The Woman in White* in a discussion of a number of mid-Victorian novels which, he argues, might be included in Camus's category of a 'literature of rebellion'[10] on the grounds that beneath the 'ordered, civilised world of conventional beliefs' (p. 60), based on the 'collective ethic of love' (p. 59), which was constantly invoked to provide the official morality of the Victorian novel, there 'lurks a vital "counterworld" that is asocial and amoral, unbound by the restraints of the socialised superego' (p. 59). Knoepflmacher suggests that, unlike his more successful contemporary Dickens, Collins made no attempt to disguise his fascination with the amorality of this counterworld, and repeatedly antagonised reviewers with his lively and sympathetic portrayal of outspoken villains and villainesses such as Captain Wragge in *No Name* and Lydia Gwilt in *Armadale*. *The Woman in White*, Knoepflmacher argues, is a more than usually self-conscious acknowledgement by a mid-Victorian novelist of the powerful attractions of the anarchic and asocial counterworld, and an unusually subtle undermining of the 'claptrap morality of the present day'.[11] Like Jenny Taylor (in essay 7), Knoepflmacher focuses on Collins's preoccupation with questions of identity, and examines the way in which *The Woman in White* stages a contest between a 'lawful order in which identities are fixed and an anarchic lawlessness in which these social identities can be erased and destroyed' (p. 61). Like the other writers on *The Woman in White* represented in this volume (and in common with many other recent commentators on this novel), Knoepflmacher is also concerned with the narrative sleights of hand in which Collins engages, and with the issue of the supposed (but illusory) objectivity of the dispersal of the narration to a range of narrators, who are presented in the novel's Preamble as if they were witnesses testifying in a court of law (see p. 10 below).

Knoepflmacher locates the subversiveness of *The Woman in White* in its endorsement of the 'licentious', transgressive, anarchic counterworld of Count Fosco and of his belief in the fragility of social and moral identity.[12] However, in appropriating Fosco as a positive representation of the subversive nihilist in order to further his project of locating Collins in the literature of rebellion (rather than the literature of consent), Knoepflmacher ignores the economy of the novel's gender politics, in which Fosco is represented *negatively* as the oppressor of strong women such as Marian and his wife (an outspoken, independent feminist sympathiser before her marriage), and an exploiter of weak women such as Laura Fairlie and Anne Catherick. Another aspect of Knoepflmacher's account of the novel's subversiveness has similarly been opened to question by later readings of the politics of Collins's fiction. Knoepflmacher sees a subversive vision at work in Collins's representation of the process by which the civilised social order is renewed and secured by the deviousness and cunning first developed by Walter Hartright in order to survive in the Brazilian jungle. In essay 5, on the other hand, Ann Cvetkovich reads Walter's route to securing the bourgeois order as conservative rather than subversive, by locating it in the context of an economy of sensation and a rhetoric of fate and the uncanny in which Walter's deviousness functions to mask the material and class determinants of his social rise.

Walter Kendrick (essay 3) regards *The Woman in White* as neither conservative nor subversive, but rather as 'a landmark of ambivalence' which 'marks a tentative breach' (p. 85) – rather than a crisis, as Brantlinger argues – of the contract of mid-Victorian realism. Kendrick's critical methodology (which is implicit rather than specified) is eclectic. He combines a literary-historical contextual approach with a formalist (narratological) interest in the relation between plot, events, and narration. Kendrick examines the sensationalism of *The Woman in White* in the context of the sensation genre's challenge to the mid-Victorian distinction between the novel of plot (or incident) and the realist novel of character, and also in relation to the way in which mid-Victorian literary theory figured plot and character as a chain or a road (plot), or a drawing or portrait (character). Echoing some contemporary reviewers of the genre, Kendrick argues that the sensation novel foregrounded the chains of plot to such an extent that it became a kind of crossword puzzle, a language game with its own rules and with a merely arbitrary relation to the real world. Kendrick distinguishes *The Woman in White* from run-of-the-mill sensation productions, however, arguing that it is a self-consciously innovatory text which exploits the techniques of sensationalism whilst, at the same time, demanding to be read as if it were realistic. In Kendrick's reading Collins's novel is seen as deriving many of its sensation effects from its self-referential play with its own textuality (and with the nature of texts and textuality more generally), but ultimately its narrative chain depends (Kendrick suggests) upon the belief that there is a truth of experience which texts may either verify or falsify. As read by Kendrick, *The Woman in White* displays a positively poststructuralist preoccupation with texts and documents – with their production, reproduction, rewriting, and their construction and deconstruction. Both the hero and villains of this novel are manipulators of texts: 'the villains are rhetorical criminals, whose principal crime is the distortion of the written word', and Hartright is a 'rhetorical hero, who engages in a long campaign of textual reconstruction' whose end is the novel which we are reading (both quotations p. 79). However, despite the centrality of texts and textuality to their various schemes, both hero and villains (like the novel itself) work on the assumption that there is a world outside texts; this is vividly demonstrated in the sensation scene in which Laura, standing beside the textual proof of her own death, belies the language on the gravestone and becomes the motive for Hartright's campaign of textual reconstruction.

In his close scrutiny of the novel's preoccupation with the relationship between texts, events, and narration, Kendrick notes that despite Hartright's assertion that events, narration, and the reading of the novel make a single sequence – a 'chain' which 'reaches fairly from the outset of the story to the close'[13] – in fact the chain of narrators does not correspond with the chain of events as they occurred. Rather than gradually unfolding a sequential narrative, the sequence of narrators provides a series of sudden revelations or sensations, played out in sensation scenes, which result in a radical revision of the character's and reader's perspective. Although Kendrick does not use the term, his analysis of the operation of Collins's sensation scenes seem to be working towards an analysis of what Ann Cvetkovich (essay 5) calls the 'sensation economy' of the novel.

Mark M. Hennelly Jr's account of the process of reading detection in *The Woman in White* (essay 4) begins with one of the sensation scenes discussed by Kendrick: the novel's '"primal scene"',[14] the 'emblematic mystery of blank metaphysical whiteness' (p. 88) of the meeting of Walter Hartright and Anne Catherick. Hennelly's critical methodology is based on Wolfgang Iser's reader-response criticism, which assumes that 'the reading process involves a dynamic *interaction* between text and reader'.[15] Hennelly argues that such an approach is particularly apt for the two 'genres' which mutually inform *The Woman in White*: detective fiction and Victorian fiction, both of which invite participatory reading.

Hennelly sees Walter Hartright as the reader-in-the-text ('the reader-identification journeyman through fictional time and space', p. 88), through whom the reader undertakes a journey through the bodily and emotional as well as the intellectual pleasures of detection. This journey moves through various overlapping stages or levels from 'exciting escape into sensationalism and melodrama', through 'purely intellectual exercise', to 'a final level of enlightened entrapment' in which, by trying to fathom the enigma of Marian Halcombe, the reader becomes involved in a 'detection paradox': the fact that detection fiction is simultaneously a self-reflective game and a serious inquiry into the nature of reality and identity (all quotations p. 88). As a consequence of this paradox, Hennelly argues, the process of reading detection cannot be simply escapist; the armchair pleasures of melodrama give way to the painful pleasures of engaging with the extratextual mystery of 'Life itself' (p. 89).

Hennelly attempts to solve one of the main problems of reader-response theory – the question of who 'the reader' is assumed to be – by positing two overlapping readers: for the most part he emphasises the response of the 'Victorian' who was the text's first reader, but he also works on the assumption that the modern reader's pattern of reader-identification will not differ radically from that of his or her Victorian predecessor. The patterns of reader-identification which Hennelly discovers are complex. They involve an elaborate process of doubling and self-division, one effect of which is to require the reader to reconcile the experiences of both the criminal and the victim, and to recognise elements of each in him or herself. This emphasis on the role of doubling and division in the reading process leads Hennelly to employ both spatial and temporal metaphors to figure that process: the characters and/or the reader are required to occupy two places (or positions of identification), either simultaneously or at different points in the development of the narrative.

Several recent critics have focused on the ways in which *The Woman in White* involves the reader emotionally, affectively or somatically (through bodily sensations) in its economy of sensation.[16] Hennelly, on the other hand, focuses on the way in which the novel engages the reader in an emotional economy of detection. He follows T. S. Eliot's influential assessment of Collins's fiction as belonging to a moment of literary production in which 'the best novels *were* thrilling',[17] and satisfied their readers' perennial craving for melodramatic emotion. Hennelly distinguishes *The Woman in White* from the type of detection fiction written by Edgar Allan Poe and Sir Arthur Conan Doyle, whose detectives require only intellectual skills, and whose readerly pleasures are also mainly intellectual. He argues that Collins's detectives require emotion and imagination as well as intelligence, and that the pleasures of reading detection are emotional and therapeutic as well as cerebral. Ann Cvetkovich (essay 5) is also interested in the emotional and therapeutic effects of reading and writing detection, but largely in so far as they contribute to the politics of affect which she sees at work in *The Woman in White*. Cvetkovich links the novel's economy of detection to its economy of sensation and reads both in terms of a 'hermeneutics of suspicion', in which 'every fact that excites a sensation merits investigation' (p. 110).

Like Kendrick (essay 3) Cvetkovich focuses on the discrepant relationship of Walter Hartright's Preamble to the narratives which it precedes and authorises, looking particularly closely at the discrepancy between Walter's rhetoric of narration and what is narrated. She suggests that the Preamble foregrounds objectivity and rationality, and suppresses sensation, and argues that this suppression is at the centre of a network of displacement strategies by means of which bodily sensations and emotional/psychological responses are substituted for social and political realities. Cvetkovich's close examination of the novel's representation of the bodily sensations of fear, excitement and suspense follows D. A. Miller, whose influential essay '*Cages aux folles*: Sensation and Gender in *The Woman in White*' (which is too long to reproduce in this volume), has been an important reference point for most discussions of this novel published since 1986. Cvetkovich's reading is, in part, offered as a corrective to Miller's. She agrees with his contention that the sensation novel has to be read in terms of its production of bodily sensation and 'nervousness', but disputes his reading of nervousness as invariably a signifier of feminity, and also takes issue with his argument that the somatic (or bodily) experience in the sensation novel is simply a threat to be defended against. Unlike Miller she does not separate 'thematic sensation' and 'bodily sensation', but takes the view that the somatic nature of sensation has to be read in relation to its projection onto a text. Read thus, she argues, sensation may be seen as functioning as both a route to (patriarchal) power and a screen for the class and gender politics involved in such a journey.

Cvetkovich, like several of the writers whose work is reproduced here (for example, David, Miller, Heller, and Taylor), is concerned with the ideology of narrative form.[18] She offers a persuasive account of the manner in which Walter's rhetoric of fate and chance combines with some of the novel's more sensational moments – his first meeting with Anne Catherick, his recognition of the close physical resemblance between Anne and Laura Fairlie, the appearance (which is presented as an apparition) of Laura next to the gravestone which bears her name – to 'enable the more materially determined narrative of [his] accession to power to be represented as though it were the product of chance occurrences, [and] uncanny repetitions' (p. 111), rather than of social convention. Cvetkovich also argues that Walter's narration of the process of detection masks the fact (as she sees it) that what he represents as a fight against injustice is also his own route to power. In this essay Walter's detective work is read as a form of paranoid projection; his narration of his efforts to discover the secrets of the men who threaten his position is constructed, in part, so as to defend against the discovery of his own secret – the socially transgressive ambition of his love for Laura Fairlie.

Cvetkovich is interested in both the psychology and politics of sensation in *The Woman in White*, and her critical approach borrows from both psychoanalytic and political theory; it is an eclectic mixing of Freud and Marx, Foucault and feminism. Her reading of the novel, and particularly her attempt to account for the meaning of its representation of Walter's falling more or less instantly in love with Laura Fairlie (rather than with her 'double'

Anne Catherick with whom he meets first), centres on its representation of Walter's fetishisation of women's bodies (particularly, but not exclusively, Laura's). She reads this fetishisation in terms of the different concepts of fetishism elaborated by Freud and Marx. Using the Freudian conception of fetishism, as a process by which men triumph over the threat of castration, Cvetkovich reads Walter's fetishising of Laura's beauty as a means by which he wards off the social and sexual threat posed by the mysterious woman in white, and also (and here she echoes Miller) the threat of feminisation posed by his susceptibility to nervousness or sensation. She also reads Walter's glorification of Laura's physical appearance as a version of the commodity fetishism which Marx described as, at once, a process of sensationalising objects and mystifying the social and economic relations by which they are produced and which are the real source of their power. The appearances of Anne and Laura – like Marx's description of the commodity – ultimately stand as a sign of social relations; the differences in their appearance signify their different social positions. It is this latter difference which is crucial in determining Walter's preference for Laura, and which Walter's narrative is at pains to suppress. Freud is also used to read the significance of the way both the novel and Walter repeatedly substitute Laura for Anne (and vice versa). Freud's concept of deferred action, in which meaning is retroactively projected onto a primal event, is used to read the significance of the way in which Anne and Laura become entangled in Walter's mind: the meaning of his response to Anne is imposed retrospectively through his response to Laura, just as his initial response to Anne is, in part, a projection of his anticipation about Laura, the young heiress who is his prospective pupil.

Like D. A. Miller, Cvetkovich reads *The Woman in White* symptomatically as a narrative of the social construction of gender and sexuality. However, whereas Miller reads this as a narrative about homosexuality, Cvetkovich reads it as a narrative which both reproduces and mystifies the construction of ruling class heterosexual masculinity. Using the nineteenth-century discourse which represents the male homosexual as having a woman's spirit caught within a male body, Miller reads the sensationalism of Hartright's meetings with Anne and Laura as figuring the threat of homosexuality as a dissolution of gender boundaries and a contamination by 'feminine' nervousness. Cvetkovich's reading incorporates Miller's, but, by foregrounding class, moves beyond it to examine the politics of heterosexual romance. In her analysis, the novel's management of heterosexual desire (like that of the wider culture) is seen as an important mechanism for reproducing class division.

II

The link between fictional form and gender politics is also at the centre of Deirdre David's essay on *No Name* (essay 6). Unlike some other recent critics (for example Barickman, and Phillip O'Neill, cited in the Further Reading section), David is not concerned to claim Collins as a feminist, rather she is interested in exploring what she sees as an 'informing link between restlessness with dominant modes of literary form and fictional critique of dominant modes of gender politics' (p. 136). In the case of the 'baroquely plotted' *No Name*, David sees a link between the novel's sympathy for its rebellious heroine's search for subjectivity and the subversion of narratorial omniscience implied in the 'intense dialogism' and 'insistent relativism' of Collins's form with its range of narrating voices and texts – such as letters, journal entries and newspaper reports. David's deconstructive reading is built on the contention that in *No Name* 'mimesis' is 'always simultaneous with semiosis' (p. 137); that is to say, it is impossible to separate what is represented in the novel from the forms and manner in which it is represented. In this reading the *absence* of a particular mode of representation has as much significance as the *presence* of other modes. Thus the absence of suspense (an absence to which Collins draws the reader's attention in his Preface) is seen as a subversive break with tradition, and a means by which the reader is involved collaboratively in an experience of plot-as-process rather than as plot-as-product.

David's deconstructive turn is also evident in her preoccupation with the novel's fictive self-reflexiveness. Wragge and his down-at-heel wife are at the centre of her account of the novel's textual play. Wragge, one of several spectacular rogues and swindlers created by Collins – the creator and manipulator of Magdalen's acting career, and the keeper of a collection of minutely accurate notebooks detailing his confidence tricks – is seen as a parodic representation of the omniscient narrator of traditional Victorian fiction. In the figure of Wragge Collins literalises the metaphor of the narrator as puppet master which Thackeray uses in the 'Before the Curtain' section of *Vanity Fair*,[19] and interrogates all forms of textual authority. If Wragge, who compares his own cultivation of the field of human sympathy with that of the great writers, is one of the chief means of advancing Collins's critique of mid-Victorian fictional practices, his wife, as a confused, deviant and subversive reader of texts, is a vehicle for his critique of dominant modes of gender politics. In a reading which foregrounds the disruptive nature of Collins's text and its indictment of patriarchal law, Mrs Wragge is placed at the centre of a disruptive episode in which, in the manner of Lewis Carroll's White Queen, she interrogates arbitrary systems of signification by deconstructing the recipe for an omelette. Another source of disruption is Collins's foregrounding of the gender politics of the heroine's story: the motive force of this narrative is Magdalen's exile from and by patriarchy, and its conclusion is her reincorporation into its embrace. This is a common enough journey for the heroine of a Victorian novel, and one traced by D. A. Miller in his reading (in '*Cages aux folles*') of the route taken by Laura in *The Woman in White*. However, David argues that, unlike the passive Laura, Magdalen (like her deviant 'double' Mrs Wragge) is, in the greater part of the narrative, actively in rebellion against the social order which ordains that journey.

Like Winifred Hughes, Phillip O'Neill, and Tamar Heller (among others), David notes the issues of social identity and subjectivity raised by Magdalen's historionic character, her acting career and the story of her movement from a daughter with no name to a wife with a new name. Collins's investigation of social, sexual and psychological identity is at the very centre of Jenny Taylor's study of his fiction, from which I have taken the chapter on *Armadale* (essay 7). Taylor's book, which is widely cited as one of the most comprehensive studies of Collins's engagement with theories of subjectivity and issues of identity, is informed by feminist cultural history and theory, and also by Michel Foucault's work on the history of sexuality and on the history of the construction and treatment of madness.[20] However, Taylor seeks to avoid the monolithic nature of much of Foucault's work by exploring Collins's fiction in relation to 'the more equivocal aspects'[21] of the conceptualisation and management of psychological 'deviance' in the nineteenth century. To this end she has done a great deal of 'archaeology'[22] of her own, and her reading of Collins is undertaken in the context of a kind of 'new historicism' of the nineteenth century in which novels are read alongside other cultural products, such as medical texts, the texts of the emergent 'science' of psychology, and the writings of nineteenth-century literary theorists. Taylor reads Collins's fiction in the context of contemporary literary, medical and psychological theories of sensation, and focuses particularly closely on contemporary theories of psychology and the management of psychological 'deviance' or 'moral insanity'. Like much recent work on Collins, Taylor's study challenges the traditional literary-historical distinction between serious and popular fiction. She examines Collins's fiction in relation to the sensation fiction of the 1860s, offering a succinct and authoritative account of the history of this genre, an account which is more sympathetic than the one given by Patrick Brantlinger (essay 1), and which includes a useful discussion of mid-nineteenth-century theories of pleasure. This is a thoroughly historicised reading of Collins, but it is also definitely a reading of and for the late twentieth century. Taylor's Collins is (re)inserted in the discursive history of the nineteenth century, but he is also, as he is in Deirdre David's deconstructive reading, 'our contemporary'. Indeed, Taylor suggests that Collins now reads as 'one of the most "modern" (even postmodern) of nineteenth-century novelists', in a comment that goes some way towards explaining the reasons for the renewed critical interest in his fiction in the last twenty years:

> [Collins] emphasises play, doubling, and duplicity. His labyrinthine narratives are dialogic and self-reflexive. His heroines can be transgressive and his villains engaging ... Moreover, his stories involve not only complex explorations of forms of perception, of consciousness and cognition, but also of the shaping of social identity, above all within that simultaneously psychic and economic institution the family; they investigate the relationship between ways of seeing and forms of power.[23]

The Collins produced in Taylor's reading certainly displays a postmodernist preoccupation with the instability of identity. Collins's version of the self, Taylor argues, is 'a collection of physical signs' whose meaning is shifting and uncertain, a 'screen' onto which the perceptions of others are projected.[24] At the same time she indicates that Collins's theories of the self also owe a great deal to nineteenth-century theories of evolution, inheritance and degeneration, and that he develops the stock conventions of Victorian fiction (family secrets, hidden connections, plots involving duplicitous characters, deception, fraud and the transmission of property) to explore wider questions of inheritance and heredity, and of the nature of the relationship between past and present.

Taylor's Collins, like Knoepflmacher's (essay 2), is a subversive; in this case one who subverts the familiarity and stability of the world of middle-class domesticity by both assimilating and resisting a range of contradictory discourses about consciousness, the formation of the self, the operations of the unconscious and the interactions of mind and body. Like Deirdre David (essay 6) and Walter Kendrick (essay 3), Taylor also sees Collins as subverting or challenging the dominant realist conventions of nineteenth-century fiction. In a sense what all these writers are trying to do is to think through that aspect of Collins's work which has preoccupied critics ever since Charles Dickens described *The Moonstone* as 'wild yet domestic'.[25] Taylor does this by locating Collins's fiction in a 'borderland state between the mimetic and the fantastic',[26] which she examines in relation to Tzvetan Todorov's theory of the fantastic and Freud's theory of the uncanny.[27]

The uncanny elements which are most closely examined in Taylor's chapter on *Armadale* are the novel's use of two pairs of doubles (the two fathers and their sons who use the name Alan Armadale), and its use of a premonitory dream. This use of the uncanny within the fantastic and extraordinarily complex plot of *Armadale* is seen as a vehicle for an elaborate (and risky) play with ideas about the ways in which the various inheritances of one generation are passed on to the next, psychologically internalised, and then transmitted or projected through 'psychic' phenomena such as the dream. Collins's use of the device of doubling and of the complications of the relationship between names and identity results, Taylor argues, in an interrogation of the stability of the boundaries of the self and of the processes involved in the social construction of subjectivity. Similar issues are raised by Collins's representation of deviants and outcasts, who are seen in Taylor's account not simply as vital inhabitants of an anarchic counterworld (as they are in essay 2), but as projections (or self-projections) of the fears and fantasies of otherness.

The two 'deviants' at the centre of Taylor's discussion of *Armadale* are Ozias Midwinter (who has disowned his given name of Alan Armadale) and Lydia Gwilt, the transgressive *femme fatale* who links the two generations of the novel. Nineteenth-century dream theory, and theories of psychological development and moral insanity are used to illuminate Collins's treatment of these two characters. Midwinter, the 'sensitive subject as palimpsest' of Taylor's subtitle, is a complex representation of a morbid and feminised subjectivity shaped by a particular social and psychological inheritance. The legacy of the past is also explored in the plotting of Lydia Gwilt, probably Collins's most shockingly transgressive female protagonist, seen in Taylor's psychoanalytic reading as a figure in whom 'fear of the father and his legacy of male violence becomes transformed into the threat of the castrating woman' (p. 166).

Taylor would no doubt dispute Deirdre David's claim that *No Name* has the most baroque plot of all Collins's novels, since she contends that *Armadale* combines in a 'bizarrely kaleidoscopic way' (p. 150) many of Collins's characteristic narrative and psychological methods. Echoing Collins's own assertion (in his Preface to *Armadale*) that his 'writing overstepped in more than one direction, the narrow limits within which [critics and reviewers] have been disposed to restrict the development of modern fiction',[28] Taylor argues that *Armadale* pushes the conventions of the sensation novel to its limits, and as a 'palimpsest of the traces of the past', it anticipates Collins's most ambitious attempt to 'investigate the process of investigation, set within a psychological context that incorporates an analysis of the unconscious' (p. 171) in *The Moonstone*.

III

As the last quotation might indicate, *The Moonstone*, more than any other of Collins's novels, has been the subject (or object) of psychoanalytic readings. I have included a relatively early example of a self-consciously psychoanalytic approach as the first of the group of four essays on this novel. The approach taken in the extract from Albert Hutter's essay on 'the implications of detective fiction' (essay 8) may seem rather unsophisticated to those readers who have grappled with Lacan's revisions of Freudian theory and with the efforts of Lacanian critics to apply them to literary texts. However, although it may now, in some respects, seem almost as reductive as the 'unrevised' psychoanalytic theories that it is attempting to replace, I thought it important to include Hutter's essay on the grounds that it offers many useful observations on Collins's novel, and has been much cited by later writers both on *The Moonstone* and on the psychology of detective fiction.

Hutter's argument turns on his contention that detective fiction and psychoanalysis have a significant structural relationship and a close historical connection. Both are stories of mysteries and their solution, which involve the transformation of a fragmented and incomplete set of events into an ostensibly more ordered and complete understanding, and both reorder our perception of the past through language. Similarly, psychoanalysis and the detective story are both cultural products of the latter half of the nineteenth century. Hutter not only uses post-Freudian psychoanalytic theories to develop a model of reading detection, but he also anticipates Jenny Taylor's attempt to read Collins in the context of specific nineteenth-century ideas of and about psychology and psychologists. Thus he examines *The Moonstone* in the context of Dr William Benjamin Carpenter's and Dr John Elliotson's work on preconscious thought, memory, and the related effects of drugs and mesmerism or hypnosis, all of which are crucial in providing Collins with the central mystery and the resolution of his plot. Hutter not only demonstrates how Ezra Jennings uses the theories and methods of Carpenter and Elliotson to such sensational effect, but he also offers an extremely thought-provoking discussion of Jennings as the novel's most significant detective – a view of Jennings which D. A. Miller and Tamar Heller later developed further (see essays 9 and 11). In the present essay Jennings is seen as a sort of psychoanalyst in his ability to interpret Dr Candy's disjointed, dreamlike utterances, but a psychoanalyst possessed of a synthesising and transforming Romantic imagination (Hutter invokes Coleridge here). Jennings is the 'ultimate detective' (p. 183) because (to borrow the phrase Taylor uses of Midwinter in essay 7) he is a 'sensitive subject' with a capacity to allow his mind to wander past the boundaries of rational thought and to perceive the significance of the most trivial of details.

Hutter's essay is also noteworthy for its substantial and influential discussion of the sexual symbolism and implications of the theft of Rachel's diamond, and for its reading of the narrative structure of *The Moonstone* in terms of the enactment of primal scene wishes and fears.[29] In both cases Hutter moves beyond a reductive psychoanalytic reading in which the literary text might be seen simply as an enactment of the author's or reader's unresolved Oedipal fears, and opens up a space for exploring how Collins's text develops a symbolic way of discussing contemporary sexual politics.

Like Mark Hennelly (essay 4) Hutter is concerned to distinguish Collins's work in the genre of detective fiction from that of his contemporaries Edgar Alan Poe and Sir Arthur Conan Doyle. Hutter suggests that the Poe–Doyle version of the genre calls into question objective and rational modes of perception by means of its valorising of the subjective and intuitive vision of the detective, ultimately revealing the objective/rational and the subjective/intuitive to be two sides of the same coin. The narrative structure of *The Moonstone*, on the other hand, is said to be 'thoroughly subjective and unreliable', forcing the reader 'to build a rational solution from the distorted and fragmented visions of [the] individual narrators' (p. 176). This is one of several of Hutter's contentions about *The Moonstone* which is disputed by D. A. Miller (in essay 9), as I indicate below. Hutter links the rise of the detective novel to the failure of 'the older forms of self-policing' that existed in rural areas or earlier forms of urban life when towns were smaller and communities more 'knowable'.[30] Like many historians of detective fiction he sees the genre as one of the characteristic cultural products of urban modernity: 'the new detective police were needed to "read" a city which had grown far beyond the easy knowledge of its inhabitants' (p. 178).[31] D. A. Miller, on the other hand, argues that one of the most important aspects of *The Moonstone* is precisely the failure of the new detective police, in the person of the renowned Sergeant Cuff. This failure, Miller suggests, is integral to the ideology of the form of the detective story, which is constructed so as to produce a 'social innocence' which is based on the perception that everyday life is 'fundamentally "outside" the network of policing power' (both quotations, p. 200). In fact, Miller argues, the narrative of *The Moonstone* not only *portrays*, but also *enacts* a process of self-policing. Miller's reading is based on the Foucauldian conception of the surveillance society in which every individual polices him or herself and everyone polices every one else;[32] the detective fever that breaks out in the novel is, thus, only an extension of 'normative social practices and models of conduct' (p. 211).

Miller's version of the narrative-ideological 'economy' of the detective story is very similar to the 'sensation economy' of *The Woman in White* which Ann Cvetkovich analyses in essay 5 (indeed, Cvetkovich acknowledges that her own essay is, in some respects, a response to Miller's work on Collins). Like the sensation economy, the narrative economy of the detective story is a 'hermeneutics of suspicion' (Cvetkovich, p. 110), which is based on the hypothesis that every event or detail might count as evidence, but ultimately it works so as to isolate those few signs that really do signify; the narrative dynamic of the detective story thus transforms universal suspicion into a highly specific guilt. Miller takes issue with the widely shared view that Collins's use of multiple narration makes for subjectivity, unreliability and relativism. Referring explicitly to Hutter's assertion that the narrative structure of *The Moonstone* is 'thoroughly subjective and unreliable' Miller (using Mikhail Bakhtin's term)[33] argues that, on the contrary, it is thoroughly monological: Collins may use a series of different narrators each with his or her own partial (i.e. both subjective and limited) perspective, but there is only *one narrative* on which 'all readers pass *the same judgement* (p. 215). This is the narrative of the novel's 'master voice' that 'corrects, overrides, subordinates, or sublates all other voices it allows to speak' (p. 216). In short, *The Moonstone* is a novel which inscribes 'the *effects* of monologism in the text without ascribing them to the *agency* of an actual monologist' (p. 218). This form of monologism, Miller suggests, is analogous to the work of detection itself; both produce the illusion of the resolution of difficulties and ambiguities as a process of 'quasi-automatic self-regulation' (p. 218), an illusion and a process which Miller sees as integral to the novel's discourse on and of power.

Miller concludes that *The Moonstone* is ultimately a novel about the securities rather than the uncertainties of perception, and one which reinscribes 'the irresistible positivities of words and things "as they are"' (p. 219). He suggests that in this respect it is no different from any other traditional novel, since all such novels – no matter what kinds of stories they tell – always 'repeat and reimpose the same story of power' (p. 219). Elisabeth Rose Gruner (essay 10), on the other hand, makes *The Moonstone* tell quite a different story; a story which is posited on and reinforces the 'instability of the respectable' (p. 237). Unlike Miller, who sees *The Moonstone* as reproducing bourgeois ideology, Gruner sees it as engaging in a critique of the status quo. She expands Hutter's argument about the sexual symbolism of the theft of Rachel's diamond by locating the diamond and its various thefts in the context of the novel's critique of nineteenth-century class, gender and imperial ideologies. Gruner argues that although *The Moonstone* is not usually grouped with Collins's novels-with-a-purpose (which are usually seen as belonging to the years of his decline), it is dominated by a 'message' about the social, sexual and psychological organisation of the Victorian family; it calls into question the very nature of the Victorian family and asks fundamental questions about whose interests it serves. Gruner pursues some of the implications of *The Moonstone's* similarities to another story of crime within the family, the Road murder case of 1860, and suggests that the mysteries of both are based on the family's impulse to conceal, and on the secrecy which is integral to the nineteenth-century conception of privacy. The sensation novel's peculiar obsession with skeletons in the family cupboard – indeed, its tendency to represent the family as nothing but a cupboard of skeletons – has preoccupied commentators ever since the 1860s.[34] More recently, Elaine Showalter has argued that secrecy within the family is precisely the enabling condition of the sensation novel.[35] Gruner's reading of *The Moonstone* is based on a similar premise. She sees Collins's novel as modifying the ideological structure and meaning of the detective story, or, perhaps more accurately, as calling into question the conventional view that the detective story – and especially the country house mystery – is about stable conservative societies invaded by dangerous foreign elements. In *The Moonstone* robbery and murder are not invasions from without, but are produced within the family and by its tensions, dissensions and desires. In this novel (as in many Victorian novels) the family is represented as being the source of danger, rather than the means of protection from it. Similarly the concept of privacy around which the Victorian middle-class family is constructed is seen as one which serves to protect it from the discovery of its own dangerous forces, rather than from contamination by the alien public world.

Tamar Heller (essay 11) also sees *The Moonstone* as offering a critique of the gender and class distinctions that structured Victorian society. Like Gruner, Heller reads this novel as a narrative which articulates and explores the material and discursive interconnections of class, gender, and imperialism. The novel's central image, the triple theft of the Moonstone, and the novel's juxtaposing of its plots of colonialism and courtship, are seen as offering 'an exposé of Victorian culture that recognises the links between types of domination – of the colonisers over the colonised ... men over women ... the upper over the lower classes' (p. 245). Heller places Franklin Blake, the commissioner and editor of the various narratives that constitute the novel, at the centre of these links. His unconscious theft of the diamond, an act of dispossession which is revealed to have a subconsciously 'good', protective motive, is seen as analogous to the rationalisations of imperial domination and gender ideology.

This concluding extract (and *Dead Secrets*, the book from which it is taken) is almost a textbook example of the way in which Collins has been appropriated by 'new types' of literary scholarship and criticism that 'seek to evaluate the political and social dimensions of literature' and expand their areas of interest 'beyond the boundaries of the traditional literary canon'.[36] Heller's study is the product of the feminist interest in 'low' genres and genres particularly associated with woman writers and/or readers. Her project in *Dead Secrets* is to demonstrate how Collins's fiction of the late 1850s and 60s transformed the conventions of the traditionally female genre of Gothic, and to explore some of the implications of the fact that his association with female Gothic and sensation fiction linked Collins to women writers and hence to literary and social marginality during a period when 'novel writing was increasingly becoming a male-defined and male-dominated profession'.[37]

In the chapter reproduced here, Heller examines the implications of the 'feminine' traces that remain in Collins's most radical revision of a feminine form, the novel in which he transforms the female Gothic into what is traditionally perceived as the masculine genre of detective fiction. These feminine traces are evident in the double narrative of *The Moonstone* (a variant of *The Woman in White*'s two stories of a man's resolution and a woman's patient endurance): the 'masculine' story about the triumph of male reason, and a 'feminine' story about buried writing, the latter of which Heller associates with the subversive discourses of the Gothic and radical Romanticism. Heller is particularly interested in exploring how and with what effects the masculine narrative of 'revelation and rational interpretation' (p. 245) in this novel that 'fathered' the masculine detective novel, is punctuated (and thus, so to speak punctured) by the 'thematics of blankness and silence' (p. 245) that it shares with the female Gothic. Heller's reading focuses on the novel's buried or silenced feminine or feminised voices. The two most important of these are the voice of Rosanna's letter, which is only heard after her death, and the feminised voice of the 'Victorian Romantic' Ezra Jennings. Like Hutter (essay 8), and like Jenny Taylor (whose chapter on *The Moonstone* in *In The Secret Theatre of Home* she discusses extensively), Heller assigns to Jennings a key role in both the detection process and the broader narrative economy. Jennings is the novel's most scientific detective, but he is also one of its most Gothic figures; he is an outcast, and an image of *ressentiment* like the monster in Mary Shelley's *Frankenstein*. He is the ultimate detective (as Hutter suggests), the one who solves the mystery, but in refusing to reveal the mystery of his own story Jennings also becomes a 'figure for authorial self-censorship' (p. 257). Authorial self-censorship is another form of buried writing which Heller detects in *The Moonstone*, and one (as I indicate below) which is extremely important in her reading of its political meanings.

Citing both Freud and Hélène Cixous (on silence as the mark of hysteria[38]), Heller locates another site of buried or silenced femininity in the 'thematics of hysteria' (p. 254), which is evident in the representation of Rachel, Rosanna, and Limping Lucy; a thematics which, she argues, conveys a 'reductive message about gender'. Heller concedes that her reading of the novel's use of the discourse of hysteria as a means of silencing or invalidating women's voices might seem to support D. A. Miller's Foucauldian reading of *The Moonstone* as a monologic text (essay 9), but she argues that the model of the 'master voice' which Miller invokes is not, in the end, as useful for understanding how this text works as is the model of the double-voiced discourse which feminist theorists have developed to account for what they see as a characteristic pattern in nineteenth-century writing by women, in which the significations of the conventional or traditional plot pattern are undercut by a subversive subtext whose vehicle is irony and indirection.[39]

In using the feminist concept of the double-voiced discourse to read the double narrative of *The Moonstone*, Heller finds a means of negotiating one of the most persistent questions debated in recent criticism of Collins (and very much in evidence in the essays reproduced in this volume). This is the question – which I raised at the beginning of this introduction – of whether Collins is a subversive who engages in a radical social critique, or a writer who avoids or retreats from radical critique and/or who simply reinscribes dominant values. Heller's answer is to argue that Collins, too, is persistently negotiating this problematic: he is *both* a radical and a 'conservative', but he is neither *simply* a radical or a conservative. Ultimately Heller's reading of *The Moonstone* is a reading of its 'political unconscious',[40] as revealed in the complex operations of its double-voiced discourse. Heller argues that the silencing of women's voices (and the silencing or burying of 'the feminine') in this text can be seen as an example of the textual containment of radical tendencies which many critics have noted in Collins's novels. This process of textual containment is, however, incomplete. *The Moonstone* continues to speak with two voices, Heller suggests; the masculine voice of the detective story (the official version of events) is fissured by the ironies and indirections of the feminine voice. Heller's reading of the meanings of Ezra Jennings is crucial to this interpretation. Jennings as a 'figure for authorial self-censorship' is seen as Collins's representative in the text; a figure for both the non-canonical (and hence feminised) writer, and for the radicalism that cannot or dare not speak its name in the mid-Victorian literary marketplace. Like the marginalised woman writer Collins tells his (radical) truth, but he tells it aslant, working by indirection and even by obfuscation; as Heller reminds us, Collins deliberately draws his readers' attention to the fact that *The Moonstone*, like Jennings's solution of its central mystery which leads to the restoration of normative familial and gender roles, was produced by an opium addict.

As these introductory comments suggest, and as the essays and extracts which follow will demonstrate, the 'Wilkie Collins' produced by recent literary criticism is a contradictory, even schizoid figure. He is, on the one hand, the deconstructor of secure perceptions and of normative class and gender identities (as read by Jenny Taylor, and Deirdre David for example), or, on the other, the scribe or reinscriber of the bourgeois, surveillance society (as read by D. A. Miller). How is the reader who is relatively new to these debates to make sense of them? Even more important, perhaps, is the question of how such a reader might position him or herself in relation to them. Is it a question simply of choosing sides, or do we need to think beyond the current terms of engagement? John Kucich has recently intervened to challenge what he sees as the polarisation of late-twentieth-century debates about Collins and other nineteenth-century novelists. He is particularly concerned to re-examine the 'political nervousness' of some recent literary criticism, which has 'hurried to demystify the oppositional postures of even the most virulent Victorian rebels'.[41] Kucich refers particularly to D. A. Miller's influential readings of Collins and other Victorian novelists in the essay reproduced here and in his book, *The Novel and the Police* (see Further Reading). Kucich sees much merit in Miller's efforts (along with those of Nancy Armstrong and Mary Poovey)[42] to expose the critical and political naïvety of many of the attempts of left-leaning and feminist criticism to justify the continuing critical relevance of certain Victorian novelists on the grounds of their supposed transgressiveness and deviance. However, Kucich usefully tries to move beyond this initial act of demystification to seek other, less polarised, ways of exploring the cultural and political meanings of Victorian fiction. Kucich suggests that it is worth looking again, and more closely, at the ways in which certain Victorian writers deployed or exploited the insider/outsider rhetoric of their culture. This approach to Collins's deployment of this rhetoric and his positioning of himself in relation to the profession of writing in the nineteenth century is not dissimilar to Tamar Heller's, nor (in some respects) to Jenny Taylor's. In the end, however, Kucich probably produces a more assertive version of Collins than they do: Kucich's Collins is a writer who intervened quite aggressively in a struggle to redefine the middle class and to claim power for cultural intellectuals. Thus, Kucich reads Collins as a self-conscious outsider whose novels produce and validate a sophisticated middle-class elite of cultural intellectuals, a proto-bohemian class struggling for cultural, social and political authority against newly elevated bourgeois professions such as the law and medicine. The debate continues.

NOTES

1. Sue Lonoff, *Wilkie Collins and his Victorian Readers: A Study in the Rhetoric of Authorship* (New York, 1982), p. 76.

2. See Lyn Pykett, *The Improper Feminine: The Women's Sensation Novel and the New Woman Writing* (London, 1992), and Tamar Heller, *Dead Secrets: Wilkie Collins and the Female Gothic* (New Haven, CT, and London 1992).

3. Peter Thoms, *The Windings of the Labyrinth: Quest and Structure in the Major Novels of Wilkie Collins* (Athens, OH, 1992), p. 3.

4. This is one of the central concerns of Nicholas Rance in *Wilkie Collins and Other Sensation Novelists: Walking the Moral Hospital* (London, 1991).

5. Richard Barickman, Susan MacDonald and Myra Stark, *Corrupt Relations: Dickens, Thackeray, Trollope, Collins, and the Victorian Sexual System* (New York, 1982), pp. 111, 113. See also Philip O'Neill, *Wilkie Collins: Women, Property and Propriety* (London, 1988).

6. For accounts of providential plotting in Victorian fiction, see Thomas Vargish, *The Providential Aesthetic in Victorian Fiction* (Charlottesville, VA, 1985) and Barry Qualls, *The Secular Pilgrims of Victorian Fiction* (Cambridge, 1982).

7. Jerome Meckier, *Hidden Rivalries in Victorian Fiction: Dickens, Realism and Revaluation* (Lexington, KY, 1987), p. 97, and Winifred Hughes, *The Maniac in the Cellar: Sensation Novels of the 1860s* (Princeton, NJ, 1980), p. 137. Peter Thoms, who also reads these novels as a 'quest for design', argues that providence is indeed the

'ultimate order' in *The Woman in White* and *No Name*, but that it is questioned in *Armadale*, and entirely dispensed with in *The Moonstone*; the 'final created order' in these last two novels is revealed as a human construct, rather than a providential design (*The Windings of the Labyrinth*, pp. 8, 9).

8. Jacques Derrida, 'The Law of Genre', trans. Avital Ronell, *Critical Inquiry*, 7 (1980), 55–81, p. 57.

9. For an alternative view, Brantlinger refers his readers to John R. Reed, 'English Imperialism and the Unacknowledged Crime of *The Moonstone*', *Clio*, 2 (1973), 81–90.

10. See Albert Camus, *The Rebel* (New York, 1956), pp. 258, 259, 263.

11. Wilkie Collins, *Armadale*, ed. and intro. Catherine Peters (Oxford, 1989), p. xxxix.

12. Although making a somewhat different sort of case, Mark M. Hennelly (essay 4) similarly sees the novel as valorising the vitality and risk-taking of Fosco.

13. Wilkie Collins, *The Woman in White*, ed. and intro. John Sutherland (Oxford, 1996), p. 636.

14. D. A. Miller, '*Cages aux folles*: Sensation and Gender in Wilkie Collins's *The Woman in White*, *Representations*, 14 (1986), 107–36, p. 99. This essay can also be found in Jeremy Hawthorn (ed.), *The Nineteenth-Century British Novel* (London, 1986), pp. 95–125.

15. Wolfgang Iser, *The Act of Reading: A Theory of Aesthetic Response* (Baltimore, MD, 1978), quoted in Hennelly, 'Reading Detection in *The Woman in White*', *Texas Studies in Literature and Language*, 22 (1980), 449–67, p. 450.

16. See Miller, '*Cages aux folles*', and Ann Cvetkovich in essay 5 and in her *Mixed Feelings: Feminism, Mass Culture and Victorian Sensationalism* (New Brunswick, NJ, 1992).

17. T. S. Eliot, 'Wilkie Collins and Dickens', in *Selected Essays of T. S. Eliot* (London, 1932), quoted by Hennelly, 'Reading Detection', p. 451.

18. For another account of the ideology of the narrative form of the sensation novel see Jonathan Loesberg, 'The Ideology of Narrative Form in Sensation Fiction', *Representations*, 13 (1986), 115–38. Loesberg links sensation scenes to images of a loss of class identity, which he sees as symptomatic of a wider problematisation of social identity in the debates about social and political reform in the 1850s and 1860s.

19. See W. M. Thackeray, *Vanity Fair*, ed. and intro. John Sutherland (Oxford, 1983), pp. 1–2.

20. Taylor, like other writers represented in this volume, makes use of Foucault's work on the history of sexuality and on the conceptualisation and treatment of madness and crime. See Michel Foucault, *Madness and Civilization: a History of Insanity in the Age of Reason*, trans. Richard Howard (London, 1971); *The Birth of the Clinic: an Archaeology of Medical Perception*, trans. A. M. Sheridan Smith (London, 1989); *Discipline and Punish: The Birth of the Prison*, trans. Alan Sheridan (Harmondsworth, 1977); *The History of Sexuality*, Vol. 1, *An Introduction*, trans. Robert Hurley (Harmondsworth, 1981).

21. Jenny Taylor, *In the Secret Theatre of Home: Wilkie Collins, Sensation Narrative and Nineteenth-Century Psychology* (London, 1988), p. 30.

22. 'Archaeology' is one of the key terms used by Michel Foucault in *The Archaeology of Knowledge*, trans. A. M. Sheridan Smith (London, 1989) and *The Order of Things: An Archaeology of the Human Sciences* (London, 1992). Foucault uses the term 'archaeology' to denote a way of doing historical analysis of systems of thought or 'discourse'. As Barry Smart puts it in *Michel Foucault* (London, 1985), archaeology 'seeks to describe the *archive*, the term employed by Foucault to refer to "the general system of the formation and transformation" of statements existent at a given period within a given society ... The objective of archaeological analysis is ... a description of the archive, literally what may be spoken of in discourse ... The ultimate objective of such an analysis of discourse is ... to document its conditions of existence and the practical field in which it is deployed' (p. 48).

23. Taylor, *In The Secret Theatre of Home*, p. 1.

24. Taylor, ibid., p. 63.

25. Dickens wrote to W. H. Wills (30 June 1867): 'It is a very curious story, wild yet domestic ... nothing belonging to disguised women and the like.' See Norman Page (ed.), *Dickens: The Critical Heritage* (London, 1974), p. 169.

26. Taylor, *In The Secret Theatre of Home*, p. 15.

27. Taylor locates Collins's fiction in the Todorovian 'fantastic-uncanny' mode. In *The Fantastic: A Structural Approach to a Literary Genre* (trans. Richard Howard, Ithaca, NY, 1987), Tzvetan Todorov distinguishes four kinds of the fantastic: the 'marvellous', in which there is a complete break from the real; the 'fantastic-marvellous' in which inexplicable occurrences are associated with a supernatural cause; the 'fantastic-uncanny' in which such occurrences have a subjective origin; and the 'uncanny', in which inexplicable occurrences are associated with unconscious projection. Taylor also reads Collins's deployment of the

fantastic-uncanny in terms of Freud's theory of the uncanny (see Sigmund Freud's 1919 essay, 'The Uncanny', in *The Standard Edition of the Complete Psychological Works of Sigmund Freud*, Vol. XVII, trans. and ed. James Strachey [London, 1955]). Freud described as 'uncanny' such elements in fiction as an undefinable sense of dread or horror, madness, double selves, figures returning from the dead or other obsessively repeated figures, which enact forms of self-projection and repression. He argued that the uncanny (*unheimlich*) was not simply the opposite of the homely (*heimlich*) or familiar, but that each was a replication of the other 'which develop[s] in the direction of ambivalence' (Freud, *Works*, Vol. XVII, pp. 224–5). In order to produce an uncanny effect in a story something had to be added to the novel and unfamiliar, and that something, Freud argues, was the familiar or *heimlich*, which he defined as cosy, knowable, and domestic, but also as hidden and secret.

28. *Armadale*, p. xxxix.

29. Hutter is referring to Freud's description of the conflicts of the child who witnesses parental intercourse.

30. I am borrowing the term Raymond Williams used to describe the 'customary society' which was being eroded by urbanism and industrialism in the nineteenth century. See Raymond Williams, *The Country and the City* (London, 1973).

31. See also Walter Benjamin, *Charles Baudelaire: A Lyric Poet in the Era of High Capitalism* (London, 1973), p. 40.

32. See Michel Foucault, *Discipline and Punish: The Birth of the Prison*, trans. Alan Sheridan (Harmondsworth, 1977). In comparing the arguments of Hutter and Miller on the failure or pervasiveness of the self-policing community, it is important to note that the setting of *The Moonstone* pre-dates by some 20 years its date of publication. Collins, an inhabitant of the modern metropolitan city (London), is writing about the confrontation of a London detective with a quasi-feudal Yorkshire society which has its own very effective system of self-surveillance networks: gossip, an almost institutionalised observation by servants of each other and of the activities of their masters and mistresses, the organisational regime of the country house with its written records such as the washing book.

33. Mikhail Bakhtin, *The Dialogic Imagination*, trans. Carl Emerson and Michael Holquist (Austin, TX, 1981).

34. W. Fraser Rae, 'Sensation Novelists: Miss Braddon', *North British Review*, 43 (1865), 180–204.

35. Elaine Showalter, 'Family Secrets and Domestic Subversion', in A. Wohl (ed.), *The Victorian Family: Structure and Stresses* (London,

1978). See also Anthea Trodd, *Domestic Crime and the Victorian Novel* (London, 1989).

36. Tamar Heller, *Dead Secrets*, p. 5.

37. See Gaye Tuchman, *Edging Women Out: Victorian Novelists, Publishers and Social Change* (London, 1989), and John Kucich (on professional elites) in *The Power of Lies: Transgression and Victorian Fiction* (Ithaca, NY, 1994).

38. Hélène Cixous, 'Castration or Decapitation?', trans. Annette Kuhn, *Signs*, 7 (1981), 49, quoted by Heller, *Dead Secrets*, on p. 153.

39. See Elaine Showalter, 'Feminist Criticism in the Wilderness', in Showalter (ed.), *The New Feminist Criticism* (London, 1986), p. 266, and Nancy K. Miller, 'Emphasis Added: Plots and Plausibilities in Women's Fiction', *PMLA*, 96 (1981), 36–48.

40. This term is taken from Fredric Jameson, *The Political Unconscious: Narrative as a Socially Symbolic Act* (London, 1981).

41. Kucich, *The Power of Lies*, p. 75.

42. See Nancy Armstrong, *Desire and Domestic Fiction: A Political History of the Novel* (Oxford, 1987), and Mary Poovey, *Uneven Developments: The Ideological Work of Gender in Mid-Victorian England* (Chicago, 1988).

1

What Is 'Sensational' about the 'Sensation Novel'?

PATRICK BRANTLINGER

Even though 'sensation novels' were a minor subgenre of British fiction that flourished in the 1860s only to die out a decade or two later, they live on in several forms of popular culture, obviously so in their most direct offspring – modern mystery, detective, and suspense fiction and films. The sensation novel was and is sensational partly because of content: it deals with crime, often murder as an outcome of adultery and sometimes of bigamy, in apparently proper, bourgeois, domestic settings. But the fictions of Wilkie Collins, Sheridan Le Fanu, Mary Elizabeth Braddon, Charles Reade, Mrs Henry Wood, and some other popular authors of the 1860s have special structural qualities as well, which can perhaps be summed up historically as their unique mixture of contemporary domestic realism with elements of the Gothic romance, the Newgate novel of criminal 'low life', and the 'silver fork' novel of scandalous and sometimes criminal 'high life'.

The best sensation novels are also, as Kathleen Tillotson points out, 'novels with a secret', or sometimes several secrets, in which new narrative strategies were developed to tantalise the reader by withholding information rather than divulging it.[1] The forthright declarative statements of realistic fiction are, in a sense, now punctuated by question marks. This structural feature is crucial for the later development of the mystery novel, though it also points backward to both Gothic and Newgate fictions. Crimes do not always involve mysteries in earlier fictions, but sometimes they do, as in

30

Oliver Twist and *The Mysteries of Udolpho*. The emergence of the protagonist as detective or of the detective as an aid to the protagonist – most obviously in the case of Sergeant Cuff in *The Moonstone* – marks the evolution of a genre of popular fiction which refuses to follow the path of direct revelation prescribed by realism but instead hides as much as it reveals. Jacques Derrida argues that it may be 'impossible not to mix genres' because 'lodged within the heart of the law [of genre] itself [is] a law of impurity or a principle of contamination'.[2] Derrida suggests that the peculiar mark or structural feature that defines any genre can never belong exclusively to that genre but always falls partly outside it. The element of mystery in a sensation novel I take to be such a distinguishing feature, one that both sets sensation novels apart from more realistic fictions and points to their relatedness to some other romantic and popular forms.

Without drawing hard-and-fast lines between it and earlier Gothic romances or later detective fictions, the sensation novel can be defined from at least three different but complementary perspectives. The most familiar is historical, involving the situating of certain novels and novelists in their 1860s context of Gothic and domestic realism in fiction, the powerful influence of Dickens, stage melodrama, 'sensational' journalism, and bigamy trials and divorce law reform. A second perspective involves isolating those structural features of the sensation novel genre that, in Derrida's terms, represent its peculiar mark or marks, even while recognising that such features may partially characterise some other genres as well – or in other words, that it may be 'impossible not to mix genres'. In the second section, I argue that an apparent disintegration of narrative authority, caused by the introduction of secular mystery as a main ingredient of plots, is an especially significant trait of the sensation novel. The third perspective is psychological. Perhaps no genre of high or popular culture has so often been subjected to psychoanalytic scrutiny as the mystery novel. I shall suggest in the final section that, as a forebear of modern detective fiction, the sensation novel shares several of its psychological properties. Taken together, these perspectives should provide a fairly comprehensive definition of a genre of fiction that stands midway between romanticism and realism, Gothic 'mysteries' and modern mysteries, and popular and high culture forms – a genre, in other words, that like all genres is itself a mixture of sometimes contradictory forms, styles, and conventions.

I

In a review entitled 'The Enigma Novel', a writer in *The Spectator* for 28 December 1861 declared: 'We are threatened with a new variety of the sensation novel, a host of cleverly complicated stories, the whole interest of which consists in the gradual unravelling of some carefully prepared enigma.'[3] Although not every tale that has come to be labelled a sensation novel involves a mystery – Charles Reade, for example, rarely withholds the sources of villainy from his readers, qualifying as a sensationalist chiefly on the grounds of content – many imply by their very structures that domestic tranquillity conceals heinous desires and deeds. And although its subject is no more sensational than those of *The Woman in White* (1860), *No Name* (1862), and *Armadale* (1866), Collins's *The Moonstone* (1868) is often called the first mystery-cum-detective novel which, according to Dorothy Sayers, set a standard of perfection that later mystery writers have failed to meet.[4]

Just as much as the introduction of sex and violence, about which the first reviewers of sensation novels raised a great hue and cry, the introduction of mystery into a novel form that seems otherwise to follow the conventions of domestic realism posed disturbing questions. These questions arise on both the thematic and structural levels. On the former level, there is the problem of the relation of mysteries of crime, adultery, skeletons in family closets to religious mystery. By a kind of metaphoric sleight of hand, the Gothic romance had managed to make secular mystery seem like a version of religious mystery. *The Monk*, for example, straddles the fence between a gruesome, sadomasochistic thriller and a religious fantasy with horrific but just religious penalties visited upon Ambrosio at the end. The mysteries in *Uncle Silas* (1864), *Lady Audley's Secret* (1862), *East Lynne* (1861), and *The Moonstone*, however, have not even a quasi-religious content. Le Fanu perpetuates the supernatural elements of Gothic as metaphors (Silas Ruthvyn as werewolf or vampire), and Collins links speculations about fate to the accidental turnings of his multiple plots. Everything that happens in *The Moonstone*, for example, can be interpreted as the fulfilment of the curse that follows the diamond, while everything that happens in *Armadale* seems predestined either because it is wildly coincidental or because it has been predicted by Allan Armadale's dream. But the sensation novel involves both the secularisation and the domestication of the apparently higher (or at any rate, more romantic) mysteries of the Gothic romance. Ironically, just as novel-writing seems to be growing more 'sensational' in the 1860s, it is also growing tamer. From one perspective, the sensation novel represents an infusion of romantic elements into realism. From another, it represents the reduction of romance to fit Biedermeier frames.

During the 1860s 'sensation' and 'sensational' were attached – usually with more than a dash of sarcasm – to artifacts other than novels. There were 'sensation dramas' at least as early as Dion Boucicault's melodramatic hit of 1861, *The Colleen Bawn*, and also 'sensational' advertisements, products, journals, crimes, and scandals. Theatrical 'sensations' like Boucicault's or like Tom Taylor's *The Ticket-of-Leave Man* (1863), which features the professional detective and master disguise artist Hawkshaw, suggest the connection between stage melodrama and the sensation novel that foreshadows the relationship between best sellers and the cinema today.[5] Most of the writers of sensation novels also wrote melodramas, and best sellers like *East Lynne* and *Lady Audley's Secret* were quickly dramatised. With his enthusiasm for all things theatrical, Dickens set the pattern. 'Every writer of fiction,' he declared, '... writes, in effect, for the stage.'[6] In the preface to his early novel, *Basil* (1852), Collins asserted that 'the Novel and the Play are twin-sisters in the family of Fiction' and invoked the poetic licence for 'extraordinary accidents and events' that he associated with the theatre.[7] And Charles Reade thought of himself as a 'philosophical melodramatist' first, a novelist second. Any piece of fiction – his own, Smollett's *Peregrine Pickle*, Trollope's *Ralph the Heir*, Zola's *L'Assommoir* – was grist for Reade's melodramatic mill. In more than one instance he even converted a play into a novel, rewriting *Masks and Faces* (1852) as *Peg Woffington* (1853) and extracting *White Lies* (1857) from an earlier script.[8] In his analysis of sensation fiction for the *Spectator*, Richard Holt Hutton states what was often literally the case: 'The melodrama of the cheap theatres is an acted sensational novel.'[9]

As with melodrama, so with the sensation novel: violent and thrilling action, astonishing coincidences, stereotypic heroes, heroines, and villains, much sentimentality, and virtue rewarded and vice apparently punished at the end. As Winifred Hughes argues, however, 'With the rise of the sensation novel, melodrama ... lost its innocence.' Partly because of its moral ambiguity, the sensation novel was felt to be dangerous by many of its first critics, while stage melodrama seemed less threatening. Traditional melodrama celebrated virtue and domesticity, but the sensation novel questions them, at least by implication. Of course the subversive qualities of novels like *Lady Audley's Secret* are not overt. As Hughes points out, bigamy – that favourite 'sensation' crime (next to murder) – 'has the advantage of making sexual offence' or 'vice' punishable. And it also validates the institution of marriage in a backhanded way.[10]

Bigamy, adultery, and the problem of divorce law were much on the minds of Victorians in the 1860s. Jeanne Fahnestock has shown the influence of – among other 'sensational' events – the 1861 Yelverton bigamy–divorce trial on the fiction of Braddon, Reade, and others. 'After the Yelverton revelations, the public was painfully aware of the disgraceful accumulation of laws governing marriage ... which made bigamy legally possible' (Captain Yelverton himself escaped without serious legal penalty).[11] Even in those sensation novels whose plots do not hinge upon bigamy, there is a strong interest in sexual irregularities, adultery, forced marriages, and marriages formed under false pretences. But rather than striking forthright blows in favour of divorce law reform and greater sexual freedom, sensation novels usually tend merely to exploit public interest in these issues. Wilkie Collins's concern with marriage and divorce law in *No Name* and *Man and Wife* (1870) is exceptional, as are Charles Reade's themes of social reform and sexual conflict in stories like *Hard Cash* (1863) and *Griffith Gaunt* (1866).

Partly because of its generally exploitative approach to controversial issues like bigamy and adultery, the sensation novel was felt to be disreputable by most contemporary reviewers. Henry James, for example, writes about *Aurora Floyd* and *Lady Audley's Secret* with half-contemptuous admiration, as 'clever' and 'audacious' literary tricks that their author has managed to bring off by applying a 'thoroughgoing-realism' to the 'romance' of 'vice'.[12] Especially when they dealt with bigamy, sensation novels seemed to be a British equivalent of the suspect 'French novels' that Robert Audley carries about with him and sometimes reads in *Lady Audley's Secret* (or, as *Punch* called it, *Lady Disorderly's Secret*). One reviewer of Collins's *No Name* mistakenly declared the sensation novel to be 'a plant of foreign growth':

> It comes to us from France, and it can only be imported in a mutilated condition. Without entering on the relative morality or immorality of

French and English novelists, one may say generally that, with us, novels turn upon the vicissitudes of legitimate love and decorous affection; while in France they are based upon the working of those loves and passions which are not in accordance with our rules of respectability.[13]

This hardly gives British fiction prior to the 1860s its due with regard to the illegitimate and indecorous. But subjects were broached in sensation novels that many good Victorians thought inappropriate, and the fact that these subjects seemed not to be addressed seriously but merely 'sensationally' made them all the more disreputable. No doubt the greatest sensation of all was the discovery by many respectable readers in the 1860s (though hardly unknown in prior decades) that crime paid in fiction, as Count Fosco in *The Woman in White* says it pays in life. James understands this; as he says in his review of *Aurora Floyd*, 'The novelist who interprets the illegitimate world to a legitimate world, commands from the nature of his position a certain popularity.'[14]

James is content to analyse the clever though shallow artistry by which Braddon produces best sellers, but other reviewers saw in the sensation novel something much more disturbing. The Archbishop of York preached a sermon against sensation novels in the Huddersfield Church Institute in 1864, in which he declared that 'sensational stories were tales which aimed at this effect simply – of exciting in the mind some deep feeling of overwrought interest by the means of some terrible passion or crime. They want to persuade people that in almost every one of the well-ordered houses of their neighbours there [is] a skeleton shut up in some cupboard.' W. Fraser Rae, who quotes the Archbishop in the *North British Review* (September 1865), describes sensation novels as 'one of the abominations of the age'.[15]

Negative responses to the sensation novel often echo negative responses to Dickens. What Thackeray said in *Catherine* – that Dickens romanticises crime and dwells upon the most sordid and 'extravagant' aspects of life – was repeated many times over in the reviews of Collins, Braddon, Wood, and Ouida. And just as the sensation novel was felt to exercise a corrupting influence on higher culture, Dickens's novels were often similarly viewed, as when Dr Thomas Arnold told Wordsworth that 'his lads seemed to care for nothing but Bozzy's next No., and the Classics suffered accordingly'.[16] All of Dickens's major novels involve crime and detection at least tangentially, and many of the other ingredients of sensation fiction are present in his work at least as early as *Oliver Twist* and *Barnaby Rudge*. Thus, the former comes close to being both a Newgate and a mystery novel: in unravelling the secret of Oliver's parentage and thwarting Monks, Mr Brownlow plays the role of the full-fledged detectives in later novels. *Oliver Twist* also contains foreshadowings of professional detectives in the Bow Street runners, Blathers and Duff. Moreover, at least the metaphors in *Oliver Twist* give it a magical, quasi-Gothic colouring, albeit more probably derived from such sources as *Grimm's Fairy Tales* than from *The Mysteries of Udolpho* or *Melmoth the Wanderer*. Oliver's entrapment in the underworld slums of the thieves is in one way not so different from the entrapment of Mrs Radcliffe's heroines in their picturesque alpine castles and abbeys, for despite the changes of location, sex, and social message, they share the archetypal pattern of youthful innocence threatened by deviltry. In any case, next to Dickens's fiction, the Gothic tales of mystery, suspense, erotic awakening, and quasi-supernatural terror of Mrs Radcliffe and her successors were the most important antecedents of the sensation novel of the 1860s.

Some sensation novels are indistinguishable from Gothic romances. Many of Le Fanu's stories of terror and the occult should perhaps be categorised as Gothic rather than sensation fictions, if only because of dominance of supernatural over realistic elements. In the preface to *Uncle Silas*, Le Fanu rejects the new label and invokes an older tradition:

> May [the author] be permitted a few words ... of remonstrance against the promiscuous application of the term 'sensation' to that large school of fiction which transgresses no one of those canons of construction and morality which, in producing the unapproachable 'Waverley Novels', their great author imposed upon himself? No one, it is assumed, would describe Sir Walter Scott's romances as 'sensation novels'; yet in that marvellous series there is not a single tale in which death, crime, and, in some form, mystery, have not a place.[17]

Scott may be the ancestor whom Le Fanu would most like to claim, but his thinly veiled sadomasochistic tale of the captivity, deception, near-seduction, and near-murder of an adolescent heroine points more directly to Mrs Radcliffe. Maud Ruthvyn suggests as much when, about to explore the decaying mansion of her Uncle

Silas, she tells her maid: 'I feel so like Adelaide, in the "Romance of the Forest", the book I was reading to you last night, when she commenced her delightful rambles through the interminable ruined abbey in the forest' (ch. 54, p. 358).

In the sensation novel, the Gothic is brought up to date and so mixed with the conventions of realism as to make its events seem possible if not exactly probable. In 'sensationalising' modern life, however, the novelists paradoxically discovered that they were making fictions out of the stuff that filled the newspapers every day. Indeed, on one level they could even claim that to sensationalise was to be realistic. In *Victorian Studies in Scarlet*, Richard D. Altick points out that 'every good new Victorian murder helped legitimise, and prolong the fashion of sensational plots'.[18] Historically there is a direct relationship between the sensation novel and sensational journalism, from the extensive crime reporting in the *Times* and the *Daily Telegraph* to such early crime tabloids as the *Illustrated Police News*. Collins based some of the details of *The Moonstone* on the sensational news stories of the Constance Kent murder in 1860 and the Northumberland Street murder in 1861. As Dickens modelled Bucket on Inspector Field, so Collins modelled Sergeant Cuff on Inspector Whicher, the chief detective in the Kent Affair. And Henry James writes of *Lady Audley's Secret*:

> The novelty lay in the heroine being, not a picturesque Italian of the fourteenth century, but an English gentlewoman of the current year, familiar with the use of the railway and the telegraph. The intense probability of the story is constantly reiterated. Modern England – the England of today's newspaper – crops up at every step.[19]

Much more disparagingly, Henry Mansel complained about the emergence of 'the criminal variety of the Newspaper Novel, a class of fiction having about the same relation to the genuine historical novel that the police reports of the "Times" have to the pages of Thycydides or Clarendon'. All a writer of a sensation novel needed to do, said Mansel, was to 'keep an eye on the criminal reports of the daily newspapers', which would virtually write his fiction for him.[20]

Mansel's outcry against 'the Newspaper Novel' comes especially close to Charles Reade. Of all the sensation novelists, Reade was most dependent on the newspapers, just as he was also the most involved in stage melodrama. When the *Times* criticised his *A Terrible Temptation* (1871), partly for its portrayal of the 'scarlet woman' Rhoda Somerset, Reade wrote two letters to the editor protesting that he had merely 'dramatised' facts reported by the *Times*. Indeed, all of his best novels, he said, were inspired by the *Times*: 'For 18 years, at least, the journal you conduct so ably has been my preceptor, and the main source of my works – at all events of the most approved.' Reade proceeds to list several of his works inspired by the *Times*. Of *It Is Never Too Late to Mend*, he says, 'a noble passage in the *Times* of September 7 or 8, 1853, touched my heart [and] inflamed my imagination'. Of *Hard Cash*, he says that 'an able and eloquent leader on private asylums' gave him the main theme for his exposé novel. And *Put Yourself in His Place* grew out of Reade's perusal of *Times* articles 'upon trades unions and trade outrages'.[21] Reade is incensed that his favourite paper should complain about the subjects of his novels when he takes those subjects straight from that paper. He could argue that his novels were based upon the 'great facts' of the age and were therefore thoroughly realistic. As he frequently declared, he was a writer of 'romances founded on facts'. Those who wanted to dismiss his novels as melodramatic, crude, or worse, had first to show that the facts were not melodramatic or crude.

II

Winifred Hughes points out that Reade's obsessive insistence on the factual basis of his stories implies a lack of faith in the authority of fictive imagination.[22] A similar difficulty in claiming authority marks the narrative structures of many sensation novels. Because they blended romance with realism, the sensational with the domestic and contemporary, improbable or at least infrequent events with probable settings and characters, sensation novels posed difficulties for their writers as well as their first readers. Murders and conspiracies do not lurk down every dark street, in the shadows of every dark house. Or do they? Newspapers suggested otherwise, and how could a sensation novelist who imitated the newspapers fail to be realistic? Here is one way in which the conventions of fictional realism come to be punctuated with question marks. Mary Elizabeth Braddon states part of the creed of the sensation novelist when she makes her amateur detective-hero, Robert Audley, tell his villainous aunt:

> What do we know of the mysteries that may hang about the houses we enter? If I were to go tomorrow into that commonplace, plebeian,

eight-roomed house in which Maria Manning and her husband murdered their guest, I should have no awful prescience of that bygone horror. Foul deeds have been done under the most hospitable roofs; terrible crimes have been committed amid the fairest scenes, and have left no trace upon the spot where they were done. ... I believe that we may look into the smiling face of a murderer, and admire its tranquil beauty.[23]

The reference to Maria Manning emphasises the credibility of such a character as Lady Audley, who is herself an incarnation of this creed: her outward beauty – the blonde, blue-eyed, childlike but also coquettish stereotype of female loveliness and innocence – masks insanity, bigamy, homicide.

The plots of sensation novels lead to the unmasking of extreme evil behind fair appearances. In doing so, they threatened their first readers' cherished assumptions about women, marriage, and the fair appearances of the Victorian scene. 'Bigamy novels' clearly played upon their readers' own marital frustrations and disillusionments. As James explains, an author like Braddon – aggressive, clever, familiar with the ways of the world – herself represents an antithesis to the Victorian ideal of innocent and unchallenging womanhood: 'Miss Braddon deals familiarly with gamblers, and betting-men, and flashy reprobates of every description. She knows much that ladies are not accustomed to know, but that they are apparently very glad to learn.'[24] Braddon could be taken as going beyond the genteel realism of a Trollope or a Thackeray to unlock the true mysteries of life – those that more proper Victorians thought should be walled off from the reader.

Perhaps the overriding feature of both melodrama and the sensation novel is the subordination of character to plot; in the novel, not just plot but also descriptive detail and setting can deduct from character. Collins seems to belie this when, in the preface to the first edition of *The Moonstone*, he says:

> In some of my former novels, the object proposed has been to trace the influence of circumstances upon character. In the present story I have reversed the process. The attempt made, here, is to trace the influence of character on circumstances. The conduct pursued, under a sudden emergency, by a young girl, supplies the foundation on which I have built this book.[25]

The 'young girl' is undoubtedly Rachel Verinder, though Collins might also mean Rosanna Spearman, who hides the chief clue –

Franklin Blake's paint-smeared nightgown – in the quicksand. But Collins's point is hardly persuasive. Rachel's failure to confront Franklin with what she has seen prolongs the mystery, but the mystery itself is largely independent of character. If character were really central, her rejection of Franklin should serve as a tip-off to a clever detective like Cuff, who instead suspects Rachel. The initial 'circumstance' is the bequest of the diamond to Rachel by her uncle, from which everything else follows. The lives of all the characters are dramatically – indeed, melodramatically – altered by this circumstance; the accursed diamond casts a spell on everyone, only broken by the unravelling of the mystery and the sensational events at the end.

In fiction as in melodrama, the sensational derives much more from plot than from character. Boucicault's plays were famous for their 'sensation scenes', like the rescue from drowning in *The Colleen Bawn* and the explosion on the steamboat in *The Octoroon*, and sensation novels contain equivalent episodes, like the arson scenes in *The Woman in White* and *Lady Audley's Secret*. Only a well-conceived villain or villainess – Collins's Count Fosco, Braddon's Lady Audley, Le Fanu's Uncle Silas – seems strong enough both to shape circumstances and to rival sensational events in interest. But even they are doomed to fall prey to circumstances: an inadvertent clue, a startling coincidence is all that melodramatic justice seems to need to unravel their secrets. The world of melodrama and of the sensation novel is very much one in which circumstances rule characters, propelling them through the intricate machinations of plots that act like fate. 'A hand that is stronger than my own is beckoning me onward upon the dark road', says Robert Audley, several times over, in Braddon's tale (ch. 23, p. 131). He is the amateur detective of the story, but he performs that role reluctantly, contradicting both his placid character and some of his better inclinations.

Early in her story, Braddon intrudes as narrator to make the same point that her hero makes about crime and mystery 'amid the fairest scenes'. What is remarkable about this narrative interpolation is that it seems itself out of context, coming along before the reader is certain that any crime has occurred, and even well before the disappearance of Lady Audley's first husband, George Talboys. On one side of the intrusion, Talboys and Robert Audley are peacefully fishing. On the other side, they return peacefully to their rustic inn. The narrative interruption seems therefore abrupt, gratuitous, shocking, like its subject matter:

We hear every day of murders committed in the country. Brutal and treacherous murders; slow, protracted agonies from poisons administered by some kindred hand; sudden and violent deaths by cruel blows, inflicted with a stake cut from some spreading oak, whose every shadow promised – peace. In the county of which I write, I have been shown a meadow in which, on a quiet summer Sunday evening, a young farmer murdered the girl who had loved and trusted him; and yet, even now, with the stain of that foul deed upon it, the aspect of the spot is – peace. No species of crime has ever been committed in the worst rookeries about Seven Dials that has not been also done in the face of that rustic calm which still, in spite of all, we look on with a tender, half-mournful yearning, and associate with – peace.

(ch. 7, p. 36)

This passage is a microcosm of the sensation novel – indeed, of all mystery novels – not just in its content, but in its structure of abrupt revelation. And not merely fiction but life is like this, Braddon says: peace masks violence; innocent appearances cloak evil intentions; reality itself functions as a mystery until the sudden revelation of guilt, which is always lurking in the shadows. The passage also serves as a foreshadowing; even before we are aware of specific crimes, Braddon makes us listen to the jingling of the keys to the mystery, all of which are in the narrator's possession. We learn at the outset how ignorant we are about the story to come – and consequently about life and the nature of evil – and how much knowledge and power the narrator has.

Sensation novels involve not radically new techniques but manneristic extensions of features from earlier novels. Braddon's key jingling is a case in point. Without any consciously experimental intention, she pushes third-person omniscient narration to its logical limits. The narrator, even while foreshadowing with fatalistic implications, ceases to convey all information and begins to disguise much of it as hints, clues, hiatuses, as when Lady Audley orders her maid to send what would be, if revealed, an incriminating telegram: '"And now listen, Phoebe. What I want you to do is very simple." It was so simple that it was told in five minutes, and then Lady Audley retired into her bed-room' (ch. 7, p. 39). The central mystery, the disappearance of George Talboys, involves the same pattern. We sense that the narrator is being wilful and even capricious when George and Robert view Lady Audley's portrait, but George – and the narrator – give no sign of recognition. And when George wanders away from Robert and from us, not to reappear until the end of the novel, the same feeling of narrative wilfulness arises.

In *The Woman in White* and *The Moonstone*, Collins escapes from the logical awkwardness of Braddon's narrative hide-and-seek by a pattern of multiple first-person narrations roughly similar, as Kathleen Tillotson suggests, to the overlapping and conflicting voices of *The Ring and the Book* (itself almost a versified sensation novel, though set in the past). But it would be a mistake to overemphasise the uniqueness of this pattern or to fail to recognise the many aspects of Collins's novels that are quite familiar within the general context of Victorian fiction. T. S. Eliot suggests as much when he says that the distinction of genre between *East Lynne* and *The Mill on the Floss* is much less than the modern distinction between 'highbrow' and detective fiction.[26] Nevertheless, to some extent sensation novels represent extreme elaborations and almost parodic inversions of works like *Middlemarch* and *Barchester Towers*. The distinction is not sharp one, but it approximates Trollope's description in his *Autobiography*:

> Among English novels of the present day, and among English novelists, a great division is made. There are sensational novels and anti-sensational, sensational novelists and anti-sensational. ... The novelists who are considered to be anti-sensational are generally called realistic. I am realistic. My friend Wilkie Collins is generally supposed to be sensational.[27]

Trollope goes on to say that he thinks this division a mistake on the part of the critics; 'a good novel should be both' realistic and sensational, 'and both in the highest degree'. But realism and sensationalism are still antithetical in his usage, and he clearly prefers the probable and commonplace to their opposites. *The Eustace Diamonds* (1873), for example, may itself parody *The Moonstone*, partly by removing the mystery and keeping no secrets from the reader.[28]

At the same time that the narrator of a sensation novel seems to acquire authority by withholding the solution to a mystery, he or she also loses authority or at least innocence, becoming a figure no longer to be trusted. Just as character is subordinated to plot in the sensation novel, so the narrator is diminished by no longer communicating with the reliability of the tellers of more forthright tales. From a presiding mentor, sage, or worldly wise ironist guiding us through the story as in *Middlemarch* or *Barchester Towers*, the narrative persona must now become either secretive or something less than omniscient, perhaps slipping back into the interstices of the story as unobtrusively as possible. If the content of the sensation novel represented a challenge to bourgeois morality, one way that challenge shows up structurally is in the undermining of the narrator's credibility. When the story is still told through third-person omniscient narration, as in *Lady Audley's Secret* and *Armadale*, the problem is most acute: the narrative persona shares the knowledge of the crime with the criminal characters but does not share it directly with the reader. The narrator therefore takes on a shady, perhaps even criminal look reminiscent of the old idea that a detective must be in secret sympathy with criminals in order to catch them (and metaphorically, at least, detectives are often portrayed as being in league with the devil).[29] This moral ambiguity is a bit like the relationship between Vautrin and the narrator of *Père Goriot*: both are men of the world, both have penetrated the 'mysteries' of Paris in ways undreamt of by Eugène Rastignac, and both are interested in Eugène's journey from innocence to experience. Vautrin, of course, is a diabolical tempter, but it is also clear that the narrator's variety of experience is not exactly angelic.

Structurally the detective emerges in the sensation novel as a substitute for the forthright narrative personae of more realistic novels, or as a personification of the morally ambivalent role of the narrator. Like their prototypes, Inspector Bucket and Sergeant Cuff, most fictional detectives have at the outset a kind of reduced omniscience, similar to Vautrin's worldly knowledge: they are familiar with society, crime, and criminals, but about the causes of the particular crime in a story they are at first as much in doubt as the reader. They do not have a solution but they know how to arrive at one. They can follow the clues that the no longer trustworthy narrator-author places in their path, leading towards a restoration both of social order and of some semblance of narrative omniscience, both through a recapitulation of the hidden events by the detective, at the end of the story.

Of course the emergence of the detective in fiction can be explained historically as well as structurally. Walter Benjamin has analysed the evolution of detective fiction as a corollary of the growth of urban anonymity and alienation.[30] To such a general analysis must be added the more specific details of the creation of the police and detective forces in nineteenth-century cities and of the fascination of Dickens, Collins, and other writers with them.

Bucket and Cuff represent a penetration of criminal low life and of 'the mysteries of London' that their creators both envied and identified as part of their own novelistic equipment. Mystery and detection in nineteenth-century fiction also appear to be correlatives of the growth of professional and technical specialisation. As the specialist – like the detective – acquires knowledge in one area, other areas become opaque, mysterious. The detective as a specialist who unravels criminal mysteries expresses a wish fulfilment shared by all of us, to be able to know or to read just a few things very well, like clues, but through reading them very well to penetrate the deepest mysteries of life.

The early, naïve development of omniscient narration in fiction breaks down partly from the intrusion of mystery into it, but partly also from the recognition of the conventional – and logically pre-posterous – nature of omniscience. Within Jane Austen's compass of 'two or three families in a country village', omniscient narration proceeds without apparent difficulty. Within Dickens's London it begins to seem more artificial, both because the idea of a narrative persona knowing everything about such a vast place implies something close to supernatural authority (clearly an uneasy fit in fiction purporting to be realistic) and because from the outset Dickens wants to show us the 'mysteries' of the city while still rendering them mysterious. Dickens's occasional experiments with narrative structure – the double narration of *Bleak House*, for example – can be seen as attempts to deal with these contradictions. So, too, can the even more radical experiments in Wilkie Collins's novels: the multiple narrations of *The Woman in White* and *The Moonstone*, the odd mixture of narrative patterns and effects in *No Name* and *Armadale*. In the latter, Collins achieves something close to multiple narration by interjecting correspondence without authorial comment (the letters between Lydia Gwilt and Maria Oldershaw), long passages of dialogue in which characters recount their life stories (the opening confession of Allan Armdale), condensations of long periods of time as viewed through the memories of a single character (the Rev. Mr Brock's recollections in the first chapter of the second book), and Lydia's diary at the end of the tale. At the same time, the supposedly omniscient narrator of *Armadale* does not often intrude into the story either to moralise or to speculate about events.

The strange world of the Armadale 'doubles' and of the dream which comes true seems thus to exist in a kind of vacuum. Because of the dream and the heavy doses of coincidence, everything in *Armadale* seems to be laden with a preternatural – if not quite supernatural – significance. Because of the unobtrusiveness of the narrator, however, this potential significance is never explained, even while the reader – in common with the characters – witnesses the unravelling of the secular mysteries that constitute the plot. The story's emphasis on 'fate' or 'destiny' does not finally point beyond the labyrinthine windings of its plot to something more than accident or chance. When Collins does at last intrude as narrator, presumably to explain the higher mysteries to which the secular mysteries seem to point, it is only in an appendix in which he gives no answers: 'My readers will perceive that I have purposely left them, with reference to the Dream in this story, in the position which they would occupy in the case of a dream in real life – they are free to interpret it by the natural or the supernatural theory, as the bent of their own minds may incline them.'[31] Of course Collins is only dodging the questions about dreams and predestination that his novel has so elaborately raised. The passage thus represents an abdication of omniscience and a backhanded acknowledgement of the diminished stature of the narrative persona in contrast to, say, those in George Eliot's novels.

As in *Armadale*, the introduction of mystery – the self-conscious withholding of any important information from the reader – necessarily both diminishes and complicates the role of narrator. The narrator must seem either to connive with criminals, thereby sacrificing moral legitimacy, or to suffer a kind of structural amnesia, only recovering something close to omniscience as a version of memory or recapitulation at the end of the story. The detective – in the sensation novel, often the protagonist like Walter Hartright of *The Woman in White* rather than a professional – appears to fill the vacuum created by the at least partial abdication of authority by the narrator. Even when the conventions of third-person omniscient narration are maintained, as in *Armadale* and *Lady Audley's Secret*, once detection begins the information supplied to the reader tends to be reduced to the information possessed or discovered by the detective. The mystery acts like a story which the narrator refuses or has forgotten how to tell; the detective must now 'put the pieces together'. The plot unwinds through the gradual discovery – or, better, recovery – of knowledge, until at the end what detective and reader know coincides with what the secretive or somewhat remiss narrator-author has presumably known all along. But this coincidence of knowledge is no longer 'omniscience' of the kind present, say, in *Middlemarch*. The diminution – indeed, perhaps even criminalisation – of the narrator is also linked to a diminution of the kind of knowledge hidden and recovered: he or she can now hold the keys only to a secular mystery, ordinarily of the criminal, most sordid kind, and can no longer make any very credible or consistent claim to be able to unlock the higher mysteries of life, nature, society, God. The equivocations and silences of Collins's narrative personae suggest these transformations of metaphysical-religious knowledge into the solution of a crime puzzle and of the omniscient narrator into a collaborator with his disreputable character doubles, the criminal and the detective.

The detective, moreover, is not so much the antithesis of the narrator, trying to recover what the narrator secretes, as one of his personifications in the text, presiding over the plot and leading the reader down several false paths before discovering – or recovering – the true one. That is, just as the narrator in the sensation novel must simultaneously reveal and withhold information, so the detective: his knowledge is usually greater than the reader's, but it is incomplete; he may finally know even less than the reader. Sergeant Cuff, for example, solves only parts of the mystery in *The Moonstone*, sets up some false leads, and then leaves the scene until near the end; he is not exactly more successful at providing information than the missing third-person narrator. In W. S. Gilbert's comic opera spoof, *A Sensation Novel in Three Volumes*, the Scotland Yard investigator, Gripper, seems mainly bent on delaying the solution of mysteries and allowing criminals to escape. Disguised as a North American Indian, Gripper says:

> When information I receive that Jones has been a-forging,
> And on the proceeds of his crime is prodigally gorging,
> Do you suppose I collar my friend and take him to the beak, m'm?
> Why, bless your heart, they wouldn't retain me in the force a week, m'm.
>
> In curious wig and quaint disguise, and strangely altered face, m'm,
> Unrecognised I follow my prey about from place to place, m'm;
> I note his hair, his eyes, his nose, his clothing and complexion,
> And when I have got 'em all into my head, I set about detection.[32]

And thus Jones slips through Gripper's fingers. Gilbert is right: fictional detectives seem often to be in collusion with both criminals and narrators, functioning as much to blow smoke in the reader's eyes as to provide solutions. They mimic the ambivalence of their at least partially abdicated narrators. Their roles are largely dictated by the central structural ambiguity upon which all mystery and detective fiction is based, an ambiguity suggested by the idea of 'telling a secret' – you must first be a party to holding the secret in order to tell it.

III

Despite the air of preternatural significance in a novel like *Armadale*, mysteries in most sensation novels do not clearly connect with anything higher than a particular case of arson or bigamy or murder. The mysteries in *Bleak House* point to the large mysteries of community and isolation, love and selfishness in the society that Dickens anatomises. But the mystery of *The Moonstone*, even though serious attitudes about crime and poverty, religious hypocrisy, the law, and the empire can be inferred from it, does not explicitly point beyond itself to larger issues.[33] And unlike the Dedlocks and their followers in *Bleak House*, who represent everything that Dickens thinks is wrong with the decaying aristocracy of the 1850s, Sir Percival Glyde and Count Fosco in *The Woman in White* are not bearers of social or even very weighty moral messages. Sir Percival is a stereotypic melodrama villain from whose career of deceit and crime Collins asks us to draw only the most obvious of morals. Count Fosco is much more interesting as a character, but the shadowy Italian politics that destroy him at the end of the novel are only a deus ex machina to bring on his just deserts. Collins is not interested in saying anything about secret societies, or Mazzini, or the Orsini affair. He does not even take the occasion to deplore the terrible conditions in private insane asylums, as Charles Reade does in *Hard Cash*. Several of Collins's other novels – *No Name* and *Man and Wife* with their treatment of the injustice of the marriage laws, for example – take up social reform themes in the Dickens manner. And no matter how melodramatic, Charles Reade's novels put social reform in the forefront.

The mysteries in *Lady Audley's Secret, Uncle Silas, The Woman in White*, and *The Moonstone*, however, function like those in later mystery novels and do not connect with anything outside themselves. In each case, though much that is violent and terrifying happens along the way, the mystery turns out to be soluble, unlike the larger mysteries raised by *Bleak House* and *Our Mutual Friend*. The worst evils that can be perpetrated by individuals are un-masked, but the instant of their revelation is usually also the instant of their exorcism. The paradox is that sensation novels – and mystery novels after them – conclude in ways that liquidate mystery: they are not finally mysterious at all. The insoluble is reduced to the soluble, just as the social evils that most concern Dickens are reduced to the level of personal villainy. Guilt is dis-placed onto others, which is to say onto scapegoat characters whom we are quite glad to see punished, and the good characters with whom we most strongly identify 'come out clean' and are rewarded with happy endings. W. H. Auden describes the process in his essay on mysteries, 'The Guilty Vicarage':

> The magic formula is an innocence which is discovered to contain guilt; then a suspicion of being the guilty one; and finally a real inno-cence from which the guilty other has been expelled, a cure effected, not by me or my neighbours, but by the miraculous intervention of a genius from outside who removes guilt by giving knowledge of guilt. (The detective story subscribes, in fact, to the Socratic daydream: 'Sin is ignorance.')[34]

Auden suggests the ritual nature of detective fiction, with the detec-tive as the priest who performs the exorcism. But the pattern is not fully developed in sensation novels, which are more flexible and various than modern detective novels and, as T. S. Eliot points out, closer to serious fiction.[35] Their structures are consequently less re-assuring; the detectives in them, for example, are usually not Auden's 'genius from outside' but a character or characters directly involved in the story. Indeed, Sergeant Cuff, the prototype of later professional sleuths, is not the chief detective in *The Moonstone*. That role belongs to Franklin Blake, the protagonist, who turns out also to have stolen the diamond. And the piecemeal process of de-tection depends heavily on luck and coincidence, as in *Oliver Twist* (the most striking coincidence in *The Moonstone*, of course, is also the most baffling: that Franklin Blake himself is the thief).

The paradox of Franklin Blake, or of the detective in pursuit of himself, points to the essence of later mystery novels. Most serious novels – manifestly in a *Bildungsroman*, for example – involve a search for the self, the attempt of at least one character to stake out a career or an identity in the social wilderness. In sensation and mystery novels, however, just as the intractable problem of evil is reduced to a neatly soluble puzzle on a personal level, so the search for self is short-circuited. The unravelling of the mystery, as in *The Moonstone* where Franklin Blake works his way through the labyrinth of clues and false leads only to discover that he himself has stolen the diamond, mimics self-revelation but points the other way. The mystery revealed exonerates both the protagonist and the reader from guilt: Franklin's act was unconscious; the real villain is his rival, Godfrey Ablewhite, whom we are only too glad to have murdered by the convenient Indians, the rightful owners of the gem.

Few works of fiction have been more psychoanalysed – as opposed to criticised and admired for their serious qualities – than *The Moonstone*. This is due partly to its approximation to fullness and seriousness. It is a big novel, with many characters, with an unusual narrative structure, and with an intricate plot – nearly as full and complicated, say, as *Bleak House*. But it is a big novel with a hole in the middle, tunnel vision; represented symbolically by the obsessive object named in its title: only find the Moonstone and all questions are answered. *Bleak House* is among other things a murder mystery, but the noose of guilt is ultimately drawn around everyone, around society at large, as symbolised by the upward spreading smallpox and by the all-engulfing Chancery suit. For its victims, there is usually no way out of Chancery, just as there is no escape from guilt and the law in *The Trial*. But in *The Moonstone*, the short circuit from Franklin Blake the detective to Franklin Blake the unconscious thief (albeit after many pages of twists and implications) and thence to Franklin Blake the rewarded and happy protagonist is eminently satisfying and finally too neat. Collins makes brilliant use of the conventions of the best Victorian novels while undercutting their most serious implications. In much the same way, other sensation novels and mysteries mimic serious fiction.

In the best of the psychoanalytic essays on *The Moonstone*, Albert D. Hutter grants too much to detective fiction when he likens it to the process of psychoanalysis itself:

> Detective fiction involves the transformation of a fragmented and incomplete set of events into a more ordered and complete understanding. As such it seems to bridge a private psychological experience, like dreaming, and literary experience in general. And like a psychoanalysis, the detective story reorders our perception of the past through language.[36]

The idea that detective fiction acts as a bridge between dreams 'and literary experience in general' may be correct, but Hutter's next sentence seems to contradict what I have just said about the reduction of mystery to a soluble level and the short-circuiting of the search for the self. Leo Löwenthal's dictum that 'mass culture is psychoanalysis in reverse' is closer to the mark than the idea that detective fiction acts like a psychoanalysis.[37] Detective fiction only mimics the processes that are like psychoanalysis in serious fiction; it is both diverting and diversionary, and inevitably reductive. Hutter appears to recognise this when he says that Collins 'adopts ... the device so common to the Victorian novel of splitting hero and villain and giving one the crime and punishment so that the other may be free to enjoy his rewards without guilt'.[38] While this may call into question the analytic power of all fiction where such character splitting occurs, it also suggests why it means very little to say that detective fiction follows the pattern of a psychoanalysis. It only mimics that pattern, just as it mimics aspects of serious fiction.

A distinction must be made between trait or character splitting in sensation novelists like Collins and in more realistic novelists like George Eliot. In the former, character splitting is more pronounced, again partly reflecting the influence of the Gothic romance. The two Allan Armadales, Anne Catherick as ghostly double-goer in *The Woman in White*, and the two lives, two husbands, and two personalities of Lady Audley hark back to the patterns of doubling in a Gothic tale like James Hogg's *Confessions of a Justified Sinner*. These patterns can be partly explained psychoanalytically as expressive of narcissistic regression. Such tendencies exist mainly on a metaphoric level in most realistic novels, whereas they are given much more literal expression in romantic fiction, including the sensation novel. As Winifred Hughes says, sensation novels 'reveal a recurrent preoccupation with the loss or duplication of identity. ... Everywhere in the lesser sensation novels the unwitting protagonists experience their strange encounters with the empty form of the *doppelgänger*.'[39]

Hughes goes on to point out that 'incident as well as character is subject to the principle of duality'. The plots of sensation novels 'are typically structured around a recurrence of similar or identical situations, not infrequently in the shape of dreams or omens and their ultimate fulfilment'.[40] A structural explanation for this doubling of incidents emerges from the realisation that mystery stories are necessarily two-fold. Hutter points to Tzvetan Todorov's essay on detective novels in *The Poetics of Prose*, in which Todorov shows that they are always double narratives. The first narrative concerns the past and the crime that has been committed; it is wound up and unravelled in the second narrative, which concerns the present and recounts the detection of the cause of the crime. Todorov relates this pattern of double narration to the Formalist distinction between 'fable', which corresponds to 'what happened in life', and 'subject' or plot, which corresponds to 'the way the author presents it to us'.[41] But in the detective novel 'what happens in life' is virtually reduced to a variant of 'the way the author presents it to us'. Whereas serious literature imitates life partly by reducing and simplifying its scale and complexity, the mystery novel imitates serious literature by carrying its reductive and simplifying tendencies to extremes. Like the sensation novel from which it evolved, the mystery novel shrinks 'fable' to a single event or a few related ones (a crime or crimes, murder or theft often combined in sensation novels with bigamy and the assumption of false identities), just as it also shrinks mystery to a soluble level and diverts the problem of self-identity into a pattern of exorcism or of the projection of guilt onto another. 'Plot' then follows the path of detection through conveniently placed clues to the final explanation of this simplified version of 'fable', correctly identifying the culprit – the personified cause of the 'fable' – and dishing out punishment and rewards. Like the fatal 'hand' that keeps pointing Robert Audley down the path of detection, or like the pattern of improbable coincidences in most melodramas and sensation novels, the unravelling of the plot seems dimly to represent the working out of destiny: everything is put back in order at the end, all questions have been answered.

Hutter proceeds to analyse the unconscious sexual symbolism in *The Moonstone* and to consider both the oedipal theory of mystery stories and the more interesting – because less obvious and perhaps less reductive – theory that mysteries are symbolic re-creations of the primal scene. No doubt both theories can help to explain all fictions, but the primal scene idea seems especially relevant to mysteries, and perhaps even more to sensation novels, in which the mysteries occur within families, than to many later detective novels. The theory, as Hutter explains it, 'reads detective fiction as an expression of primal scene fears and wishes, that is, as an expression of the conflicts of the child who witnesses parental intercourse'. Hutter's application of this theory to *The Moonstone* is especially

insightful, partly because it is a novel 'built around a visual tension
... the characters watching a crime committed in a bedroom at
night, not understanding it, and suffering because they are forced
into a new view of a loved object'.[42] Obsessive curiosity and
voyeurism characterise all mystery stories, but the theory fits best
where the mystery is confined to a family and the voyeurism is a
matter of life and death to the voyeur, as in both *Lady Audley's
Secret* and *Uncle Silas*, for example, and also in much Gothic
fiction. Such a thesis involves interpreting both the victims or
corpses and the villains as surrogate parent figures, seen dimly
through the childhood memory of the fearful vision (whether real
or imagined) which both misconstrues the parental intercourse as
an act of violence and secretly wishes it to be such an act. In *Uncle
Silas*, which has, if anything, even more 'visual tension' and horror
related to that tension than *The Moonstone*, the Bluebeard and
vampire-werewolf metaphors attached to Maud Ruthvyn's terrifying uncle point towards the regressive pattern suggested by the
primal scene theory, although it is Silas's son, Dudley, who aims at
marrying Maud, seducing her, or having her any way he can. The
terrific finale points even more clearly in the same direction: Maud
watches from the shadows as Dudley drives home the strange pick
axe, with its 'longish tapering spike', meant for Maud herself, time
after time into the breast of the apparently sleeping Mme de la
Rougierre, whose body heaves with 'a horrible tremor' and 'convul-
sions', 'the arms drumming on the bed', until 'the diabolical surgery
was ended' (ch. 64, pp. 426–7). It is a 'sensation scene' to match
anything in Boucicault's plays – anything in the entire literature of
sensation, in fact – for its combination of grisly terror with erotic
suggestion. The regressive quality of *Uncle Silas* and Le Fanu's
other fiction is unmistakable, whether it is better explained by the
primal scene idea or some other psychological theory; that quality is
the chief source of its very considerable power.

Most sensation novels confine their voyeuristic, primal scene revelations to family circles, but the family itself was the mainstay of
Victorian bourgeois values. Sensation novels were therefore subversive without ordinarily addressing political issues. They stripped the
veils from Victorian respectability and prudery, exposing bigamists
and adulterers, vampires and murderesses. They did so not by
pushing the conventions of realistic fiction to the limits, as Zola was
soon to do in France, but by subverting those conventions themselves, importing romantic elements back into contemporary

settings, reinvesting the ordinary with mystery (albeit only of the secular, criminal variety), and undoing narrative omniscience to let in kinds of knowledge that realistic fiction had often excluded. In place of the empiricist realism that strives for objective, direct mimesis, the sensation novel seems to substitute a different measure of reality, based on primal scene psychology, that now reads objective appearances as question marks or clues to mysteries and insists that the truth has been hidden, buried, smuggled away behind the appearances. But this subversive attitude is also felt to be regressive, inferior to traditional realism: the sensation novel never directly challenged the dominance of more serious, more realistic fiction, and sensational authors and narrators seem forever to be backing away from the deepest truths in their stories, abdicating or undermining their own authority. Precisely because of their reductive and regressive properties, however, sensation novels often approach the quality and complexity of more serious Victorian fiction. Perhaps it would be best to say that sensation novels seize upon and exaggerate the reductive properties that are already present in serious fiction. In terms like Derrida's on the impurity of genres, T. S. Eliot writes:

> You cannot define Drama and Melodrama so that they shall be reciprocally exclusive; great drama has something melodramatic in it, and the best melodrama partakes of the greatness of drama. *The Moonstone* is very near to *Bleak House*. The theft of a diamond has some of the same blighting effect on the lives about it as the suit in Chancery.[43]

The development of the sensation novel marks a crisis in the history of literary realism. At the same time that George Eliot was investing the novel with a new philosophical gravity, the sensationalists were breaking down the conventions of realistic fiction and pointing the way to the emergence of later popular forms and perhaps also to later, more conscious assertions of the need to go beyond realism into all those mysterious areas of life and art that supposedly omniscient narrators often seem not to know. Although anything 'sensational' is by definition not to be taken too seriously, the word itself points to a source of immediate excitement or surprise, the realm of the unexpected. As T. S. Eliot remarks, 'we cannot afford to forget that the first – and not one of the least difficult – requirements of either prose or verse is that it should be interesting'.[44] Whatever else they are, sensation novels are certainly that. In his defence of literary sensationalism in *Belgravia* (a journal edited by none other than Mary Elizabeth Braddon) George Augustus Sala launched an assault on 'the dolts and dullards and envious backbiters' for whom 'everything is "sensational" that is vivid, and nervous, and forcible, and graphic, and true'. If these 'anti-sensationalists' had their way, Sala declared in his final terrific sentence, then life itself would be a sorry affair, for they would establish a new reign of dullness: 'Don't let us move, don't let us travel, don't let us hear or see anything; but let us write sonnets to Chloe, and play madrigals on the spinet, and dance minuets, and pray to Heaven against Sensationalism, the Pope, the Devil, and the Pretender; and then let Dulness reign triumphant, and Universal Darkness cover all.'[45] Sala's sensational protest points forward to the fuller, more profound rebellions of the decadent and modernist writers who wrote the final epitaphs for the safer kinds of realism and for the Victorian pieties of hearth and home.

From *Nineteenth-Century Fiction*, 37 (1982), 1–28.

NOTES

[Patrick Brantlinger's widely cited essay locates Collins's fiction in one of its generic contexts, the sensation novel. It synthesises and revises several accounts of the sensation genre which appeared between 1969 and 1980. Brantlinger argues that the term 'sensational' partly designates a specific kind of fictional content (murder, adultery, bigamy, blackmail and fraud), and partly a range of special structural qualities (among others, the subordination of character to plot, the mixing of domestic realism with Gothic romance, and the development of particular forms of narrative secrecy). Brantlinger examines the sensation novel from three perspectives: historical, structural and psychological. He also considers the much discussed question of the sensation novel's relationship to the tradition of realism which dominated the nineteenth-century novel, and concludes that the techniques of the sensation novel are symptomatic of a crisis in realism. Ed.]

   1. Kathleen Tillotson, 'The Lighter Reading of the Eighteen Sixties', Introduction to Wilkie Collins, *The Woman in White*, Riverside edn (Boston, 1969), p. xv.

   2. Jacques Derrida, 'The Law of Genre', trans. Avitall Ronell, *Critical Inquiry*, 7 (1980), 57.

   3. 'The Enigma Novel', rpt. in *Wilkie Collins, The Critical Heritage*, ed. Norman Page (London and Boston, 1974), p. 25.

4. Dorothy L. Sayers, Introduction, *The Omnibus of Crime*, ed. Dorothy L. Sayers (New York, 1992), p. 25.

5. There is a brilliant exposition of this idea in T. S. Eliot, 'Wilkie Collins and Dickens', *Selected Essays*, new edn (New York, 1960), pp. 409–18; originally published in *TLS*, 4 August 1927, pp. 535–26.

6. Dickens, quoted by J. W. T. Ley, *The Dickens Circle* (New York, 1919), p. 87.

7. Willie Collins, 'Letter of Dedication', *Basil* (3 vols, London, 1852), I, xiii. Also see *Basil* (1862) rev. edn; rpt. New York, 1980), p.v.

8. According to Wayne Burns, Reade thought of fiction 'as a lesser form of drama' (*Charles Reade: A Study in Victorian Authorship* [New York, 1961], p. 113; see esp. ch. 4).

9. Richard Holt Hutton, 'Sensation Novels', *Spectator*, 8 August 1868, p. 932.

10. Winifred Hughes, *The Maniac in the Cellar: Sensation Novels of the 1860s* (Princeton, NJ, 1980), pp. 71, 31.

11. Jeanne Fahnestock, 'Bigamy: The Rise and Fall of a Convention', *NCF*, 36 (1981), 58. See also Arvel B. Erickson and Fr. John McCarthy, 'The Yelverton Case: Civil Legislation and Marriage', *Victorian Studies*, 14 (1971); and Mary Lyndon Shanley, '"One Must Ride Behind": Married Women's Rights and the Divorce Act of 1857', *Victorian Studies*, 25 (1982), 355–76.

12. Henry James, 'Miss Braddon', rev. of *Aurora Floyd*, in *Notes and Reviews* (Cambridge, MA, 1921), pp. 108–16; originally published in the *Nation*, 9 November 1865, pp. 593–4.

13. Unsigned review, rpt. in *Wilkie Collins: The Critical Heritage*, pp. 134–5; originally published in the opening number of the *Reader*, 3 January 1863, pp. 14–15.

14. James, 'Miss Braddon', p. 115.

15. The Archbishop of York's sermon is quoted by W. Fraser Rae in 'Sensation Novelists: Miss Braddon', *North British Review*, NS 4 (1865), 203 (British edn).

16. Wordsworth to Edward Moxon, April 1842, excerpted in *Charles Dickens: A Critical Anthology*, ed. Stephen Wall (Harmondsworth, 1970), p. 61. See also George Ford, *Dickens and His Readers: Aspects of Novel-Criticism since 1836* (New York, 1965), pp. 39–43 and 177–9.

17. Joseph Sheridan Le Fanu, 'A Preliminary Word', *Uncle Silas: A Tale of Bartram-Haugh*, intro. Frederick Shroyer (New York, 1966); p. xvii; further citations in the text are to this edition.

18. Richard D. Altick, *Victorian Studies in Scarlet* (New York, 1970), p. 79.

19. James, 'Miss Braddon', pp. 112–13.

20. Henry Mansel, 'Sensation Novels', *Quarterly Review*, 113 (1863), 501.

21. *Readiana* in *The Works of Charles Reade*, 9 vols (New York, n.d), IX, 377–8.

22. Hughes, *The Maniac in the Cellar*, p. 75.

23. *Lady Audley's Secret*, intro. Norman Donaldson (New York, 1974), ch. 18, p. 94; subsequent references in the text are to this edition. An excellent study of Braddon is Robert Lee Woolff, *Sensational Victorian: The Life and Fiction of Mary Elizabeth Braddon* (New York and London, 1979).

24. James, 'Miss Braddon', pp. 115–16.

25. Preface to the First Edition, rpt. in *The Moonstone*, ed. J. I. M. Stewart (Harmondsworth, 1966), p. 27.

26. Eliot, *Selected Essays*, pp. 409–10.

27. Anthony Trollope, *An Autobiography*, intro. Bradford Allen Booth (Berkeley, CA, and Los Angeles, 1947), p. 189.

28. H. J. W. Milley, '*The Eustace Diamonds* and *The Moonstone*', *Studies in Philology*, 36 (1939), 651–63.

29. Ian Ousby, *Bloodhounds of Heaven: The Detective in English Fiction from Godwin to Doyle* (Cambridge, MA, 1976), pp. 3–18.

30. Walter Benjamin, *Charles Baudelaire: A Lyric Poet in the Era of High Capitalism*, trans. Harry Zohn (London, 1973), pp. 40–8.

31. Appendix, *Armadale* (New York, 1977), p. 597.

32. W. S. Gilbert, *A Sensation Novel in Three Volumes* (London, 1912), pp. 22, 23.

33. For a contrasting argument see John R. Reed, 'English Imperialism and the Unacknowledged Crime of *The Moonstone*', *Clio*, 2 (1973), 281–90.

34. W. H. Auden, *The Dyer's Hand and Other Essays* (New York, 1968), p. 158.

35. Eliot, *Selected Essays*, pp. 417–18.

36. Albert D. Hutter, 'Dreams, Transformations, and Literature: The Implications of Detective Fiction', *Victorian Studies*, 19 (1975), 191. [See p. 175 below. Ed.]

37. Lowenthal, quoted by Martin Jay, *The Dialectical Imagination* (Boston, 1973), p. 173.

38. Hutter, 'Dreams, Transformations, and Literature', pp. 202–3.

39. Hughes, *The Maniac in the Cellar*, p. 21.

40. Ibid.

41. Tzvetan Todorov, *The Poetics of Prose*, trans. Richard Howard (Ithaca, NY, 1977), p. 45.

42. Hutter, 'Dreams, Transformations, and Literature', pp. 203–4. The first crude version of this theory is Geraldine Pederson-Krag, 'Detective Stories and the Primal Scene', *Psychoanalytic Quarterly*, 18 (1949), 207–14. See also Charles Rycroft, 'The Analysis of a Detective Story', *Imagination and Reality*, intro. M. Masud R. Khan and John D. Sutherland (New York, 1968), pp. 114–28.

43. Eliot, *Selected Essays*, pp. 417–18.

44. Ibid., p. 418.

45. George Augustus Sala, 'On the "Sensational" in Literature and Art', *Belgravia*, 4 (1868), 457, 458.

2

The Counterworld of Victorian Fiction and *The Woman in White*

U. C. KNOEPFLMACHER

'The novel is born at the same time as the spirit of rebellion and expresses, on the aesthetic plane, the same ambition.' In *The Rebel*, Albert Camus devotes a special section to the novel as the archetypal form of 'the literature of rebellion, which begins in modern times'. Pointing to the scarcity of works of fiction found in 'the literature of consent, which coincides, by and large, with ancient history and the classical period', Camus regards the novel as the product of a more recent and more defiant romantic imagination: 'there are no more fascinating heroes than those who indulge their passions to the fullest'. Camus's specimens of rebellion in the novel are taken, unsurprisingly, from Russian, French, and modern American fiction. Beyond a brief allusion to Heathcliff, 'who wanted to go beyond death in order to reach the very depths of hell', the English Victorian novel is pointedly ignored.[1]

At first glance, Camus's omission seems justified. There are no Stavrogins or Julien Sorels in the masterpieces of Victorian fiction; those few heroes and heroines who do 'indulge their passions to the fullest' are handled with circumspection by novelists who insist on dissociating themselves from their creatures' excesses. Recent critics such as Raymond Williams and J. Hillis Miller have correctly stressed the communal emphasis of Victorian fiction, its exaltation of a collective conscience, its distrust of escapism, isolation, and defiance – those same impulses which Camus regards as endemic to creative rebellion. The Victorian novel is uneasy about revolt; *Mary Barton, The Tale of Two Cities, Felix Holt* attest to that uneasiness. Dickens and George Eliot disarm all that threatens to undermine their precarious faith in a beneficent social order bonded by love: Oliver Twist must be preserved from his contaminating contact with Fagin's anarchic underworld; Maggie the rebel must expiate her desire to flee St Ogg's. One side of the Victorian novelist rejects the escapism or aggression that the other side indulges. Even Heathcliff, the sole English representative of that romantic 'intelligence in the service of nostalgia or rebellious sensibilities' which Camus claims to find in all novels,[2] is muted in his Manichaean role when replaced by the tamer Hareton and the second Catherine.

Does the Victorian novel, then, belong to Camus's 'literature of consent' rather than to his 'literature of rebellion'? I think not. It will be my contention in this essay that beneath the moralism and the collective ethic of love invoked by most Victorian novelists to protect themselves and their readers from impulses antagonistic to society lurks a vital 'counterworld' that is asocial and amoral, unbound by the restraints of the socialised superego. Just as the figures of Heathcliff and the first Catherine dominate *Wuthering Heights* despite Brontë's attempts at counterbalance, so does the power of most other great Victorian novels reside in the sometimes concealed, sometimes more overt traces of an anarchic 'intelligence' (or emotional affect) opposed to the lawful, ordered Victorian values to which novelist and reader tacitly agreed to subscribe.

This subversive counterworld (usually restricted to characters whom the novelist tries to keep at a distance either by casting them in the role of villains or by placing them in subsidiary roles) does not merely exist as a sanctioned vehicle for the criticism of established values and institutions. Mrs Gaskell may enlist the figure of John Barton in her polemic against the unfairness of the Manchester masters, yet her interest in the quasi-Dostoevskian mentality of this dark, rebellious, homicidal figure of negation clearly outweighs his serviceability as a spokesman for the oppressed. George Eliot and Trollope are hardly uncritical of the provincial societies whose strong communal bonds they nonetheless endorse; yet it is in their treatment of figures that both they and their invented societies reject – a Bulstrode or a Melmotte – that each author reveals a paradoxical fascination, even empathy, with the ruthlessness of a power-hungry and unrestrained egotism.

Dickens's well-documented attraction to criminal minds and Thackeray's empathy with the destructive logic of Becky Sharp are inevitably checked, but the asocial energies of such creatures survive despite the attempts at dissociation made through a protesting narrator or through the blunting effects of characterisation and plot.

In the ensuing discussion, I intend first to sample some of the ways in which nineteenth-century English novelists repudiate yet indulge rebellious attitudes at odds with the dictates of accepted behaviour, and then shall analyse Wilkie Collins's *The Woman in White* (1859–60) as a unique instance of a mid-Victorian novel in which the author openly acknowledges an anarchic and asocial counterworld as a powerfully attractive alternative to the ordered, civilised world of conventional beliefs. [...]

[There follows a discussion of Scott, Dickens and Thackeray at this point in the essay which deals with rebels and outsiders in Victorian fiction.]

To Collins, who began his career with a historical romance entitled *Antonina; or, The Fall of Rome* (1850), a portrait of a decadent society unable to withstand the more vital barbarians who live outside the bounds of Roman law, Scott remained 'beyond all comparison the greatest novelist that has ever written ... the Prince, the King, the God Almighty of novelists'.[3] Yet in his second full-length novel, *Basil: A Story of Modern Life* (1852), Collins aligned himself with the more recent revival of Newgate fiction. Accusing those critics who had deplored the prurience of *Antonina* of practising a morality that 'stops at the tongue', Collins provided his detractors with further fuel by openly defying convention in his characterisation of the all-powerful Robert Manion, the master criminal who dominates the lurid plot of his second novel. The critics responded by charging that *Basil* illustrated the 'aesthetics of old Bailey' in its 'vicious atmosphere'.[4]

Unlike Dickens, who would later urge his friend to respect the sensibilities of his Victorian audience,[5] Collins never disguised his fascination with the amorality of the counterworld. In *A Rogue's Life: From His Birth to His Marriage*, a five-part novella published in *Household Words* in 1856, three years before the serialisation of *The Woman in White* in *All the Year Round*, he depicted with great relish a transported young convict's supposed confessions. Like the satirical Becky Sharp, Frank Softly (who starts his career as the caricaturist Thersites Junior) shares his creator's delight in puncturing the pretensions of conventional society. Like Becky also, this remorseless pícaro goes unpunished: although transported to Australia, he becomes 'a convict aristocrat – a prosperous, wealthy, highly respectable mercantile man'.[6] His memoirs end abruptly at this point, for, as he explains, he cannot 'be expected to communicate any further autobiographical particulars' now that his identity has merged with that of his readers: 'No, no, my friends! I am no longer interesting – I am only respectable like yourselves.'[7]

In *A Rogue's Life*, Collins follows Thackeray's precedent whenever he teases the appetite for sensationalism of readers who belong to the same middle-class society that exiles Frank. Yet unlike the Showman who discourages us from empathising with Becky Sharp or the moralist who asks us to look askance at the misconduct of Arthur Pendennis (like Frank Softly, the ne'er-do-well son of a respectable physician), Collins delightedly enters into Frank's shady activities, his contact with underworld figures such as Mr Ishmael Pickup, a Jewish art dealer who commissions the young man to forge old masters, and Doctor Dulcifer, a suave coiner who has advanced from the adulteration of wine to 'The more refined pursuit of adulterating gold and silver'.[8] Like Captain Wragge in *No Name* (1862), another colourful confidence man, Dulcifer easily evades the punitive retribution he would have received at the hands of most other Victorian novelists.

In his later career Collins continued to antagonise reviewers offended by his markedly sympathetic treatment of the villains and villainesses who had become his trademark. Increasingly sarcastic, he defended the characterisation of figures such as the voluptuous Miss Gwilt in *Armadale* (1866) by protesting that his work could be considered 'daring' only if 'estimated by the clap-trap morality of the present day'.[9] The clumsiness of such pronouncements, however, belies the subtlety with which he had undermined this morality in the counterworld of his masterpiece, *The Woman in White*.

The Woman in White depicts a collision between a lawful order in which identities are fixed and an anarchic lawlessness in which these social identities can be erased and destroyed. In the novel's 'Preamble', the chief narrator, Walter Hartright, draws an analogy between his chronological documentation of 'an offence against the laws' and the presentation through successive witnesses made by a prosecutor in a court of justice.[10] The reader of the novel's strands of narrative is thus invited to preside as judge and juror; we are asked to sift and assess the depositions made by a series of witnesses. Hartright's intended analogy between legal truth and his narrative truth, however, is subverted as soon as we are drawn into the story's incidents. A trial involves the knowledge of the offence and the offender; it relies on a detached, ex post facto analysis of events. But the narrative strips that Hartright has assembled draw us into the same time scheme of characters wholly unaware of their future; for a long time we share their ignorance of the offence alluded to in the 'Preamble' and adopt their false surmises, their uncertainties, their surprise. We become engaged in the narrative, not as impartial and objective judges but as subjective participants in a mystery – a mystery based on the irrational suspicions of the same figure who has posed in the 'Preamble' as a rational accuser before a rational court of law.

Hartright is the novel's prime orderer. Determined to restore Laura Fairlie's identity, he fulfils the same function as Scott's Richard [in *Ivanhoe*] and Dickens's Mr Brownlow [in *Oliver Twist*], those other agents for social reintegration. But Hartright's role is strangely qualified. Near the end of the novel, this fighter for the cause of truth admits that he has resorted to fiction in his presentation of the facts: to protect all characters, including himself, he has assigned them fictive names. The admission is significant: by giving the name of Petrarch's beloved to Laura Fairlie, the conventional, blonde, disingenuous heroine so unfairly treated by the villainous Sir Percival Glyde, and by calling attention to his own sound heart, Hartright resorts to obvious conventional precedents.[11] The stereotypes he adopts, however, are as inadequate as his analogy to a trial. The dutiful Laura who respects her father's wishes when she renounces Walter soon ceases to fit her assigned part as she becomes engulfed in the anarchic reality that prevails at Blackwater Park; she becomes so like the deranged outcast Anne Catherick that the keeper of the insane asylum cannot tell the two apart. Even Hartright ruefully admits that Laura no longer resembles the conventional beauty he fell in love with at Limmeridge House: the 'terror' that she has undergone has set its 'profaning marks' on her face; her 'fatal resemblance' to the madwoman who proves to be her sister has become 'real and living' (p. 341).

Laura's disenfranchisement converts her into Anne Catherick's double, a persecuted alien. But Hartright's own belief in 'law and reason' is affected by the madwoman whose touch sends an illicit thrill through his 'bosom'. On first meeting the apparition in white,

Walter so identifies with her plight that he lies to the lawmen who want to return her to the asylum. On meeting her again in the churchyard, he reads in the 'dark deformity of her expression' his own irrational feelings of hatred for Sir Percival (p. 77). His alienation is hers: she hides to escape confinement by those who brand her as insane; he flees to Honduras to avoid being overcome by madness and despair. Away from the civilised world he survives fever, murder, and drowning – all emblems of the death wish that almost destroys the less hardy Laura.

When Hartright returns to England to restore Laura's identity, he must resort to methods that lie outside the 'law and reason' to which Collins's Victorian readers presumably gave their assent. He considers wearing a disguise; he resorts to intimidation. Sir Percival the hunter of Anne and Hartright the hunter of Sir Percival's Secret resemble each other more and more. But Walter's true antagonist turns out to be Count Fosco, like himself an avenger with genuine motives for his revenge. Fosco taunts Marian Halcombe: 'Warn Mr. Hartright! ... He has a man of brains to deal with, a man who snaps his big fingers at the laws and conventions of society, when he measures himself with ME' (p. 433). Yet the count fails to reckon with Hartright's own alienation, his ability to operate outside 'the laws and conventions of society'. Walter soon learns that to reinstate Laura he cannot work within the legal fabric of society; it is the villains, Glyde and Fosco, who can avail themselves of the law. He therefore relies on the primitive habits he has acquired by walking with stealth: 'I had first learnt to use this stratagem against suspected treachery in the wilds of Central America – and now I was practising it again, with the same purpose and with even greater caution, in the heart of civilised London!' (p. 357). At the end Hartright resorts to even more uncivilised tactics: by betraying Fosco to members of the counterworld, the anarchists who belong to a secret terrorist society, he not only succeeds in dislodging the count but also becomes responsible for his assassination.

Hartright's confederate and fellow guardian of the sentimental Laura, the ugly, dark-haired Marian Halcombe, is also led to adopt the lawless tactics of the outsider. Although it is she who first invokes convention to part the young drawing master from her half-sister, she is herself unconventional, a descendant of both Scott's and Thackeray's Rebecca, whose passionate intelligence always breaks through the observances of etiquette. After she forces herself to acknowledge Sir Percival's handsome looks and his seemingly 'considerate and unselfish' behaviour, she immediately disclaims, 'I hate Sir Percival! I flatly deny his good looks. I consider him to be eminently disagreeable' (p. 147). Aggressive and direct, she displays none of Laura's submissive acquiescence. Incensed at a fat servant who tells her that the keeper shot a wounded dog, she exclaims, 'I was almost wicked enough to wish that Baxter had shot the housemaid instead' (p. 158). On seeing the marks on Laura's wrists, she does not shrink from the thought of murdering Sir Percival: 'They say we are either better than men, or worse. If the temptation that has fallen in some women's way, and made them worse, had fallen in mine, at that moment – Thank God! my face betrayed nothing' (p. 232).

If the Walter Hartright who skulks around London is hardly the civilised man of feeling who renounced Laura Fairlie to Sir Percival, the Marian Halcombe who spies on Fosco and Sir Percival by lying on a roof in a dark, rain-drenched cape is hardly the same Victorian lady whose delicacy prevented her from further inquiry into Sir Percival's reputation. Collins delights in portraying the metamorphoses of beings forced to shed their civilised identities. But just as Walter and Laura revert to their stereotypical roles after Fosco's defeat, so does Marian Halcombe again become a subsidiary figure, the kindly maiden aunt of Laura's and Walter's child. Collins deliberately toys with the artificiality of this return to convention; he makes it clear that the unconventional sensibility that Marian displayed makes her a potential fellow rebel of Count Fosco, Marian's stout admirer. If Laura, the sentimental heroine with the Petrarchan name, is the heroine of Hartright's narrative, a narrative that concludes on the side of convention and law and order, Marian Halcombe is the heroine of the novel that Fosco would have written if his notion of 'truth', and not that of Hartright, were allowed to dominate. The Italian count, too, knows his Petrarch when he calls Marian 'my adored enemy'.

Long before we sense Fosco's infatuation with Marian, an infatuation that prompts his only acts of imprudence, we are made aware of Marian's acute interest in the foreign nobleman: 'he excites my strongest interest ... I wonder if he will ever come to England? I wonder if I shall like him?' (p. 147). When Laura describes Madame Fosco, her aunt, Marian deplores the absence of any allusion to the count, 'who interests me infinitely more'. When the party arrives at Blackwater Park, Marian records her impressions, quickly disposing of the wife as a mere example of the count's power of taming this 'once wayward Englishwoman'. She is mesmerised by the husband who 'has interested me, has attracted me, has forced me to like him' (p. 167), and her elaborately detailed description of the count, his pet animals, his vests, his corpulence, permits the reader to share her fascination as well as her flattered response to his quick recognition of her own fine intelligence.

Collins skilfully encourages the reader to regard this unconventional pair as the true protagonists of his novel, far more deserving of our sympathy and interest than Hartright and his insipid Laura. We are made to entertain the union between these two characters far more seriously than the union between Rebecca and Bois-Gilbert [in Scott's *Ivanhoe*]. Like Scott, Collins has Marian reject her kinship with the Rebel; unlike Scott, however, Collins does not endorse the rejection. Quite the contrary, he makes it clear that Marian's sudden revulsion over the count's 'horrible admiration' (p. 432) involves a repression of her own asocial impulses. It is neither Fosco's actions against Laura nor the 'glib cynicism' she professes to find in his philosophy that causes Marian to recoil; what so unsettles her is the discovery that Fosco has invaded the privacy of her diary, read her innermost thoughts, and concluded that a civilised English lady is a fellow anarchist, 'a person of similar sensibility' (p. 262). She denies this judgement and insists that she be vindicated, that Hartright pursue revenge for her sake. She prefers the safety of the stereotype of self-renouncing friend, Hartright's desexualised 'sister'.

Through the figure of Fosco, however, Collins makes the reader see that Marian is only a step away from the count's licentious counterworld. To Fosco, renunciation is a meaningless act, at odds with true instinct: he deplores that his lawful wife should but get 'the shillings and pennies' of his affection, while 'the gold of my rich nature' is poured hopelessly at Marian's feet, but he accepts his faithless impulses with ease: 'Such is the world, such Man; such Love. What are we (I ask) but puppets in a show-box?' (pp. 475–6). Regarding moral strictures as but an artificial superimposition on the true nature of human beings, Fosco considers a ménage à trois; he views the ugly woman whom Hartright can see only in a formal and socialised role as a 'magnificent creature who is inscribed in my heart as "Marian" – who is known in the colder atmosphere of Society, as "Miss Halcombe"' (p. 475).

In *The Woman in White* that colder atmosphere prevails, but not until Collins has given a fuller hearing than any of his English predecessors to the antisocial voice of the Rebel. Fosco's long exposition of his philosophy to Marian stresses a logic that Dickens had suppressed in *Oliver Twist* and that Thackeray had employed only for satirical purposes in *Vanity Fair*, namely, that crime can pay. Fosco asks Marian: 'Which gets on the best, do you think, of two poor starving dressmakers – the woman who resists temptation, and is honest, or the woman who falls under temptation, and steals? You all know that the stealing is the making of that second woman's fortune – it advertises her from length to breadth of good-humoured, charitable England – and she is relieved, as the breaker of a commandment, when she would have been left to starve, as the keeper of it' (p. 181).

Fosco's point is borne out by Anne Catherick's mother. She has yielded to the money of Sir Percival and to the good looks of Philip Fairlie, the blond father absurdly trusted by Laura as the truest and best of men. But her goal is respectability. Like Becky Sharp standing in her booth in the charity bazaar, Mrs Catherick exults in her acceptance by the same society that denies Laura her identity: 'I stand high enough in this town, to be out of your reach. The clergyman bows to me' (pp. 383–4). Yet this prospective member of the Dorcas Society can also write to Hartright, 'If I was a young woman still, I might say "Come! put your arm round my waist, and kiss me, if you like." … and you would have accepted my invitation' (p. 417). As Fosco recognises, social decorum is but a veneer.

There is much of Collins' own bohemianism in Fosco's quick rejection of Hartright's high-sounding words; using the same vocabulary that Collins employed in the diatribes against his reviewers, the count vows: 'Your moral clap-traps have an excellent effect in England – keep them for yourself and your countrymen, if you please' (p. 467). The name Fosco may mean 'dark' or 'sinister', but there nonetheless is a clear logic in the man who delights in stripping Laura Fairlie of her respectable identity. Like Scott and Dickens before him, Collins kills off his version of the rebel. Significantly, though, the forces of law and reason cannot punish the count; he is murdered by the anarchists that Hartright has unleashed. The enormous corpse is surrounded by a wailing group of Frenchwomen who lift their 'hands in admiration, and [cry], in shrill chorus, "Ah, what a handsome man!"' (p. 495). Madame Fosco pays her own tribute when she writes a biography which, like Collins's own 'public' biography of his father, contains only praise of the dead man's 'domestic virtues, the assertion of his rare abilities'. On the last page she writes: 'His life was one long assertion of the rights of the aristocracy, and the sacred principles of Order' (p. 496).

Despite Collins's irony, Madame Fosco's tribute is not incorrect: the aristocratic Fosco has asserted certain principles of order at variance with middle-class Victorian morality. Fosco sees a universe that is not governed by the Providence that Hartright and Marian invoke after the fashion of Dickens and Scott: 'Mind, they say, rules the world. But what rules the mind? The body. The body (follow me closely here) lies at the mercy of the most omnipotent of all mortal potentates – the Chemist. Give me – Fosco – chemistry; and when Shakespeare has conceived Hamlet, and sits down to execute the conception – with a few grains of powder dropped into his daily food, I will reduce his mind, by the action of the body, till his pen pours out the most abject drivel that has ever degraded paper. Under similar circumstances, revive me the illustrious Newton' (pp. 477–8).

In *The Woman in White* Collins deftly undermines the fictional conventions he purports to follow. Although, like his predecessors, he portrays the eventual triumph of order, he forces the reader to admit the justice of Fosco's anarchic belief in the frailty of our social identities. Only through evasion and incomprehension can men and women manage to resist the truths of a darker counterworld: like so many Conradian heroines, the well-meaning Mrs Michaelson stays protected in her orderly world; surrounded by her husband's sermons, she never sees the truths that Marian Halcombe rejects.

Collins compels us to empathise with the man who so clearly prefers animals to humans. (Fosco's horse is called Isaac of York; his favourite white mouse may well be called Rebecca.) The foreign count's denial of the Victorian morality of renunciation and his absolute freedom from scruples are those of Bois-Gilbert, Fagin, and Becky Sharp. But it is noteworthy that Collins also had to go outside English fiction for a precedent: the eccentric Isidor Ottavio Baldassare Fosco is an adaptation of Count Mosca of [Stendhal's] *The Charterhouse of Parma*, another middle-aged nihilist who openly defies conventional morality. In *The Rebel* Camus asks why a figure like Count Mosca should appear so much more familiar than 'our professional moralists'.[12] The answer, clearly understood by Collins though rejected by Marian Halcombe, is obvious:

beneath our acceptance of the social codes by which we live lurks the nihilism of the amoralist.

From *The Worlds of Victorian Fiction*, ed. J. H. Buckley (Cambridge, MA, 1975), pp. 351–69.

NOTES

[This is an extract from an influential essay in which U. C. Knoepflmacher makes the case for reading Collins as a subversive writer. This case is made in the context of a wider discussion of a number of mid-Victorian novels which, it is argued, might be included in Albert Camus's category of a 'literature of rebellion' on the grounds that they all suggest the existence of an asocial and amoral 'counterworld' lurking beneath the ordered, civilised world on which the official morality of the Victorian novel was posited. Knoepflmacher suggests that, unlike his more successful contemporary Dickens, Collins made no attempt to disguise his fascination with the amorality of this counterworld, and repeatedly antagonised reviewers with his lively and sympathetic portrayal of outspoken villains and villainesses such as the transgressive, anarchic Count Fosco with his belief in the fragility of social and moral identity. Knoepflmacher explores various aspects of Collins's preoccupation with questions of identity, and he also examines the narrative sleights of hand in which Collins engages, and addresses the issue of the supposed objectivity of the dispersal of the narration to a range of narrators who tell their stories as if testifying in a court of law. Omitted from the extract reprinted here is Knoepflmacher's discussion of the way in which rebellious social attitudes are repudiated yet indulged in Sir Walter Scott's *Ivanhoe*, Charles Dickens's *Oliver Twist*, and William Makepeace Thackeray's *Vanity Fair*. Ed.]

1. Albert Camus, *The Rebel* (New York, 1956), pp. 258, 259, 263.

2. Ibid., p. 264.

3. Quoted in Robert Ashley, *Wilkie Collins* (London, 1952), p. 109.

4. Quoted in Kenneth Robinson, *Wilkie Collins: A Biography* (New York, 1952), p. 71.

5. See, for instance, Dickens's concern about Collins's proposed dramatisation of *Armadale*: 'Almost every situation in it is dangerous. I do not think any English audience would accept the scene in which Miss Gwilt in widow's dress renounces Midwinter' (9 July 1866, *Letters of Charles Dickens to Wilkie Collins: 1851–1870*, ed. Laurence Hutton [London, 1982], p. 132). Collins, in turn, felt misgivings about Dickens's prudery: he claimed that since the portrayal of Nancy in

Oliver Twist Dickens 'never afterwards saw all sides of a woman's character – saw all round her' (Robinson, *Wilkie Collins*, p. 258).

6. *A Rogue's Life: From His Birth to His Marriage* (New York, n.d.), p. 202.

7. Ibid., pp. 302–4.

8. Ibid., pp. 121–2.

9. *Armadale* (New York, 1874), p. 9.

10. *The Woman in White*, ed. Kathleen Tillotson and Anthea Trodd (Boston, 1969), p. 1. Further references to this work are given in the text.

11. Hartright's unsubtle use of Petrarch differs markedly from Collins's subtle use of Dante, traced by Peter Caracciolo in 'Wilkie Collins' "Divine Comedy": The Use of Dante in *The Woman in White*', *Nineteenth-Century Fiction*, 25 (1971), 383–404.

12. *The Rebel*, p. 260.

3

The Sensationalism of
The Woman in White

WALTER M. KENDRICK

One aim of Henry James's 'The Art of Fiction' (1884) is to dispose of some misconceptions which have obscured the understanding of what novels are. Prominent among these hindrances to clarity is the 'old-fashioned' distinction between the 'novel of incident' and the 'novel of character'. No practising novelist, according to James, can ever have paid much attention to this clumsy separation. It must have been devised by critics and readers to help them out of the 'queer predicaments' into which they sometimes stumble.

> It appears to me as little to the point as the equally celebrated distinction between the novel and the romance – to answer as little to any reality. There are bad novels and good novels, as there are bad pictures and good pictures; but that is the only distinction in which I see any meaning, and I can as little imagine speaking of a novel of character as I can imagine speaking of a picture of character.[1]

In a general sense, the distinction which James dismissed in 1884 had been a topic of literary discussion since Aristotle. The particular terms which he attacked, however, were of much more recent date. The separation of novels of incident from novels of character had been devised to deal with the queer predicament of British criticism in the 1860s, when the sudden popularity of the 'sensation novel' seemed to challenge the supremacy of fictional realism.[2]

The sensation novel had a long and various literary ancestry.[3] But its major significance for mid-Victorian novel theory was the

70

demonstration that novels could be successfully, even brilliantly written according to principles which seemed to contradict those of realism. The sensation novel, most prominently represented by the works of Wilkie Collins, defined the territory of the novel of incident; while the realistic novel, epitomised by the works of Trollope and George Eliot, established criteria for the novel of character. Using this distinction, critics were able to map the hectic field of the contemporary novel and also to find both types in the literature of the past. And, despite James's confident dismissal, these types have endured in criticism long past the decade of their discovery, outliving many of the novels which first made them visible.[4]

In whatever terms this distinction has been expressed, it has based, as it was for mid-Victorian critics, on the notion that all novels are composed of two elements, plot and character. If a novel favours one element, it must slight the other; and the relative preponderance of plot or character in any novel will allow one to place it among either the novels of incident or the novels of character. In its crudest form, this understanding of narrative led mid-Victorian critics to a conception of the novel as a kind of vessel into which a limited amount of compositional liquid could be poured. Plot and character, like oil and water, could be combined but never fused. Subtler critics took plot and character to be only differing functions of a single narrative enterprise, but plot remained alien or even hostile to character, and any novel which devoted itself to one had by necessity to neglect the other.

The problem is reflected in the incommensurate figures which the mid-Victorians employed in discussing these two aspects of narrative. Plot was commonly figured as a chain or a road, while character was a drawing or a portrait. There is no way in which these two figures can be conveniently combined, and the occasional attempts to do so produced some extraordinary mixed metaphors.[5] The matter is further complicated by a strong tendency to attribute the whole value of a novel to its painting of character portraits and to regard the linking together of plot as a merely mechanical business. Plot was a vehicle, and the worth of the novel resided in what it conveyed, not in the conveyance. Anthony Trollope, for example, was accustomed to speak of plot as 'a vehicle of some sort' (*An Autobiography*, ch. 7) or a thing which could be borrowed from one's brother as one might borrow a fresh pen-nib (ch. 6). In his habitual denigration of plot, Trollope was in agreement with the generality of mid-Victorian literary critics.

The complaint most commonly brought against the sensation novelists was that, because they devoted all their attention to the construction of intricate plots, they ignored the painting of character. This deficiency was seen as not only an aesthetic but also a moral flaw. As G. H. Lewes observed of M. E. Braddon, she could never attain true eminence so long as her 'grasp of character' remained inferior to her 'power over plot-interest'.[6] It was generally held that Wilkie Collins, who persistently claimed a place in the 'front rank' of novelists, could never make that claim good unless he learned how 'to create a character which the world shall recognise as an addition to the number of living beings'.[7]

The figure of character painting implies that there is a structure in the real world which pre-exists and governs its fictional representation. Because the novel is bound to the temporal succession of narrative, it must assemble its portraits stroke by stroke. But this sequence is of no more importance to the finished representation than is the order of a painter's brush strokes to the picture he turns out. For mid-Victorian critics and realistic novelists, the value of fiction depended on its cultivation of what the real world already contained. The language of which the fictional text is made and even the fact that it is a text should efface themselves before the illusion that what it represents is real. This realistic imperative motivated the works of the great mid-Victorian realists as well as their reception by critics.[8] It is apparent, for example, in George Eliot's declaration of good faith in chapter 17 of *Adam Bede*, and in Trollope's delighted approval of Hawthorne's remark that his novels are 'just as real as if some giant had hewn a great lump out of the earth and put it under a glass case' (*An Autobiography*, ch. 8).

The major sin of the sensation novelists was their breach of this realistic faith. By focusing the reader's attention on the chains that constitute a novel's plot, they made of fiction merely a game, an activity which dictates its own rules and which stands to the real world in at best an arbitrary relation. Much of the outrage inspired in mid-Victorian critics by the sensation novel came from their perception that the value of the elements in such a novel depended primarily, like that of links in a chain, on their relation to other elements in the same novel – and not, like that of the brush strokes in a portrait, on their correspondence to something in the real world. As Alexander Smith complained of Collins's novels, 'every trifling incident is charged with an oppressive importance; if a teacup is broken, it has a meaning, it is a link in a chain; you are certain to hear of it afterwards'.[9] The reader of a sensation novel engages in the discovery of an artificial pattern, and the enterprise need not teach him anything, even anything false, about the real world. At its best, the sensation novel aspired towards the condition of a crossword puzzle, a system of language which is governed only by its own design. As such, it was potentially subversive of the belief that fiction is and must be mimetic.

Most sensation novels were ephemeral productions, turned out and consumed in haste; and most sensation novelists were unaware of the implications of the genre or unable to exploit them. But in one case, sensationalism was practised by a self-conscious innovator who understood the terms of critical debate and took enthusiastic part in it. Throughout the 1860s, most critics gave dubious credit to Wilkie Collins for having 'founded' the sensation novel, and they looked to him for the best that could be done in the genre. Collins took the responsibility of his position very seriously, endeavouring to win recognition for himself as an artist and for his novels as advances in new directions. To a large extent, however, his reputation has been determined by the brief duration of the craze he helped to initiate. He was, as the *Athenaeum* called him, '*facile princeps* ... in a transient school',[10] and he is now generally remembered either as an adjunct to Dickens or as yet another candidate for the role of grandfather to the twentieth-century detective novel.

From the perspective of this essay, however, Collins's first great success, *The Woman in White*, can be seen as more than a historical artifact or a primitive precursor of Agatha Christie. The novel is very much concerned with the problems of plot and character, form and imitation, artifice and authenticity, which occupied the debate over literary sensationalism. It is a significant departure from the realism of Trollope and George Eliot, and it exploits its sensational techniques with remarkable ingenuity. At the same time, it is founded in the realistic faith which it violates. The novel exhibits a double urge towards conventionality and innovation, taking full advantage of its sensationalism but at the same time demanding that it be read as if it were realistic.

The Woman in White was first published in *All the Year Round*, appearing in forty weekly instalments between 26 November 1859 and 25 August 1860. It was revised and a preface was added for immediate publication in three volumes. Further revisions were made, including a new preface, for a second edition in February

1861. The first set of revisions had the intention, according to the 1860 Preface, of 'smoothing and consolidating' the text. Many of the later revisions, however, represent a direct response to adverse criticism of the first edition. A serious complex of errors had been uncovered by the *Times*, which reported them in its review of the novel. These Collins tried to correct, though the 1861 Preface dismisses them as 'certain technical errors' and 'little blemishes' which had no effect on the 'interest of the narrative'.[11]

Much of the third volume of *The Woman in White* is devoted to Walter Hartright's efforts to prove that Lady Glyde did not arrive in London on 25 July, the date of her supposed death, because she did not leave Hampstead until 26 July. The one weak point in the evil intrigue of Sir Percival and Count Fosco is this discrepancy in dates, the discovery of which proves that the woman buried in Limmeridge churchyard is not Lady Glyde. As the *Times* observed, however, it is possible to establish from the sequence of dates set up in the first two volumes that Lady Glyde could not have arrived in London before 9 or 10 August, leaving a gap of more than two weeks between the conspiracy and the 'truth'. This truth, furthermore, as any attentive reader might assemble it, turns the hero's discovery of a one-day discrepancy into as much a fraud as the villainous plot he reveals. In its first edition, the third volume of *The Woman in White* is, as the *Times* called it, 'a mockery, a delusion, and a snare'.[12]

For the 1861 edition, Collins attempted to correct these errors by setting all relevant dates back sixteen days. In doing so, however, he passed over Mrs Clements's testimony (pp. 414–19), which contains no numerical dating but which can be coordinated with the other narratives by phrases like 'the next day' and 'a fortnight later'. This brief section of Volume III had been 'true' according to Hartright's discovery, but in the second edition it puts Anne Catherick in London sixteen days too early. The second edition, therefore, and all subsequent editions based on it, continue to mock, delude, and snare their readers – although for more than a century no one seems to have been disturbed by the fact.

Errors of this kind would be, no doubt, of little importance for the reading of most novels, but they are of special interest in this case, because *The Woman in White* insists on its verifiable accuracy as a text and because Hartright applies to various fictional documents exactly the method of investigation employed by the *Times* reviewer. Collins had even gone so far as to request, in the 1860 Preface, that reviewers should give away none of the 'hundreds of little "connecting links", of trifling value in themselves, but of the utmost importance in maintaining the smoothness, the reality, and the probability of the entire narrative'. These little links are trifling and crucial at once. They do not guarantee the novel's correspondence to some structure outside of itself; rather, they guarantee that the novel will form a system which is consistent in all its parts. The reader will be able to validate the novel's coherence, but not by comparing it to something he has felt or seen elsewhere. Rather, he will be able to compare one part of the novel with another, using as his standard the novel's own scale of dates and durations. If the reader accepts this undertaking and if the writer constructs a system which completes its own requirements, then the contract between them is fulfilled. This is the radical contract of sensationalism, and it makes the only necessary link between the fictional world and the world of its reader.

The Woman in White is a series of documents which have been put in their present order for a specific purpose. In the brief 'Preamble' which begins the novel,[13] Hartright explains the rationale of the arrangement. The events to be narrated here should have reached public attention in a 'Court of Justice'; but, since 'the Law is still, in certain inevitable cases, the pre-engaged servant of the long purse', due process has been impossible. The novel will therefore take the form of courtroom testimony: 'As the Judge might once have heard it, so the Reader shall hear it now.' Each narrative will represent the eyewitness experiences of one participant in the case. These narratives have been placed, by Hartright, in a sequence which answers to the two criteria of immediacy and continuity:

> When the writer of these introductory lines ... happens to be more closely connected than others with the incidents to be recorded, he will describe them in his own person. When his experience fails, he will retire from the position of narrator; and his task will be continued, from the point at which he has left it off, by other persons who can speak to the circumstances under notice from their own knowledge, just as clearly and positively as he has spoken before them.

This method will attain the double object of presenting 'the truth always in its most direct and most intelligible aspect' and of tracing 'the course of one complete series of events' (p. 1).

It is evident from the start that Hartright is writing at some time after the completion of this series of events and that his understanding of the whole series has brought him to arrange the narratives in this order. Hartright's privilege is shared by no other narrator. All of them have written their testimony at a time which falls within the limits of the series as Hartright defines it, and none of them has the advantage of knowing what events will follow those which he himself describes. As the editor of the collection of documents called *The Woman in White*, Hartright sees the story whole, from the beginning, and he has arranged its components so that they form at once a temporal and a causal continuity. He figures the course of the novel as a 'dark road' (p. 373) which advances 'to an appointed and an inevitable end' (p. 253), and as a 'chain' which 'reaches fairly from the outset of the story to the close' (p. 564).

The criteria of immediacy and continuity are, as Hartright establishes them, apparently complementary. In its two stages of revision, the novel was made to look more and more like a continuous whole. In the serial, each section was labelled only with the name of its narrator, but in the first book-edition these titles were changed so that we read from 'The Story Begun by Walter Hartright' through 'The Story Continued' by the other narrators, to 'The Story Concluded' by Hartright again. In both the serial and the 1860 edition, the novel was divided into two unequal parts, but in 1861 this division was replaced by three 'Epochs', each corresponding to one volume. In its final form, the novel attempts not only to smooth over the discontinuous appearance of a story told by several narrators but to minimise even the interruptions made by putting down one volume and picking up another.

Hartright's 'Preamble' maintains that events, narration, and the reading of the novel make a single sequence. Changes in the name of the narrator should not affect this triple unity. In practice, however, the chain of narrators does not correspond to the chain of events: nothing in the events requires that their progress should be told by the sequence of voices which Hartright has chosen. These voices make their own sequence, superimposed upon and not always in close touch with the sequence of events. Reading *The Woman in White* is an experience quite unlike living it, though Hartright's rhetoric of continuity insists throughout that the two experiences are one. The sequence of narrators provides no step-by-step development of events, but rather a series of sudden revelations. Each time a narrator belatedly uncovers some fragment of the truth, there is an abrupt adjustment of his and the reader's vision. These adjustments produce what for mid-Victorian critics was the real aim of a novel like this one – a series of 'sensations'.

Margaret Oliphant's 1862 review of *The Woman in White*, which prophetically names it the founder of a new 'school' in fiction, picks out two 'sensation scenes' for special notice. The first occurs early in Hartright's initial narrative; it is, in Mrs Oliphant's estimation, 'a sensation scene of the most delicate and skilful kind'.[14]

> I ... was strolling along the lonely high-road – idly wondering, I remember, what the Cumberland young ladies would look like – when, in one moment, every drop of blood in my body was brought to a stop by the touch of a hand laid lightly and suddenly on my shoulder from behind me.
>
> (p. 14)

This touch marks Hartright's first encounter with the woman in white. The high-road becomes the 'road' which the novel travels, and this encounter becomes the 'cause' of others which follow it. The chain of sensational revelations leads back eventually to Anne Catherick's illegitimate conception in August 1826; and it is only when the reader has learned this fact, which is revealed some five hundred pages later, that he knows the full sequence of causes which brought the woman in white to the high-road after midnight. This chain of sensations, which leads the reader on an anti-Shandean course *ad ovum*, adds a third chain to those of narrators and of events. And again, in spite of the 'Preamble', this chain is far from coincident with the other two.

All the questions which this scene raises in Hartright's mind – how has this woman come here? why does she wear white? who is the Baronet she fears and why does she fear him? – obtain answers at some point in the novel, but only the revelations come in chronological sequence. The immediate cause of her presence is her escape from the Asylum that same evening (p. 21); she wears white because of Mrs Fairlie's kindness to her in 1837 (pp. 48–9); she fears Sir Percival Glyde (p. 90) because he had her committed a short time before her appearance on the high-road (p. 119); and he had her committed because she claims to know his Secret, which she learned about the time she took to wearing white (p. 485). The order of these answers is less like a road or a chain than a 'mosaic of evidence', as the sharp-eyed *Times* reviewer called the novel, to which pieces may be added at any time, in any sequence. The woman in white herself is a bundle of potential sensations, who exists in the novel only in order to provide them one at a time.

Mrs Oliphant's second great 'sensation scene' also occurs early in the novel, at the end of the third serial instalment. At Hartright's first meeting with Laura Fairlie, he had observed 'something wanting' in her (p. 41). With this odd idea still on his mind, he sits down to hear Marian read from Mrs Fairlie's letters the explanation of how Anne Catherick came to Limmeridge and how she began to wear white. Meanwhile, tying a 'white handkerchief' about her head, Laura goes out to walk on the terrace in the 'soft, mysterious rays' of the moon (p. 46). As Marian reads about the 'walking mystery' of Mrs Catherick (p. 47), Hartright watches Laura's figure, 'bright and soft in its snowy muslin dress – her face prettily framed by the white folds of the handkerchief which she had tied under her chin' (p. 48). As Marian asks him how old the woman on the high-road was (Laura's age) and how she was dressed ('all in white'), Hartright begins to notice something. But it takes Mrs Fairlie's comments on the resemblance between Laura and Anne to bring the truth upon him:

> I started up from the ottoman before Miss Halcombe could pro-
> nounce the next words. A thrill of the same feeling which ran
> through me when the touch was laid upon my shoulder on the lonely
> high-road chilled me again.
> There stood Miss Fairlie, a white figure, alone in the moonlight; in
> her attitude, in the turn of her head, in her complexion, in the shape
> of her face, the living image, at that distance and under those cir-
> cumstances, of the woman in white!
>
> (p. 50)

All doubt now turns to conviction, the 'something wanting' in Laura is now explained – and the effect, as Mrs Oliphant remarks, is 'pure sensation, neither more nor less' ('Sensation Novels', p. 572).

The resemblance between Laura and Anne Catherick is the pivotal device of *The Woman in White*. Fosco's evil plot consists merely in the extension of what Hartright himself has introduced to the reader: the similar appearance of the two women. Through an illegitimate synecdoche, Fosco makes whiteness stand for all there is of both; from this he moves to the fatal metaphor by which Anne is made to take Laura's place in her grave. The principal crime in *The Woman in White* is the perpetration of this false metaphor. Indeed, as Mrs Oliphant observes, Fosco is likely to strike most readers as 'rather an ill-used personage than otherwise', hardly the 'impersonation of evil' that Hartright and Marian take him to be ('Sensation

Novels', p. 567). But in the morality of *The Woman in White*, false rhetoric is the worst of crimes, and Fosco is guilty on several counts of criminal figuration. Yet he is apparently no more guilty than Hartright himself, whose tricks ought equally to be condemned by the novel which displays them. There is, however, one great difference: in order to provide sensations in plenty, Hartright must do what his archenemy does; but Hartright's victim is only the reader, and the crime is only the reader's desire to be duped.

Before Fosco decides to exchange her for Laura, Anne has been making sensational appearances in the neighbourhood of Blackwater Park, dropping hints that she knows some dire 'Secret' about Sir Percival. These appearances alternate in the novel with a clumsy conspiracy to make Laura turn over her property to her husband by signing documents which have been folded to hide all but the signature space. By sheer frequency of juxtaposition, it comes to seem that the mystery of Anne's 'Secret' must be related in some way to this intrigue over twenty thousand pounds. Until nearly the end of the novel, Hartright's investigations of Anne's past are carried on as if they will lead to a discovery about the crucial discrepancy in dates. Eventually he does find a cause for the resemblance between the two women: Anne is Laura's illegitimate half-sister (p. 502). He discovers as well the nature of the Secret: Sir Percival is illegitimate, too (p. 461). But his most striking discovery is that Anne, for all her hinting, knew only that there was a Secret, not what it amounted to. Her hints were only the repetition, 'like a parrot', of angry words her mother had once used in her presence (p. 487). With this revelation, the apparent connection between Anne's history and Laura's fortune is shown at last to be illusory. In just Fosco's manner, the novel has taken two complexes of features, some of which correspond, and implied that they all do – proving finally that the correspondence is no greater than it first appeared to be. A grand rhetorical quibble is carried on for five hundred pages, and the result is that the only traits which the women have truly in common are those accidents of dress, attitude, and complexion that Hartright noticed in the second sensation scene.

Both Hartright and his opponents deal throughout the novel in texts and documents of many kinds, continually examining, comparing, and emending them. Just as the villains are rhetorical criminals, whose principal crime is the distortion of the written word, so Hartright is a rhetorical hero, who engages in a long campaign of textual reconstruction, the final achievement of which is the novel itself. Some of the villains' tricks are crude and obvious – trying to make Laura sign a concealed document or substituting a blank sheet for Marian's letter to Mr Kyrle (p. 312). Others are more ingenious, or at least more sensational. When Marian collapses in fever after a strenuous session with her diary, her writing trails off. The next page, however, contains a 'Postscript by a Sincere Friend', a statement by Fosco, who has doubly violated this text by reading it and then by writing upon it himself (pp. 302–4). When Laura arrives at the Asylum, dazed and drugged, she is dressed in Anne's clothes, and her feeble efforts to convince the matron that there has been an error are met by the latter's bland exclamation, on reading her labelled linen: 'Anne Catherick, as plain as print!' (p. 385).

The most evil false text in the novel is the inscription on the Fairlie tombstone, which declares in letters of stone that Laura is buried there and that she died on 25 July. The 'Narrative of the Tombstone' is the only explicitly mendacious case among the 'several narratives' which conclude Volume II, and it is the culmination of Hartright's campaign when, with the whole village of Limmeridge gathered round to watch, the lying words are chipped away (p. 563). Fosco, too, is done away with by reinscription. Seeing him for the last time, in the Paris morgue, Hartright observes that the brand on his upper arm, which had marked him as a member of the Italian 'Brotherhood', has been obliterated by 'two deep cuts in the shape of the letter T'. He learns later that the T stands for 'Traditore', and with this accurate label the Count descends to the grave (p. 567).

Sir Percival's Secret is also a textual one. Led by various evidence to the vestry of Old Welmingham Church, Hartright examines the parish register book for the entry on the marriage of Sir Percival's parents. There is nothing remarkable about the entry except 'the narrowness of the space into which it was compressed at the bottom of the page' (p. 453). But, since there is a duplicate register at Knowlesbury, he resolves to examine it as well. The result is sensational.

> My heart gave a great bound, and throbbed as if it would stifle me. I looked again – I was afraid to believe the evidence of my own eyes. No! not a doubt. The marriage was not there. ... The last entry on one page recorded the marriage of the man with my Christian name. Below it there was a blank space. ... That space told the whole story!
>
> (p. 460)

Sir Percival, too late to prevent this discovery, sets fire to the church vestry and is trapped in the burning building. When Hartright and the townspeople break down the door, they can see no trace of the villain. They see 'nothing but a sheet of living fire' (p. 469).

Sir Percival begins as a blank space and ends as a blank sheet of flame. His life has been a forged document, and justice erases him. In a similar way, the white figure of Anne Catherick, so portentous in the first sensation scene, dwindles in significance with each new discovery about her – until, when all is known, she vanishes, as blankly insignificant as her own white clothing.

> So the ghostly figure which has haunted these pages, as it haunted my life, goes down into the impenetrable gloom. Like a shadow she first came to me in the loneliness of the night. Like a shadow she passes away in the loneliness of the dead.
>
> (p. 504)

Sir Percival owes his power and position to a few lines of writing where there ought to be a space; Anne Catherick is a blank, written over in life by her own delusion and in death by another woman's name. Laura herself, though she is supposed to be the novel's heroine, exists primarily as a name written on a folded parchment and inscribed on a white tombstone, both of which spaces ought to remain blank. As the champion of textual integrity, Hartright has the duty of erasing that name, and in the end he completes his mission by marrying Laura and changing her name permanently.

Villainy and heroism alike in *The Woman in White* operate on the assumption that there is such a thing as a transparent text, an ordered arrangement of words and spaces which can be taken as proof of events in the real world and even as a substitute for them. The corrupt texts of Glyde and Fosco are discredited only by other texts gathered by Hartright. In the dense rhetorical atmosphere of the novel, characters exist as collections of signatures, register entries, letters, and laundry marks. Empty spaces tell stories, and a tombstone makes a narrative. There is no way of knowing which of these texts is transparent and which corrupt except by comparison with other texts which are taken on trust to be honest. If these texts fail, then others still must be found to support them. But the endless chain of text on text cannot get beyond the fact that a true word is indistinguishable from a forged one, that all blanks are equally white. The textual chain cannot verify itself; it must be broken at some point and attached to a trust not derived from words.

For Hartright, this trust is established at the end of the second Epoch when, although chronology continues to march forward, the novel doubles back on itself. Hartright's campaign of textual renovation is set moving by an experience which cancels the similitude set up in the second sensation scene three hundred pages before. Returning to England after several months in Central America, Hartright visits Laura's tomb in Limmeridge churchyard. As he stands by the grave, a veiled woman approaches.

> She stopped on one side of the grave. We stood face to face with the tombstone between us. She was close to the inscription on the side of the pedestal. Her gown touched the black letters. ...
> The woman lifted her veil.
> 'Sacred to the Memory of Laura, Lady Glyde—'
> Laura, Lady Glyde, was standing by the inscription, and was looking at me over the grave.
>
> (p. 370)

All of Hartright's subsequent investigations of diaries, letters, and register books are anchored in this striking moment when language is negated by the sight of a living face. From this point onward, Hartright will devote himself to the correction of texts, but his entire campaign depends upon an immediate vision which transcends the lies of language – just the sort of direct felt sympathy which was the ultimate goal of mid-Victorian realism. Hartright breaks the textual chain by believing that Laura's face cannot lie. The reader of *The Woman in White* has already broken it by believing, as the novel urges him to do, that a man named Hartright has a heart which is right and writes from his heart. For Hartright, this trust leads to love and eventual happiness; for the reader, it leads to a series of sensational deceptions.

Despite the continuous chronology which makes Volume III look like a sequel to Volumes I and II, most of the third volume is a retelling of earlier matter either in word-for-word transcription by Hartright or in his paraphrase of other narrators. The period from 20 to 26 July, which has already been treated by Mrs Michelson, Hester Pinhorn, Jane Gould, Dr Goodricke, and the tombstone, is renarrated by Marian, Laura, Mrs Clements, and Count Fosco, along with earlier and subsequent information which sets the crucial period in a motivated context. Each of these renarrators fills in some omissions in earlier testimony and leaves gaps for later narrators to fill. The story is not made complete until a letter from Sir Percival and a cabman's order, both dated 26 July, are obtained. Joining these to his other texts, Hartright is at last able to announce, 'I now had in my possession all the papers that I wanted' (p. 559). These papers, brought before the sceptical lawyer, constitute 'the plainest evidence he had ever heard in his life' (p. 562). Compiled as a 'plain narrative of the conspiracy', they convince the Limmeridge townspeople of Laura's identity (p. 560). Fleshed out by Hartright's narrative and the later addition of other evidence, they make *The Woman in White*. But by this time, with Laura recognised again, her home restored, and all villainy disposed of, the pugnacious 'Preamble' has lost its motivation. The reason for the novel's existence, which it provides with great care on page one, has been used up by its end. In retrospect, it looks as if there never was any reason for the novel to exist at all.

Everything, indeed, which the 'Preamble' guarantees evaporates during the course of the novel. The technique of first-person testimony, which the 'Preamble' claims will make the events clear and positive, is the principal means by which they become blurred and ambiguous. The complex doings at Blackwater Park between 20 June and 26 July involve the simultaneous activity of several characters in different places. The apparent fullness of the early narratives conceals tricks with space behind a pretence of fidelity to time. Only when Count Fosco's confession reveals where he was during the many gaps in Marian's vision of him does spatial continuity match its temporal counterpart. In the last pages of the novel, when the same time period has been narrated eight times, the reader is at last able to construct a full narrative from the omniscient perspective which Hartright has enjoyed since the beginning – including not only how time passed during that busy month but also where each character passed it. Only at the end of the novel does its complex mosaic of corrupted words, violated spaces, broken time, and splintered space make the coherent whole which the 'Preamble' promised.

According to the 'Preamble', the three sequences of narrators, events, and reading are really one – a linear movement from moment to moment, incident to incident, and page to page. In practice, however, the novel derives its sensations from the multiple discrepancies among these three sequences. The reader's encounter with the events is limited by the very thing which is supposed to make it complete – confinement to the experience of one or another character. In this, *The Woman in White* reverses the values which mid-Victorian criticism assigned to the two components of narrative. The events which Hartright sets out to describe make a complete structure before he begins. As the narrators tell their several tales, this structure is constituted bit by bit – or, in the language of mid-Victorian criticism, stroke by stroke. Only when all aspects of this structure have been described and placed in an order which is not that of the novel's own temporality, has the reader acquired a full 'portrait' of the events.

In contrast to the complex spatiality of its plot, the characters of *The Woman in White* are bound to the sequence in which they make their narratives. They are the links in the narrative chain, reduced to the vehicular function which mid-Victorian criticism ascribed solely to 'plot'. 'Character' in *The Woman in White* has none of the pseudospatial coherence which critics sought in it – only the events have that – and its plot is not merely a means of getting from one page to the next – it is the unified structure which the novel's language imitates. The first great 'novel of incident' does fall victim, despite its author's disclaimers, to the subordination of character to plot which critics of the 1860s took to be the hallmark of sensationalism. It does so, however, not because it contains less of one element than the other, but because the narrative function of what ought to be a higher interest has been assumed by what should have been a lower.

One consequence of this reversal is the novel's demonstration that the exploitation of textuality runs counter to the achievement of mimesis. *The Woman in White* derives its sensations from tricks with its own nature as a text, but if all the world's writing were like *The Woman in White*, the truth which the novel pretends to seek would be available nowhere. In order for the novel to provide its sensations, there must somewhere be texts which are trusted to be transparent. This is the faith of mid-Victorian realism, and *The Woman in White* is as firmly grounded in it as any novel by Trollope or George Eliot. Yet, at the same time, *The Woman in White* violates the realist's faith at every turn.

This contradiction is reflected in the novel's structure as a sort of second-degree text, an arrangement of realistic writing which becomes sensational by means of the pattern which its editor has given to it. There is an odd alliance between the hero of the novel and its villain: Hartright's arrangement of narratives contains as many misleading analogies and false metaphors as Fosco's conspiracy; but Fosco imposes a deceitful pattern on people and things, while Hartright restricts himself to fictional reports of them.[15] Hartright's deceptions are forgivable, indeed they are necessary, in the world governed by the sensational contract between the writer and the reader of *The Woman in White*; but these same deceptions are crimes in the world which the novel portrays. According to its own morality, *The Woman in White* places itself one step further from the real world than the realistic novel claims to do. The morality of reading *The Woman in White* is very different from that of living in its world: reading is a separate territory, and Fosco's evil is its good.

By comparison with later sensation and detective novels, or even with the sophisticated earlier sensationalism of *Tristram Shandy*, *The Woman in White* appears as an intermediate work, a landmark of ambivalence. Perhaps also, because it cannot support its claim to be a direct vision of the real world, it and its author can never attain a place in the 'front rank', such as Collins desired for both of them. The novel does, however, suggest some provocative implications of the mid-Victorian vocabulary of chains and portraits, a vocabulary which has continued to be used throughout the past century. The 'chain' of *The Woman in White* is its own nature as language, a language which is not life; while the 'portrait', which the faith of realism made pre-eminent, is a matter of agreement between writer and reader, a contract which states that language shall efface itself before what it portrays. At the heart of *The Woman in White* stands the momentous question whether the chain might not precede the portrait, whether the language of any text might not generate the reality which it pretends to imitate. The ambivalent rhetoric of *The Woman in White* marks a tentative breach of the mid-Victorian realist contract; and this, far more than its role as precursor of the twentieth-century detective novel, makes *The Woman in White* a significant document in the history of English fiction.

From *Nineteenth-Century Fiction*, 32 (1977–8), 18–35.

NOTES

[This essay addresses the question of the ambivalent relationship of Collins's fiction to mid-Victorian realism. Kendrick combines a literary-historical contextual approach with a formalist (narratological) interest in the relation between plot, events, and narration. He examines the sensationalism of *The Woman in White* in the context of the sensation genre's challenge to the mid-Victorian distinction between the novel of plot (or incident) and the realist novel of character, and also in relation to the way in which mid-Victorian literary theory figured plot and character as a chain or a road (plot), or a drawing or portrait (character). Kendrick argues that the sensation novel foregrounded the chains of plot to such an extent that it became merely formulaic – a kind of crossword puzzle, a language game with a merely arbitrary relation to the real world. However, *The Woman in White* is distinguished from run-of-the-mill sensation productions on the grounds that it is a self-consciously innovatory text which exploits the techniques of sensationalism whilst, at the same time, demanding to be read as if it were realistic. *The Woman in White* is seen as deriving many of its sensation effects from its self-referential play with its own textuality (and with the nature of texts and textuality more generally), but ultimately its narrative chain depends (Kendrick suggests) upon the belief that there is a truth of experience which texts may either verify or falsify. Ed.]

1. Henry James, 'The Art of Fiction', *Longman's Magazine*, September 1884, pp. 511–12, rpt. in *The Future of the British Novel*, ed. Leon Edel (New York, 1956), p. 15.

2. In *British Novelists and Their Styles* (Boston, 1859), David Masson offered a list of thirteen 'rough and obvious' types of British novels since Scott, all of them derived from the milieux with which the novels dealt (pp. 221–33). In the subsequent decade, though such labels as Military, Naval, and Traveller's Novels continued to be applied, they tended to give way before the more abstract, sometimes almost ideological distinction between 'novels of incident' and 'novels of character'.

3. This subject is treated fully in Walter C. Phillips's *Dickens, Reade, and Collins, Sensation Novelists* (New York, 1919).

4. 'Novels of action' and 'novels of character' are the two largest categories of novels in Edwin Muir's *The Structure of the Novel* (New York, 1929), and a similar distinction underlies the two aspects of 'Plot' and 'people' in E. M. Forster's *Aspects of the Novel* (Wolfgang Kayser maintains the classifications of 'Handlungsroman' and 'figurenroman' in *Das Sprachliche Kunstwerk* [Bern, 1948], and Franz K. Stanzel has further elaborated them in *Typische Formen des Romans* [Gottingen, 1964]). The distinction persists, though the terms are different, in Roland Barthes's 'Introduction à l'analyse structurale des récits', *Communications*, 8 (1966), 1–27, where novels are ranged between the 'strongly functional' pole of the 'popular story' and the 'strongly indicial' pole of the '"psychological" novel'. And the distinction is still current enough for Gérard Genette to dismiss it as having no 'semiological existence' in *Figures II* (Paris, 1969).

5. For example, the reviewer of Charles H. Ross's novel *A Private Inquiry* for the *Spectator*, 15 October 1870, p. 1231, conjures up the bizarre image of 'mean and meanly-painted figures passing to and fro on scenes meant to be sensational enough to make you gasp'.

6. G. H. Lewes, 'Criticism in Relation to Novels', *Fortnightly Review*, 15 December 1865, p. 354.

7. Review of *No Name*, *Spectator*, 10 January 1863, p. 1502.

8. This 'realistic imperative' is examined from a different perspective in Walter M. Kendrick, 'Balzac and British Realism: Mid-Victorian Theories of the Novel', *Victorian Studies*, 20 (1976), 5–24.

9. Alexander Smith, 'Novels and Novelists of the Day', *North British Review*, February 1863, p. 184.

10. Review of *Poor Miss Finch*, *Athenaeum*, 17 February 1872, p. 202.

11. This (p. xi) and all subsequent references to *The Woman in White* are to the Everyman's Library edition, ed. Ernest Rhys (London, 1910) which prints the text of 1861.

12. *Times* (London), 30 October 1860, p. 6.

13. This title was replaced after serial publication by 'The Story Begun by Walter Hartright'.

14. Margaret Oliphant, 'Sensation Novels', *Blackwood's*, May 1862, p. 565.

15. In *Wilkie Collins* (New York, 1970), William Marshall points out that Hartright and Fosco agree on the principle that 'knowledge leads to power' (p. 60). The withholding of knowledge, however, is for both the primary exercise of power. Fosco is 'evil' because he withholds knowledge from other characters, while Hartright is 'good' because he withholds it only from the reader.

4

Reading Detection in
The Woman in White

MARK M. HENNELLY, JR

'There, in the middle of the broad, bright high-road – there, as if it had that moment sprung out of the earth or dropped from the heaven – stood the figure of a solitary Woman, dressed from head to foot in white garments; her face bent in grave inquiry on mine, her hand pointing to the dark cloud over London, as I faced her' (p. 15).[1] So begins the emblematic mystery of blank, metaphysical whiteness 'fac[ing]' Walter Hartright, the reader-identification journeyman through fictional time and space in Wilkie Collins's *The Woman in White* (1859–1860). And so begins the reader's own journey on the 'high-road' of detection through overlapping stages or levels of reader involvement, a journey which travels from the usual, initial motive of exciting escape into sensationalism and melodrama,[2] through a stage of purely intellectual exercise, to a final level of enlightened entrapment. In this sense, 'from the first stage of the investigation to the last' (p. 573), Hartright and the reader, especially the Victorian reader, enjoy both the 'out of the earth' and the 'from the heaven', visceral and cerebral, pleasures of detection. Moreover, they finally entrap themselves by trying to understand the enigmatic Marian Halcombe, thereby detecting a detection paradox in *The Woman in White*. Namely, the 'hand pointing', reflexive genre of detection or detective fiction is here ultimately a 'grave inquiry' into both reality and selfhood. Such an inquiry is at last self-sacrificial since it demands that Hartright and the attentive reader alike surrender the melodramatic, armchair pleasures of textual detection for the extratextual, painful pleasures of mysterious Life itself, 'the dark cloud over London'.[3] In Hartright's own words, detecting the secret paradox of detection is successful in 'forcing me to act for myself' (p. 578), and 'the way to the Secret lay through the mystery, hitherto impenetrable to all of us, of the woman in white' (p. 420).

Before specifically discussing the stages of escape, intellectual exercise, and enlightened entrapment, however, we should first consider the assumptions behind such a discussion. In the words of Wolfgang Iser, the primary assumption of reader criticism is that 'the reading process' involves 'a dynamic *interaction* between text and reader'.[4] And such an assumption is especially relevant to the two genres which mutually inform *The Woman in White* – detective fiction and Victorian fiction. For instance, after analysing *The Woman in White* and other melodramatic examples of detection, Gavin Lambert argues that the best of such works discover 'subtlety on the far side of shock by creating complex patterns of identification for the reader ..., forcing him to reconcile the experiences of criminal and victim and to perceive elements of both in himself'.[5] On the other hand, U. C. Knoepflmacher, one of the most perceptive readers of the Victorian novel, likewise emphasises his 'conviction that one of the salient features of Victorian fiction was – and still is – its participatory quality'.[6] Although Iser makes useful distinctions between contemporary and modern reactions to, say, a nineteenth-century novel, modern readers perpetuate many nineteenth-century responses to *The Woman in White* since we are certainly the inheritors of many of its Victorian moral and psychological dilemmas. Hence this essay, though often stressing the Victorian response, assumes that of the modern reader to be different only in degree, not in kind. In fact, one often feels that, as modern readers, we like to project our cultural shortcomings onto a convenient Victorian scapegoat, forgetting our own heritage and, what is worse, failing to imitate the self-critical honesty which typifies the best Victorian fiction.

Finally, whether we assume the temporal metaphor of stages or the spatial metaphor of levels to discuss reader response to *The Woman in White* really makes no difference because the two approaches constantly conflate and overlap as one reads the novel. That is, we continually look before and after in the text, all the while looking deeper within ourselves. Since this study usually employs the temporal construct, however, it is worthwhile to hear

Iser utilising the spatial metaphor. His remarks are valuable because they help to clarify the relationship, to adapt Iser's own terms, between the 'alien me' and 'real me', the criminal and citizen, in detective fiction. Moreover, they stress the significance of the act of apprehension itself, something that might be termed the 'gnostic quest' in Victorian fiction.[7] And this, as we will see, defines the direction of the reading process in *The Woman in White*. Lastly, Iser's conclusions are relevant to that resolution of the divided self for which both Victorian and twentieth-century readers yearn:

> As we read, there occurs an artificial division of our personality, because we take as a theme for ourselves something that we are not. Consequently when reading we operate on different levels. ... Thus, in reading there are these two levels – the alien 'me' and the real, virtual 'me' – which are never completely cut off from each other. Indeed, we can only make someone else's thoughts into an absorbing theme for ourselves, provided the virtual background of our own personality can adapt to it. Every text we read draws a different boundary within our personality, so that the virtual background (the real 'me') will take on a different form, according to the theme of the text concerned. This is inevitable, if only for the fact that the relationship between the alien theme and virtual background is what makes it possible for the unfamiliar to be understood.[8]

Focusing on the first level of reader appeal, H. P. Sucksmith ranks *The Woman in White* as 'the greatest melodrama ever written'.[9] And T. S. Eliot introduces his essay comparing Collins and Dickens with a celebration of melodrama and sensationalism, the same qualities which most later critics, like Sucksmith, emphasise in *The Woman in White*, but emphasise by at least implying that the 'best novels' are also thematically profound, not simply 'thrilling', or escapist. Eliot even anticipates such an un-Victorian and for him false distinction: 'Those who have lived before such terms as "high-brow fiction", "thrillers" and "detective fiction" were invented realise that melodrama is perennial and that the craving for it is perennial and must be satisfied. If we cannot get this satisfaction out of what publishers present as "literature", then we will read – with less and less pretence of concealment – what we call "thrillers". But in the golden age of melodramatic fiction there was no such distinction. The best novels *were* thrilling.'[10] And Collins himself, in his many prefaces which invariably state his joint concern with reader involvement and aesthetic integrity (for him, too, there was no contradiction in terms), emphasises the need to provoke an emotional response in his audience. In his preface to *Basil*, for example, he calls his melodrama 'this book where I have attempted to excite the suspense or pity of the reader'.[11] And again, of course, for the ratiocinative Victorian, an emotional display, an exercise of the Heart and an exorcism of the Head, is fundamental fictional therapy.

Thus this most elementary and 'escapist' appeal of *The Woman in White* is also the most crucial. It is likewise a prerequisite for the second and third stages of detection, and Collins underscores the therapeutic need for emotion in his audience by repeatedly demanding it from his characters. On this most basic level, the primary appeal of *The Woman in White* (and of detective fiction in general) is its provision of an element of sensational mystery to readers whose real lives are anything but mysterious, that is, are dull, rationally predictable, and hence unfulfilling. As we will later see, classic detective fiction demands only acute intellectual talent to solve life's mystery. In Collins's example of Victorian detection, however, unlike Sir Conan Doyle's saga of Holmes, emotion, imagination, and intelligence are all equally important talents. For the moment it is only necessary to understand that Hartright and the reader react to the melodramatic mystery (what we might facetiously call 'the albino dwarf principle' of detection), here 'the light-haired foreigner, with the scar on his cheek' (p. 543), in the same way as lawyer Gilmore: 'I live, professionally, in an atmosphere of disputation, Mr Hartright; and I am only too glad to escape from it, as I am escaping here [with the melodramatic relationships at Limmeridge House]' (p. 104). Like the repeated notion of 'the secret self', most of the novel's mysteries are hidden behind 'a perverse lock' (p. 459), that is, metaphors of enclosure and depth, 'the Secret, hidden deep under the surface' (p. 435), which conceal the solution of the mystery and the satisfaction of reader escapist 'curiosity', a curiosity which is itself ultimately entrapping. Count Fosco's corpse, for instance (like Glyde's in the church), is hidden in 'the terrible deadhouse of Paris – the Morgue. A great crowd clamoured and heaved round the door. There was evidently something inside which excited the popular curiosity, and fed the popular appetite for horror' (p. 580). And Collins's own 1860 preface to the novel underscores 'doing a service to the reader' by maintaining the 'two main elements in the attraction of all stories – the interest of curiosity, and the excitement of surprise' (p. xxxvi). Finally, the

melodrama's own breathless pace dramatises Collins's words as the
reader shares Hartright's increasing curiosity and excitement: 'The
rapid motion of the cab, the sense that every instant now was bringing me closer to the Count, the conviction that I was embarked at
last, without let or hindrance, on my hazardous enterprise, heated
me into such a fever of excitement that I shouted to the man to go
faster and faster' (p. 543).

Besides appearing to be prosaic and predictable, however, life
also seems to be mysterious and chaotic; and detective fiction vicariously solves life's mysteries by providing a perfect paradigm for im-
posing rational order on an irrational universe: 'the conviction of
an unseen Design in the long series of complications which ... fas-
tened round us' (p. 257). Thus, for David I. Grossvogel, the detective story 'redefines mystery by counterstating it; by assuming the
mystery can be overcome, it allows the reader to play at being a god
with no resonance, a little as a child might be given a plastic stetho-
scope to play doctor. Judging by the large number of its participants, this kind of elevation game is sufficient for the greatest part
of the fiction-reading public.'[12] This second level, that of intellectual
exercise, would naturally be most reinforcing and satisfying to the
Victorian reader's rational compulsions and irrational repressions,
but it is also comforting to the rage for order within each of us. In
the words of Julian Symons, 'The pleasure the intelligent reader gets
from reading detective stories is thus partly the fascination of engaging in a battle of wits with the author, something more nearly
akin to a game of chess or a crossword puzzle than to the emotional rewards commonly looked for in reading fiction.'[13] Often the
figure bent on detection assumes the role of an archetypal quester
attempting to resolve the primordial conflict between order and
chaos, to discover the golden key or clue to life's 'perfect labyrinth
of troubles' (p. 316).[14] And this is certainly part of *The Woman in
White's* appeal, especially to an age when modern police work and
forensic science were just beginning and were receiving popular
tabloid exposure.[15]

The title of our contemporary journal devoted to criticism of detection has captured this familiar role; it is *Armchair Detective. The
Woman in White* certainly gratifies such sedentary and cerebral
needs, besides demanding much more from its reader in the third
stage of its detection. Thus Hartright and the reader enjoy intellectual exercise as they together travel the symbolic road toward
'Truth' and *Knowledge* at the aptly named *Knowlesbury*; to mix

the novel's metaphors, they strive 'so the tangled web will be most speedily and most intelligibly unrolled' (p. 381), an especially difficult task when dealing with the ravelled skeins of several rather knotty narrations. As Walter M. Kendrick puts it, 'Each time a narrator belatedly uncovers some fragment of the truth, there is an abrupt adjustment of his and the reader's vision.'[16] Hartright's opening dilemma – 'These events have a meaning, these events must lead to a result. The mystery of Anne Catherick is *not* cleared up yet' (p. 165) – is solved when the successive metaphysical questions in the whodunit are systematically answered: *Who* is the Woman in White; *Why* does Glyde insist on her being committed to an asylum; *What* is the source of the eerie resemblance between Anne and Laura; and *When*, exactly, did Laura leave Blackwater Park? Thus, like the 'white chaos of paper' (p. 553) on Fosco's desk, the novel itself provides a blank universe pregnant with meaning which each reader must construct, or reconstruct, for himself.

This intellectual exercise of unravelling or 'unroll[ing]' the mystery is not only the purely cerebral one which is the normal fictional task[17] but is also the obsessive, self-conscious one defining detection's usual game of wits, complicated because here even more, as indicated, the 'terrible story of the conspiracy ... was presented in fragments, sadly incoherent in themselves, and widely detached from each other' (p. 390). In *The Woman in White* intelligence is dependent upon adopting the correct 'point of view', that which balances Head, Imagination, and Heart, or more particularly Science, Art, Law, Intuition, Trust, and Love. And Science, Art, and Law receive qualified approbation in the melodrama as long as these objective, reasonable points of view do not repress Intuition, Trust, and Love. As lawyer Gilmore philosophically points out to the immature Hartright, 'I am an old man; and I take the practical view. You are a young man; and you take the romantic view. Let us not dispute about our views' (p. 104). Thus Fosco's medical Science allows him to diagnose correctly Marian's typhus fever, while Hartright's early artistic temperament preoccupies itself with the best 'point of view' (p. 45).

Still, it is appropriately ironic that Hartright early champions a rationally disinterested, perfect 'Art' over imperfect 'Nature'; and this 'romantic view' consequently predisposes him to adopt a courtly love attitude toward the Petrarchan Laura, a 'visionary nursling of ... [his] own fancy' (p. 42).[18] Such a deluded and idealist posture is eventually the 'nursling' of his real love, which ultimately matures and becomes humanised in the third level of detection when Hartright truly learns to be involved, loving, and unbiased enough to accept 'the story of Laura and the story of Marian ... presented to me from a stranger's point of view' (p. 407). The stranger here is lawyer Kyrle, who represents the objective, disinterested 'machinery of the Law' (p. 1), that point of view which Hartright first asks the reader to share when outlining detection's fair-play agreement whereby the author or narrator agrees not to withhold evidence from his audience seeking complete intelligence from the fictional game of wits. This second level is finally unravelled, or unrolled, or resolved when Hartright reports that Kyrle's legal demands have been satisfied: 'My case was proved by the plainest evidence he had ever heard in his life' (p. 576). Chiefly Law, then, teaches the 'self-control' or 'self-mastery', to use Hartright's repeated vocabulary, necessary for total intellectual exercise; and complementary 'patience' and 'caution' are prime skills for ersatz detectives: 'It is impossible at this stage of the investigation to be too cautious' (p. 469). Together these first two stages of detection place emphasis on plot and character respectively. Consequently, Kendrick's insightful essay is certainly correct in asserting that Collins transcends the usual Victorian separation of novels into those of either plot or character and that *The Woman in White* curiously reconciles both sensationalism and realism: 'The novel exhibits a double urge toward conventionality and innovation, taking full advantage of its sensationalism but at the same time demanding that it be read as if it were realistic.'[19]

As the Victorian novelist knew so well, however, rational skills are ultimately ineffectual, in fact are obstacles to unlocking 'the secret self'. To use Hartright's corollary diction, 'risk' is the essential 'clue to discovery' (p. 435), that is, the risk taken in actualising Heart values like trusting or believing, imagining, and loving. Realisation of this very complex third level of Victorian detection, then, subtly entraps both Hartright and the reader in risk-ridden 'complete enlightenment' (p. 583) of the vital processes of Life itself. Consequently, as Hartright outlines the correct evidentiary procedure to satisfy Kyrle's empirical point of view, he simultaneously and lovingly 'put my arm around Laura, and raised her so that she was plainly visible to every one in the room' (p. 576). Thus for Victorian detection, Love must balance the Law, which, like the other sterile viewpoints of Science and Art in the novel, is abstract and unfeeling since 'the Law was not so tender-hearted' (p. 493) and 'the Law ... can dispute any human statement' (p. 117). But more significantly for detection, the Law is also untrustworthy and misleading if used alone to solve Life's mysteries because in Fosco's employ of the Law against Hartright it works 'with the customary exaggeration and the customary perversion of the truth' (p. 467). Collins believed deeply in this added Victorian stage of detection; in fact he invented it when he extended Poe's Dupin's brand of detection beyond solving 'The Mystery of Marie Rogêt' by reading newspapers in his armchair, like an armchair detective, to Hartright's throwing away 'self-control', caution, newspaper, and chair alike and 'risking' life by 'act[ing] for myself' (p. 578). Or, as T. S. Eliot explains this final level, 'the detective story, as created by Poe, is something as specialised and intellectual as a chess problem; whereas the best of English detective fiction has relied less on the beauty of the mathematical problem and much more on the *intangible human element*.'[20] Accordingly, in the preface to *The Law and The Lady*, Collins writes that 'the actions of human beings are not invariably governed by the laws of pure reason' (V.3); and he relates the worthlessness of such Kantian categories specifically to his readers in a letter to his publisher Samson Low, criticising the *Times* critic who found flaws in the calendar of *The Woman in White*: 'readers are not critics, who test an emotional book by the base rules of arithmetic'.[21]

Consequently, this complicated, last level of Collins's detection is particularly (but not exclusively) Victorian and demands the most attention in *The Woman in White* because it probes the problems of the divided self, and how this self-division exacerbates 'the struggle for existence among the men and the women about us' (p. 397).[22] In his preface to *No Name*, Collins in more general terms labels this as his major theme: 'the struggle of a human creature, under those opposing influences of Good and Evil, which we have all felt, which we have all known' (XII.5). Even here Collins implicates and traps the reader in the struggle, making him an enlightened accomplice not only in the self-discovery process of detection but also, as we shall see, in the very crime itself. In this sense the usual detection process of identification, what even Fosco, Hartright's dark alter ego, calls 'identifying the person of whom we were in search' (p. 559), becomes self-identification for the reader. This is especially true when the two major doppelgängers, Laura and Anne, merge in 'the complete transformation of two separate identities' (p. 559), just as the now self-reflected and hence trapped reader is urged to reconcile and transform his own Head and Heart. In an 1887 article in the *Globe*, Collins makes even clearer this self-discovery process when he discusses the book's divided structure: 'The destruction of ... identity represents a first division of the story; the recovery of ... identity marks a second division' (p. 596). And Hartright, the reader-identification figure, finally discovers that ratiocinative detection by itself becomes a sign of lonely repression, while he, Marian, and Laura are 'completely isolated in our place of concealment, as if the house we lived in had been a desert island' (p. 399). Most significantly, it must be joined with heartfelt love if real detection, if real self-discovery, is to succeed: 'If we had loved her [Laura] less dearly, if the instinct implanted in us by that love had not been far more certain than any exercise of reasoning, far keener than any process of observation, even then we might have hesitated' (p. 399). Gilmore, in fact, learns that 'even lawyers have hearts' (p. 129). And speaking of himself in the third person, he warns (and thus helps to trap) the readers that they, too, must share his 'experience' in order not only to understand the fictional inheritance within the novel but also to understand their own inheritance of the melodrama's detection of the riddles of life. This legacy of experience must be practised after the book is finally closed: 'I warn all readers of these lines that Miss Fairlie's inheritance is a very serious part of Miss Fairlie's story; and that Mr Gilmore's experience, in this particular, must be their experience also, if they wish to understand the narratives which are yet to come' (p. 131).

A number of apparently minor characters personify this need for self-discovery by repressing their 'inner self'. Thus all of these are negative foils for Hartright's major act of detection of 'that fallen nature we all share in common' (p. 345), which act itself is a model for the trapped and enlightened reader. Madame Fosco, for instance, 'under her outer covering of icy constraint', betrays 'her secret self', which Marian 'detected' repeatedly during her stay at Blackwater. This leads Marian 'to suspect that her [Madame Fosco's] present state of suppression may have sealed up something dangerous in her nature, which used to evaporate harmlessly in the freedom of her former life' (p. 195). Madame Fosco, however, unlike Marian herself, is hopelessly self-divided between a frozen 'female skeleton' (p. 194), as 'submissive' and well trained as her husband's white mice, and a sinister succubus who unleashes 'suppressed tigrish jealousy' whenever Fosco attends to 'any woman in the house' (p. 195). Mrs Catherick is similarly 'a walking mystery'

(p. 49), on the one hand, enduring years of shame and gossip so that a clergyman will finally bow to her out of 'common courtesy', on the other, suppressing the secret of her hatred of Glyde and the identity of Anne's father, 'like a lurking reptile' which 'stirred in its lair the serpent-hatred of years' (pp. 453, 451).

The detection of Professor Pesca's self-division, however, enlightens and entraps the reader more profoundly than that of either of these femmes fatales since 'the harmless eccentricity' (p. 3) of this dwarfish placebo is initially reminiscent of one of Dickens's comic, innocent grotesques, like Grimwig in *Oliver Twist*. He thus lulls the reader, who takes his appearance for his reality, into a sense of false, or fictional, security. Ultimately, though, Pesca warns and challenges both the reader and Hartright when the Italian, who wears the 'bright red', symbolic 'brand' of mortality (p. 537), discloses the secret self-division of the 'Brotherhood' of all humanity: 'The iron that has entered into our souls [the secret Brotherhood's] has gone too deep for *you* to find it. Leave the refugee [Fosco] alone! Laugh at him, distrust him, open your eyes in wonder at that secret self which smoulders in him, sometimes under the everyday respectability and tranquillity of a man like me' (p. 535). With his 'secret self', one capable of possible murder and subversion, thus detected, Pesca finally resembles Dickens's self-crippling grotesques, like Jenny Wren in *Our Mutual Friend*, whose abnormality shockingly spills over into the normality of a schizoid nation of suppressed shopkeepers.

Indeed, as narrator, Hartright ultimately triggers Collins's trap for the unwary reader by a textual, extratextual footnote erasing the imaginary boundary between fact and fiction and between closure and disclosure: 'It is only right to mention, here, that I repeat Pesca's statement to me, with the careful suppressions and alterations which the serious nature of the subject and my own sense of duty to my friend demand. My first and last concealments from the reader are those which caution renders absolutely necessary in this portion of the narrative' (p. 534). As character, Hartright himself escapes from his early, artificial posture as a courtly lover from afar, from a 'suppression of myself' (p. 374) which is as duplicitous as Pesca's, when he first undergoes symbolic death in 'the wilds and forests of Central America ... Death by disease, death by Indians, death by drowning – all three had approached me' (p. 373). He then tries surreptitiously to use his new self-survival skills once employed 'against suspected treachery in the wilds of Central America ... with the same purpose and with even greater caution, in the heart of civilised London!' (p. 418). And finally, risking everything and throwing such repressive 'caution' to the winds in 'defiance of all reason' (p. 478), Hartright openly acts for himself and practises these skills, not by murder like Pesca, but by redemptive self-sacrifice when, attempting to save Glyde, he braves the fire symbolising his own actualised, secret self which 'leaped out like a wild beast from its lair' (p. 477).

Following self-critical, mainstream Victorian fiction, *The Woman in White* even goes so far as to condemn the paralysis and parasitism of purely cerebral detecting, of the spectator's role in a game of wits, which classic detective fiction normally champions. As previously noted, Hartright's withdrawing postures as both lover and artist from a distance resemble the 'safe' approach to life of the armchair brand of detection required of the uncommitted reader. Sometimes this regressive fear of life drives Hartright toward paranoia, toward obsessively disbelieving and mistrusting everyone and everything as he is 'distorted by the suspicion which had become a part of myself, [when] even ... trifles ... looked too dangerous to be trusted without a guard' (p. 276). The voyeuristic reader falls a similar prey to such self-defensive suspicion when he is sure, presumably beyond a shadow of a doubt, that the sinisterly named Mrs Rubelle has been infecting Marian with typhus germs and that Fosco is trying to discredit the attending physician so that the disease can spread unchecked. Both presumptions prove false when the reader detects that sometimes appearances are realities, even in detective fiction where usually the least suspicious are the most guilty. Yet Hartright still learns that more often than not conventional appearances do cloak inner realities: 'Was it possible that appearances ... had pointed in one direction, while the truth lay, all the while, unsuspected, in another direction?' (p. 435). Consequently, both he and the reader must maintain their belief and trust, must remain committed to real life. Even the apparent digression of the schoolboy Jacob's punishment for 'imagining' he saw a real, live ghost testifies to the power of belief and the necessity of a commitment to the revealed facts of life. Hartright remarks, 'The boy's story, as I believe, has a foundation in fact', and it 'encourages me to perservere in the investigation' (p. 76).[23] Thus, 'exorcising a ghost' (p. 74), revealing the secret self, and believing in the woman in white, all ensure self-discovery, while suspicious and unimaginative doubting Thomases, like the schoolmaster Mr Dempster, will never be successful detectives in life, or of life. The 'ghost,' it turns out, is Anne Catherick and consequently is real, but the sceptical Dempster pales before Mr Fairlie, Collins's major personification of the escapist reader of detective fiction.[24] Actually, Fairlie represents an extreme version of Hartright's early posture of detachment since he too is a connoisseur of fine art, though not a creative artist like Hartright. In fact, in the Platonic scheme of things, he is not twice but thrice removed from realities because he presides only over photographs of art objects. Deprecating 'Young Persons' in anticipation of Dickens's Podsnap, Fairlie's masterfully self-ironic point of view criticises sentiment and tearful 'secretion' because of his own blind regression from emotional involvement: 'I cannot see the interest of a secretion from a sentimental point of view. Perhaps, my own secretions being all wrong together, I am a little prejudiced on the subject. No matter. I behaved, on this occasion [of Marian's entreaties to harbour Laura] with all possible propriety and feeling. I closed my eyes' (p. 312). Indeed, Fairlie's compulsive misoneism, or pathological fear of change, is revealed in his 'characteristically choosing the alternative which promised soonest to release him from all personal anxiety', as he regressively 'whine[s] and whimper[s] ... like a fretful child' (p. 574) throughout the melodrama. Consequently, Fairlie does 'not recognise' his own niece Laura when she is brought to him for redemptive identification and self-defensively 'call[s] on the law to protect him' (p. 395) from such intrusions of reality. Finally, 'Mr Fairlie's selfishness, indolence, and habitual want of feeling' (p. 395), all early snares for Hartright and continual traps for the armchair detective, are aptly emblematised when he dies after being 'struck by paralysis' (p. 583).

This third level further traps the reader in its self-enlightening process by its repetition compulsion which establishes hidden links among all the major characters: the three half-sisters, Marian, Laura, and Anne; Hartright and Glyde; Pesca and Fosco; Marian and Fosco; and especially between Hartright and Fosco, and thus Fosco and the identifying reader. Once again, all these secret sharers dramatise that favourite Victorian theme of the divided self. And the double figure reappears so obsessively throughout the text that the reader, as innocent bystander, eventually detects himself trapped by symbolic self-reflections in this fictional hall of distorted mirrors. From the first appearance of the woman in white, image patterns of disease, dream, and madness ambiguously reflect the surreal repetitions of this nightmarish ambience. For example, Laura is stricken with 'heart-disease' (p. 368), and Anne dies of a 'disease of the heart' (p. 448), signalling that both are linked by their wasting emotions. Thus, approximating the reader's reaction to much of the melodrama, Hartright incants while watching Laura's 'mystery of sleep': 'That unconscious appeal, so touching and so awful in the sacredness of her sleep, ran through me like fire' (pp. 523–4). And 'the mystery and terror of' Marian's prophetic 'dream' (p. 262) are finally duplicated in fictional real life as the novel's art of detection is meant to duplicate the trapped reader's real-life need for detection: 'The darkness closed round the pilgrim at the marble tomb; closed round the veiled woman from the grave; closed round the dreamer who looked on them' (p. 249).

The microcosm at Blackwater Park, the archetypal home of a couple (the Glydes) married on December 22, the solstice division between autumn and winter and arrived at near the summer solstice, is likewise founded upon such geminating and graven images. This monumental gargoyle of civilised self-division sports an 'allegorical leaden monster', schizoid apartments with 'two galleries', and 'two' wings built 'in the time of George the Second', and is further reflected by the environs of Blackwater Lake, a wasted Eden 'of solitude and decay'. All these images are 'live shadows themselves' (pp. 182 ff.) of the novel's splintered personalities. Marian's writing seal of 'two doves drinking out of the same cup' (p. 276) repeats the pattern more innocently, as do Laura and Anne, those recurrent, 'living reflexions of one another' (p. 84). Sometimes this doppelgänger device copies conscious resemblances; sometimes, as with Anne's madness versus her 'twin-sister' (p. 84) Laura's sanity, the one is an 'unconscious contradiction' (p. 402) of the other, that is, its repressed 'secret self'. Indeed, Hartright's later detection of a 'bridegroom's Christian name being the same as my own' (p. 462) on the Old Welmingham church registry is another textual spillover into extratextual existence, another symbolic opportunity for the trapped reader to find his own 'Christian name' on the 'pages, in manuscript' of *The Woman in White*. Even a most minor character like the coachman who drives Laura to Fosco's hideaway in London helps trigger the trap for Hartright since he remembers Lady Glyde because 'my wife's name, before she changed it for mine, was the same as the lady's – meaning the name of Glyde, sir' (pp. 572–3).

That remarkably villainous polymath Count Fosco, however, most shockingly traps the reader since Hartright, the reader-identification figure, must identify more and more with 'this strangely original man' (p. 201) in order to overcome him.[25] As Kendrick suggests from a different point of view, 'There is an odd alliance between the hero of the novel and its villain.'[26] Fosco works within the law, indeed with Glyde even uses the law to steal Laura's inheritance and achieve Glyde's illegal ends; while Hartright works outside the law, even to the point of being arrested and ultimately becoming an unwilling accomplice to Fosco's assassination, in order to secure Laura's legal rights. The significance here, as Fosco boldly testifies, is that Victorian 'detection of crime is miserably ineffective' because like most forms of detective fiction it prizes cerebral 'self-control' and punishes forbidden 'risk' taking. Consequently, the criminal becomes the 'secret self' of the repressive police force, and thus a healthy imitation of Fosco's own 'resolute' vitality, itself a parody of the resolved head and heart, is the only action that can save Hartright from ineffectual detection or compulsive self-control.[27] As Fosco asks, 'The hiding of a crime, or the detection of a crime, what is it? A trial of skill between the police on one side, and the individual on the other. When the criminal is a brutal, ignorant fool, the police, in nine cases out of ten, win. When the criminal is a resolute, educated, highly-intelligent man, the police, in nine cases out of ten, lose ... [Consequently,] English society ... is as often the accomplice, as it is the enemy of crime' (pp. 210–12). True to his boast and echoing another quester for whiteness, Melville's Ahab, only Fosco seems to muster enough self-control and risk, enough head and heart, to solve life's mysteries and detect the realities beneath appearances: 'I say what other people only think; and when all the rest of the world is in a conspiracy to accept the mask for the true face, mine is the rash hand that tears off the plump pasteboard, and shows the bare bones beneath' (p. 213). Thus Hartright, whose 'heart turns faint, [and] ... mind sinks in darkness' (p. 379), must somewhat imitate Fosco's example of balancing 'manly tenderness, with a fatherly care' and 'combin[ing] in myself the opposite characteristics of a Man of Sentiment and a Man of Business' (p. 565). In Hartright's words, 'There was no choice but to oppose cunning by cunning' (p. 411). And so in Fosco's own house, Hartright finally and crucially practises both self-control and risk: 'At that final moment, I thought with *his* mind; I felt with *his* fingers' (p. 546, Collins's emphasis). The identifying reader, no longer an innocent bystander and now trapped within the criminal's mould, must likewise imitate Fosco if he or she is to solve the mystery and, like Hartright, learn 'to act for myself'.

There is a point, however, where Fosco's exemplary model obviously ends for Hartright since the Count brutalises humans and humanises his pet brutes; and consequently his corpse is branded with 'two cuts, in the form of a T, [that] ... signified the Italian word, "Traditore"' (p. 581). Fosco thus betrays his secret self by hiding his identification with the Brotherhood under disguises in Paris; Hartright shuns 'the mere act of adopting a disguise' (p. 445), even at his own personal peril. Fosco cynically detects only 'bare bones beneath' the mask of appearances; Hartright ultimately detects the sensations of real love under his discarded courtly love pose. Fosco is a traitor to his own heart and his brotherhood with humanity. Hartright's heart is *right*; his trust and love discover the missing clues for successful detection.

But, ironically, Fosco's saving love for Marian ('in my Heart – behold, in the image of Marian Halcombe, the first and last weakness of Fosco's life,' [p. 570]) leads to the mystery of Marian herself, a mystery that Collins seems unable to solve, yet one that traps the reader perhaps more than any other.[28] Knoepflmacher is certainly correct in seeing an analogy between Marian's and Fosco's relationship and that anomalous one between Rebecca and Bois-Guilbert in *Ivanhoe*.[29] It also recalls that between Cora and Magua in *The Last of the Mohicans*. In all three instances, the liaison or potential liaison is, understandably, felt to be poisonous to the health of society. As Marian experiences it, Fosco's passion is too egocentric and domineering and thus untrustworthy: 'His voice trembled along every nerve in my body, and turned me hot and cold alternatively' (p. 262). What is not understandable, especially in light of Collins's usual candour regarding the themes of detecting and actualising the secret self and of revitalising Victorian mores, is his reluctance to satisfy the wishes of most of his readers by providing for the eventual union of Marian and Hartright. Even Laura tells Hartright, 'You will end in liking Marian better than you like me' (p. 441). Racial bias forbids such a union between Rebecca and Ivanhoe or between Cora and Uncas or Duncan, but no such impediment exists here. And even if it did, the bohemian Collins presumably would not subscribe to it. The involved reader can only assume one of three motives on Collins's part. He may simply have miscalculated Marian's 'natural energy and courage' (p. 387), her 'sensitive, vehement, passionate nature' (p. 120), which qualities far outstrip those of his passive damsel in distress, Laura, and thus which seem the fittest reward for Hartright's loving labours of detection. However, Collins's actual admiration for Marian over Laura seems quite obvious in the text. Or, it may be that he was too subjectively involved with the extratextual model for Marian, since Collins, like Hartright, was himself living in a ménage à trois,[30] and thus for personal reasons he may have wished to displace Marian's potentially sexual role. Such an argument has merit, but again I think Collins's central themes here would cancel his desire to safeguard his private life.

His real motive seems to plumb more deeply the third level of detection and the realities of Victorian living. The implication is that none of us can ever detect all the untrodden places of the heart so that when a well-rounded Victorian rebel, as Hartright finally becomes, still fails to detect the final mysteries of his own heart, or of Marian's either for that matter, his sympathetic story is all the more mysterious and insoluble, and hers all the more self-sacrificial and educating.[31] The climax of such a detection is paradoxically double-edged for the identifying, trapped reader since he detects that there always are mysteries in extratextual life which he can never detect. Yet at the same time, he has gratified his thirst for detection in *The Woman in White* by outwitting Hartright, the sympathetic, reader-identification figure. And the reader is only further trapped by trying to guess how much of the mysterious 'secret' between them Marian has herself detected. For example, when Hartright, after Glyde's death and after the three are living in a comfortable ménage à trois, intimates that he is again thinking of marriage with Laura, Marian's 'face [mysteriously] grew pale. For a while, she looked at me with a sad, hesitating interest. An unaccustomed tenderness trembled in her dark eyes and softened her firm lips' (p. 510). And once the marriage plans are settled, the momentarily insouciant Hartright does not search for clues to the melodramatic mystery that for 'the first time since the farewell morning at Limmeridge', Marian 'touched my forehead with her lips. A tear dropped on my face, as she kissed me. She turned quickly ... and left the room' (p. 522). It seems apparent, at any rate, that Marian's tutoring of Laura in the hard realities of life when she is engaged to, or trapped by, Glyde is an analogy for her education of the naïve and equally trapped reader. Her diction even anticipates Fosco's 'stripping' the mask from a mysterious world of benign illusions: 'Drop by drop, I poured the profaning bitterness of this world's wisdom into that pure heart and that innocent mind, while every higher and better feeling within me recoiled from my miserable task. It is over now. She has learnt her hard, her inevitable lesson. The simple illusions of her girlhood are gone; and my hand stripped them off' (p. 167).

Indeed, we know that many bachelor readers were certainly trapped by Marian since they wrote to Collins, detailing their desire to marry the extratextual, real-life model for Marian.[32] Furthermore, Marian earns reader sympathy by not only being the only other major narrator in the novel but by also displaying the quick wit and self-conscious humour that Hartright sadly lacks and Fosco employs only at the expense of others. Marian is perhaps the most dramatic example of the true detective, one who illustrates both risk and self-control when she crawls along the veranda roof to eavesdrop on Fosco and Glyde. This feat prompts the illness which symbolises her fortunate fall from the kind of detachment of noblesse oblige, Victorian caste consciousness which would not permit Laura's union with the commoner Hartright, to Marian's humble involvement in the self-sacrificing and self-ennobling mysteries of life. Again and again this mannish woman is described in androgynous terms which reconcile her head and heart. Hartright feels 'indebted to Marian's courage and to Marian's love' (p. 504), and Fosco likewise reveres 'this grand creature, who stands in the strength of her love and her courage' (p. 296). Consequently, Hartright's final problem, 'the consideration of Marian's future' (p. 578), is also the ultimate mystery for the trapped reader, himself personified and perpetuated in textual existence by Hartright's child, '*the Heir of Limmeridge*' (p. 584, Collins' emphasis), who is also heir to the detected mysteries of the collected narratives and who, significantly, will be reared and educated by Marian.[33] The reader, then, can well agree with Hartright that 'Marian was the good angel of our lives – let Marian end our Story' (p. 584), since she most crucially and problematically triggers the third level trap for the escapist and cerebral reader of detective fiction. She, symbolically, prompts Hartright and the reader to share the lasting 'conviction that a trap has been laid for me, and the vexation of knowing that I had fallen into it' (p. 466).

From *Texas Studies in Literature and Language*, 22 (1980), 449–67.

NOTES

[The critical methodology used in this account of the process of reading detection in *The Woman in White* is based on Wolfgang Iser's reader-response criticism, which assumes that reading is a dynamic interactive process between text and reader. It is suggested that Iser's approach is particularly apt for detective fiction and Victorian fiction, both of which invite participatory reading. Hennelly sees Walter Hartright as the reader-in-the-text, through whom the reader undertakes a journey through the bodily and emotional as well as the intellectual pleasures of detection. This journey moves through various overlapping levels: escapism (a surrender to the excitement of sensationalism and melodrama), intellectual exercise (the puzzle-solving aspect of reading detection), and, finally, 'enlightened entrapment' in which the reader becomes involved in the paradox of reading detection – the fact that detection fiction is simultaneously a self-reflexive game and a serious inquiry into the nature of reality and identity. As a consequence of this paradox, Hennelly argues, the process of reading detection cannot be simply escapist; the armchair pleasures of melodrama give way to the painful pleasures of engaging with the extratextual mystery of life itself. Ed.]

1. William Wilkie Collins, *The Woman in White*, ed. and intro. Harvey Peter Sucksmith (Oxford, 1975). All subsequent citations will be taken from this Oxford edition and noted within the text.

2. The melodramatic and sensationalistic interests of *The Woman in White* and of Collins in general have prompted the most critical response. See, for example, Bradford A. Booth, 'Wilkie Collins and the Art of Fiction', *Nineteenth-Century Fiction*, 6 (1951), 131–43; Sucksmith's introduction to the Oxford edition, pp. vii–xxii; and Kathleen Tillotson's 'Introduction' to *The Woman in White*, ed. Kathleen Tillotson and Anthea Trodd (Boston, 1969), pp. ix–xxvi. In light of our subsequent treatment of 'entrapment' in the novel, see Tillotson's brief discussion of Virginia Woolf's words recalling the past age '"when a plot was as necessary as a spring to a mouse-trap; and in these days [of the twentieth century] we have given up catching mice"' (p. xi).

3. David I. Grossvogel finds detection to be 'self-destructive' rather than self-sacrificial; see *Mystery and its Fictions* (Baltimore, MD, 1979), p. 98.

4. Wolfgang Iser, *The Act of Reading: A Theory of Aesthetic Response* (Baltimore, MD, 1978), p. 107. The emphasis is Iser's.

5. Gavin Lambert, *The Dangerous Edge* (London, 1975), p. 296. The reader should also see Robert P. Ashley's 'Wilkie Collins and the Detective Story', *Nineteenth-Century Fiction*, 6 (1951), 47–60.

6. U. C. Knoepflmacher, *Laughter and Despair: Readings in Ten Novels of the Victorian Era* (Berkeley, CA, 1971), p. ix.

7. See Mark M. Hennelly Jr, '*Dracula*: The Gnostic Quest and Victorian Wasteland', *English Literature in Transition*, 20 (1977), 13–26. Stoker admitted, by the way, that he 'borrowed' Collins's narrative technique when writing *Dracula*; see H. Ludlam, *A Biography of Dracula: The Life Story of Bram Stoker* (London, 1962), p. 101. What deserves future consideration, however, is the extent of the particular influence of *The Woman in White* on *Dracula*; especially significant are the many resemblances between Count Fosco and Count Dracula and between Marian and Mina.

8. Wolfgang Iser, *The Implied Reader: Patterns of Communication in Prose Fiction from Bunyan to Beckett* (Baltimore, MD, 1974), pp. 293–4.

9. Sucksmith, 'Introduction', p. xxii.

10. 'Wilkie Collins and Dickens', in *Selected Essays of T. S. Eliot* (New York, 1932), p. 409.

11. *The Works of Wilkie Collins* (1900; rpt. New York, 1970) X, 4. All subsequent references to Collins's Prefaces will be from this edition and noted within the text.

12. Grossvogel, *Mystery and its Fictions*, p. 40.

13. Julian Symons, *The Detective Story in Britain* (London, 1962), pp. 8–9.

14. See Mark M. Hennelly Jr, 'American Nightmare: The Underworld in Film', *The Journal of Popular Film*, 6 (1978), 258. The entire essay deals sporadically with this quest theme.

15. For accounts of the relationship between the history of the police force, journalism, pulp fiction, and detective fiction, see Eric Routley, *The Puritan Pleasures of the Detective Story, from Sherlock Holmes to Van der Valk: A Personal Monograph on the Excellences & Limitations of Detective Fiction* (London, 1972), pp. 20–1, and Larry N. Landrum, Pat Browne and Ray Browne's introduction to their collection, of essays, *Dimensions of Detective Fiction* (n.p.: Popular Press, 1976), pp. 1–6.

16. Walter M. Kendrick, 'The Sensationalism of *The Woman in White*', *Nineteenth-Century Fiction*, 32 (1977), 26 [see p. 76 above – Ed.].

17. For a significant, recent appraisal of unravelling techniques, see *Narrative Endings*, a special issue of *Nineteenth-Century Fiction*, 33 (1978).

18. See Peter Caracciolo's related discussion of Dante's influence on Collins, 'Wilkie Collins' "Divine Comedy": The Use of Dante in *The Woman in White*', *Nineteenth-Century Fiction*, 25 (1971), 383–404.

19. Kendrick, 'Sensationalism', p. 22.

20. Eliot, *Selected Essays*, p. 413, emphasis added.

21. Quoted by Tillotson and Trodd, *The Woman in White*, p. 150, n. 2.

22. As Lambert has noticed, the better examples of fictional detection, however, also like to stress a Siamese twin kind of relationship between criminal and sleuth and thereby entrap the identifying audience. See also Hennelly, 'American Nightmare: The Underworld in Film', especially p. 260.

23. This emphasis on *belief* is always important in the gnostic quest. See Hennelly, '*Dracula*: The Gnostic Quest and Victorian Wasteland', especially pp. 13–17.

24. For a discussion of this role applied to a film audience see Hennelly, 'American Nightmare: The Underworld in Film', especially pp. 240, 258.

25. See William H. Marshall's analysis of 'the colourful Fosco', who 'unique as a personality, relentlessly spreads, like evil itself, over the action', in his *Wilkie Collins* (New York, 1970), p. 57. Marshall's entire discussion of the novel, pp. 56–66, focuses primarily on Fosco.

26. Kendrick, 'Sensationalism', p. 34.

27. See U. C. Knoepflmacher's relevant treatment of the theme of the Victorian rebel in the novel, 'The Counterworld of Victorian Fiction and *The Woman in White*', in *The Worlds of Victorian Fiction*, Harvard English Studies 6, ed. Jerome H. Buckley (Cambridge, MA, 1975), pp. 351–69. [See pp 58–69 above. Ed.]

28. See Marshall's (*Wilkie Collins*) and Knoepflmacher's ('Counterworld') discussions of Marian, *passim*. Sucksmith's analysis of Marian's displaced sexuality should be consulted if only for the half-truths of an extreme view. He asserts, for example, that 'Marian is unattractive, yet that other nether-face of sexuality, with other lips and cheeks, which is secretly displaced upwards in Marian's form, is at once both ugly and attractive; body and face are unconsciously reversed in such a way as to conceal yet betray the true state of things' (p. xviii). See his entire discussion of Marian, pp. xviii–xx.

29. Knoepflmacher 'Counterworld', p. 366.

30. For an analysis of the relationships between Collins's life and the novel, see Clyde K. Hyder, 'Wilkie Collins and *The Woman in White*', *PMLA*, 54 (1939), 297–303.

31. Julian Symons suggests that 'Lesbian tendencies' perhaps motivate Marian's feelings toward Laura. See his introduction to *The Woman in White* (New York, 1974), p. 35.

32. Collins recounts this phenomenon in an interview with Edmund Yates printed in the *World* (26 December 1877), pp. 4–6.

33. Again, in *Dracula* Stoker likewise employs the Harker child, who inherits the collected manuscripts of the novel, as a personification of the innocent reader. See Hennelly, '*Dracula*: The Gnostic Quest and Victorian Wasteland', pp. 22–3, for a discussion of the child's symbolic role.

5

Ghostlier Determinations: The Economy of Sensation and *The Woman in White*

ANN CVETKOVICH

> Do you believe in dreams? I hope, for your own sake, that you do.
> See what Scripture says about dreams and their fulfilment, and take
> the warning I send you before it is too late.
>
> (the woman in white in *The Woman in White*)

> And they said unto him, We have dreamed a dream, and there is no
> interpreter of it. And Joseph said unto them, Do not interpretations
> belong to God? Tell me them, I pray you.
>
> (*Genesis* 40:8)

> When the work of interpretation has been completed, we perceive
> that a dream is the fulfilment of a wish.
>
> (Freud, *The Interpretation of Dreams*)

The 'Preamble' to Wilkie Collins's *The Woman in White* claims for
the narrative the status of a legal document whose writing is neces-
sitated by the inadequacy of the legal system in uncovering and
prosecuting all crimes. Because the 'Law is still ... the pre-engaged
servant of the long purse', operating in the service of those with
power and wealth, it remains the task of a poor man and amateur
detective, Walter Hartright, to investigate and defend the interests
of Laura Fairlie, the victim of legal loopholes that disenfranchise
her of both her inheritance and her identity. As the primary narrator of the story of crime and its investigation, Hartright aspires to

'present the truth always in its most direct and most intelligible aspect'. To carry out this project, he enlists the supporting testimony of eyewitness accounts other than his own and arranges these texts in logical order so as to 'trace the course of one complete series of events'.[1]

This description of the novel as an objective and rational document seems oddly inaccurate, given that *The Woman in White* was one of the most famous sensation novels, noted for its capacity to create suspense and excitement. Following *The Woman in White*'s publication in 1860, the sensation genre became the publishing phenomenon of the decade. Novelists such as Collins, Mary Elizabeth Braddon, Mrs Henry Wood, and Charles Reade wrote stories about bigamy, mistaken identity, and murder that sold in enormous numbers to a public clearly eager for literature that would '[preach] to the nerves.'[2] In the Preface to the 1860 edition of *The Woman in White*, Collins refers to the 'two main elements in the attraction of all stories – the interest of curiosity, and the excitement of surprise'.[3] It does not seem to be his intention that the reader listening to a story told 'as the Judge might once have heard it' should respond with impartial objectivity (p. 33). Instead, his mystery narrative invites the reader not just to participate in a process of rational inquiry but to enjoy the thrill of being shocked by the unexpected.

The absence in the Preamble of any reference to the narrative's sensationalism perhaps signals a disavowal of the way the sensation novel promotes an extension of the operation of the law by locating the private confines of the family as the domain of crime.[4] Sensational responses are central to the quasi-legal procedure of uncovering the secrets that crop up everywhere in the novel. Characters are alerted to the presence of a mystery by their own bodily sensations of fear, excitement, and suspense. Similarly, the reader who is startled by the 'excitement of surprise' is prompted to satisfy the 'interest of curiosity' that might also motivate legal inquiry. The extension of the law beyond its usual boundaries installs a hermeneutics of suspicion in which every fact that excites a sensation merits investigation.

We might suspect that Walter Hartright, the writer of the Preamble, is hiding more than just his narrative's sensational qualities. He is, after all, more central to the novel both as narrator and as character than his claims to pluralism and disinterestedness admit. The story he introduces is not only about Laura Fairlie's persecution ('what a Woman's patience can endure') but also about the way his discovery of it ('what a Man's resolution can achieve') serves as a vehicle for his accession to patriarchal power and property, making it possible for him to marry her despite their class difference. His pursuit of justice allows him to further his own interests, and by unmasking the crimes of aristocratic men like Sir Percival Glyde and Laura's sexually immoral father, he finally assumes their social position. In lamenting the fact that the legal system is not extensive enough to protect Laura Fairlie from exploitation by her husband, he fails to acknowledge that its lapses afford him the opportunity to step in where the patriarchal fathers and lawyers leave off.

I want to argue that many of *The Woman in White*'s most sensational moments – Walter's encounter with Anne Catherick on the road to London, his realisation that Laura Fairlie is identical in appearance to Anne, Laura's return from the dead – enable the more materially determined narrative of Walter's accession to power to be represented as though it were the product of chance occurrences, uncanny repetitions, and fated events. The mechanism for his rise up the social hierarchy is another kind of sensational moment – falling in love with Laura Fairlie – but this event is obscured by its links with those other sensational events (sensational both because extraordinary and because they produce bodily responses) described in the rhetoric of fate and chance. The disruptive energy of Walter's secret love for Laura is diffused by his ability to uncover other secrets, such as Sir Percival's false identity, Anne Catherick's mysterious origins, Laura's resemblance to Anne, Count Fosco's Italian past, or Sir Percival's plot against Laura, that are more criminal or repressed than his own. As his romance with Laura becomes entangled with the mystery of Anne Catherick, Walter constructs a sensational narrative about fate and chance that provides an alternative to the possibility that events are determined by social convention, and thus suggests that the unlikely event of his marriage to Laura Fairlie can become a reality.

Long before he has any evidence to do so, for example, he is obsessed with the idea of Sir Percival's secret and overcome with a foreboding sense that misfortune will come to Laura Fairlie:

> Judging by the ordinary rules of evidence, I had not the shadow of a reason, thus far, for connecting Sir Percival Glyde with the suspicious words of inquiry that had been spoken to me by the woman in white. And yet, I did connect him with them. Was it because he had now become associated in my mind with Miss Fairlie, Miss Fairlie being, in her turn, associated with Anne Catherick, since the night when I had discovered the ominous likeness between them? Had the events

of the morning so unnerved me already that I was at the mercy of any delusion which common chances and common coincidences might suggest to my imagination? ... The foreboding of some undiscoverable danger lying hid from us all in the darkness of the future was strong on me. The doubt whether I was not linked already to a chain of events which even my approaching departure from Cumberland would be powerless to snap asunder – the doubt whether we any of us saw the end as the end would really be – gathered more and more darkly over my mind.

(p. 101)

The passage maps the mental process by which Walter comes to 'associate' Sir Percival with Laura Fairlie, and Laura in turn with Anne Catherick, a process which, rather than following 'the ordinary rules of evidence' seems to be inspired by the associative powers of the unconscious. The affective charge of his relation to the two women plays itself out through the transfer of that affect to the person of Sir Percival, who becomes his rival for possession of Laura. Walter's belief that events are controlled by some invisible force, even as it renders him helpless, gives him the hope of rescue from the social position to which he is confined. Furthermore, his susceptibility to bodily sensation provokes the melodramatic conviction that 'the end' to be foreseen cannot be predicted. He describes himself as being 'at the mercy of any delusion' because of the 'unnerving' nature of his encounter with the woman in white and his uncanny recognition of her resemblance to Laura Fairlie. Bodily sensation, because it is involuntary, becomes a symptom of the self's subjection to the shock of chance or surprise events, and underwrites the process by which a sensational or melodramatic narrative can be constructed. Walter's incapacity to control his own body, even as it renders him anxious, permits him to rise to power without appearing to aspire to it. The dramatic revelation of Sir Percival's illegitimacy and Count Fosco's membership in the Brotherhood makes it possible for the bourgeois hero magically to ascend to the status of the aristocracy. However, before his confrontations with these two men, which are almost like chivalric duels, take place, Walter has a series of shocking encounters with 'the woman in white' and her double, Laura, the affective power of which needs to be explained.

In arguing that the sensational narrative, which intertwines romance, male secrets, and the rhetoric of chance and fate, mystifies the story of Walter's class mobility, I do not want simply to replace one story with the other. This would be to lapse into the logic of false consciousness, to explain away without explaining the force of sensation. Rather, it is necessary to consider what dividends might accrue by routing Walter's desire and rise to power through the sensational. As D. A. Miller has suggested, *The Woman in White* provides a locus for examining 'the value, meaning, and use that modern culture … finds in the nervous state'.[5] I want to look carefully at the early scenes in the novel that are centrally concerned with the creation of both sensation and Walter Hartright's desire in order to examine how, in addition to providing a cover for his class aspirations, they carry an affective power that seems to exceed this explanation. It does not seem accidental that this excess seems to centre on the bodies of two women, whose extraordinary effect on Walter is increased rather than dispelled by his discovery that they resemble one another. The thrill exerted by Anne's and Laura's resemblance is not demystified by the revelation that they have the same father. We don't really care what the reason is, we want an excuse to be shocked, preferring to read an interesting story rather than a legal document.[6] The rather predictable story of the young art instructor falling in love with his beautiful student is complicated by its occurrence in the midst of the mystery about Anne Catherick. Walter stresses the immediacy of his love for Laura, relying on her natural beauty as an alibi for the way that his desire transcends the economic exigencies that govern her marriage to Sir Percival Glyde and that promote her persecution. We could say that his story of 'love at first sight' is a mystification, that he reads the signs of her position as if they emanated naturally from her body rather than being a function of her social position. What's odd about his claim to love Laura at first sight.[5] is that the novel itself seems to demystify it by having Laura's appearance preceded by Anne's. Why, after all, does Walter not fall in love with Anne Catherick, given that she looks the same as Laura? The fact that he doesn't suggests that his love for Laura must be determined by her social class, but because the text itself reveals this so readily, we must consider how sensational plotting complicates any simple material or social interpretation of romance.

A reading of the sequence of events that leads to the awakening of his desire suggests that his attraction to Laura is inhabited from the start by his experience of Anne Catherick, and furthermore that the shock of his encounter with Anne Catherick is connected to his expectations of Laura. There is no primal event in which love arises naturally or instantaneously as an uncontrollable physical sensation, but rather a structure of determinations that patterns events. The forces of social determination revealed by Anne's resemblance to Laura can be mapped in relation to how the women's startling similarity plays out another kind of determination, one that follows the logic of Freud's notion of *Nachträglichkeit* or deferred action. For rather than demystifying Walter's love for Laura, the woman in white's relation to her double seems only to add further sensational intrigue to the romance, which itself sensationalises and masks Walter's class transition.

Although future events will ultimately confirm the significance of his experience, Walter Hartright's first perceptions of Laura Fairlie and Anne Catherick acquire much of their sensational force from his own investments. Walking home on the last evening before he departs for his new position at Limmeridge House, Walter indulges in a fantasy prompted by Pesca's fairy-tale story about his prospects for marrying one of the ladies of the house, the first of a series of prophecies that will ultimately be fulfilled. He loses the customary constraint required by his position as art instructor, a profession in which the sign of his class difference is his desexualisation. A male version of the female governess whose class position and relation to the family are ambiguous, Walter appears to harbour some resentment about being 'admitted among beautiful and captivating women much as a harmless domestic animal is admitted among them' (p. 89). His professional training demands that he separate himself from his body and his feelings as though they were detachable possessions: 'I had trained myself to leave all the sympathies natural to my age in my employer's outer hall, as coolly as I left my umbrella there' (p. 89). Rather than being an integral part of one's identity, the bodily sensations of desire conform to the exigencies of social position, since Walter's 'situation in life [is] considered a guarantee against any of [his] female pupils feeling more than the most ordinary interest in [him]' (p. 89). These passages remind us that one of the mechanisms for class division is the management of sexual desire, which far from being a natural entity independent of social convention, is so tied to class politics that Walter's pupils are assumed not to be susceptible to any but the 'most ordinary interest'. Rather than being forbidden or repressed by social restrictions, desire or sensation does not even appear when the social configuration is inappropriate. Thus it cannot be said that sexuality is a natural force, and that the awakening of Walter's sensations in response to Laura, and her feelings for him, represent an escape from social restrictions. The link asserted here between sexuality and social classifications reminds us that what is forbidden is not sexuality in and of itself but the class transgression that love between an instructor and his pupil might represent. Since Walter so closely associates sexuality with class here, we have to see his love for Laura as crucially tied to class mobility, rather than independent of it.

Yet Walter's encounter with the woman in white would seem to suggest that sexuality is repressed by class hierarchies rather than being a mechanism for their preservation. As he proceeds on his walk home, the return of this repressed sexuality is catalysed by his heightened sensitivity to the landscape, as if to suggest that, freed from the confines of the social world, he can recover a more natural sensibility:

> The prospect of going to bed in my airless chambers, and the prospect of gradual suffocation, seemed, in my present restless frame of mind and body, to be one and the same thing. I determined to stroll home in the purer air by the most roundabout way I could take; to follow the white winding paths across the lonely heath; ... So long as I was proceeding through this first and prettiest part of my night walk my mind remained passively open to the impressions produced by the view; and I thought but little on any subject – indeed, so far as my own sensations were concerned, I can hardly say that I thought at all.
>
> But when I had left the heath and had turned into the by-road, where there was less to see, the ideas naturally engendered by the approaching change in my habits and occupations gradually drew more and more of my attention exclusively to themselves. By the time I had arrived at the end of the road I had become completely absorbed in my own fanciful visions of Limmeridge House, of Mr Fairlie, and of the two ladies whose practice in the art of water-colour painting I was so soon to superintend.
>
> (pp. 46–7)

Walter allows himself to be carried along by the landscape, forsaking his usual rationality and direction for the 'most roundabout way' (just as the mystery story takes a detour through sensation to arrive at rational explanations). He gives himself over to the outside world, letting his mind 'remain passively open to impressions' that remain unmediated 'sensations' rather than formulated thoughts. Even when his consciousness turns inward to speculations on the

future, and his dispersed attention narrows to a single focus so that
he is 'completely absorbed' by visions that '[draw] more and more
of [his] attention exclusively to themselves', Walter's mind is still
the passive receiving medium of ideas that are 'naturally engen-
dered' rather than produced of his own volition. The taboo on 'fan-
ciful visions' is loosened by his ability to disavow any responsibility
for them.

Given the already charged relation between Walter's state of
mind and the landscape, it is hard not to read Anne Catherick's
startling appearance as though it were a response to his questions
about the future:

> I had now arrived at that particular point of my walk where four
> roads met. ... I had mechanically turned in this latter direction [back
> to London], and was strolling along the lonely high-road – idly won-
> dering, I remember, what the Cumberland young ladies would look
> like – when, in one moment, every drop of blood in my body was
> brought to a stop by the touch of a hand laid lightly and suddenly on
> my shoulder from behind me.
>
> (p. 47)

Walter's emphasis on his passivity as he 'idly' speculates about the
future and 'mechanically' proceeds towards his destination suggests
that he is subject to a determination outside his control, that the
event which occurs has not been willed or desired in any way. The
woman in white's touch abruptly returns him to his body, interrupting the flow of mental and bodily activity by bringing 'every
drop of blood ... to a stop'. Walter becomes the sentient flesh-and-
blood creature that he cannot be in the workplace. The shock of
this physical event resonates forwards and backwards across the
text, underwriting the mystery of Anne Catherick's behaviour and
demanding an explanation in part because it takes the form of a
physically traumatic experience. Yet, one possible meaning for the
event might be derived from the speculation that precedes it. The
woman in white might be seen as the harbinger of the ladies at
Limmeridge House, but in a way that allows Walter to disavow any
responsibility for his desire to form a romantic liaison with one of
them. Rather than being removed from the social world, the encounter with Anne Catherick appears magically to suggest that
Walter's fantasy might become a reality.

Walter's construction of the woman in white as a figure of
mystery can be seen as an attempt to recover from his physical

shock by explaining it as the product of an identity or a story that remains hidden from him. The single instant of his terror must be installed within a larger narrative that will locate and rationalise that fear as residing outside of himself. 'Far too seriously startled by the suddenness with which this extraordinary apparition [stands] before [him]', Walter finds himself 'quite unable to account for' the woman's presence (pp. 47–8). He describes his attempt to determine her identity or motives from her physical appearance, the illegibility of which allows him to construct her body as the sign of and potential solution to her mysteriousness: 'All I could discern distinctly by the moonlight ...'; 'The voice, little as I had yet heard of it ...'; 'her dress ... so far as I could guess' (p. 48). Anne Catherick's body provides a series of clues, which, if correctly read, might provide the explanation for her cataclysmic effect.

In describing his response to Anne Catherick, Walter seems particularly concerned to ward off any suggestion of a sexual subtext to the encounter. His guilt about the sympathy he feels when 'the loneliness and helplessness of the woman touched [him]' suggests that he fears that his response will be construed as sexual attraction. Disturbed by his own sense of helplessness, when his 'natural impulse to assist her and to spare her' overcomes 'the judgment, the caution, the worldly tact, which an older, wiser, and colder man might have summoned to help him in this strange emergency', Walter must reassure himself that he has not fallen into the clutches of a woman of ill repute (p. 49). 'The one thing of which I felt certain was, that the grossest of mankind could not have misconstrued her motive in speaking, even at that suspiciously late hour and in that suspiciously lonely place' (p. 48). The narrative is marked by retroactive justification, indicating that Walter is still haunted by uncertainty about his behaviour and its significance. His feelings of sympathy seem uncomfortably ambiguous, perhaps in part because they take the form of an uncontrollable bodily response that resembles sexual desire.

> What could I do? Here was a stranger utterly and helplessly at my mercy – and that stranger a forlorn woman. No house was near; no one was passing whom I could consult; and no earthly right existed on my part to give me a power of control over her, even if I had known how to exercise it. I trace these lines, self-distrustfully, with the shadows of after-events darkening the very paper I write on; and still I say, what could I do?
>
> (p. 50)

Walter casts his aid to Anne Catherick as the equivalent of a sexual fall, emphasising his own helplessness and lack of control as much as hers. Writing about his acquiescence to her request to be left alone, he describes his utterance of the word 'yes' as though it were as cataclysmic in its consequences as a woman's sexual consent: 'One word! ... Oh me! and I tremble, now, when I write it' (p. 50). The writing of the past causes him to re-experience his earlier sensations, while the future contaminates his account so much that 'the shadows of after-events [darken] the very paper' he writes on. Past and present grow confused, and the affect the episode conjures seems to be produced as much by subsequent events as by the encounter itself. Is Anne Catherick's significance present to Walter when he meets her, or is it only constructed retrospectively, in light of 'after-events'? He 'traces the lines' of his writing as if the script, rather than the event itself, might be the source of meaning. The physical nature of the encounter becomes both alibi and dilemma, as Walter can only describe himself as the victim of a bodily sensation that overtakes all rational considerations: 'Remember that I was young; remember that the hand which touched me was a woman's' (p. 50). This moment attains the status of an event which shapes the course of his future life, marking his break from the 'quiet, decent, conventionally domestic atmosphere of [his] mother's cottage' (p. 50).

Walter's lurid rendering of the encounter with the woman in white leaves ambiguous the question of whether its significance lies within the event itself or in its relation to future events. We are caught between body and text; is the moment charged because of the force of his physical experience of having 'every drop of blood ... brought to a stop' or because Anne Catherick will turn out to resemble Laura Fairlie and will become embroiled in Sir Percival's plot and secret past? It is not clear whether the physical shock of the event must be diffused or parried by the sense that future events are determined by it, or whether Walter is locating the affect attached to subsequent events in the single telling instance of his encounter with Anne Catherick. Walter tells the story as though his response to Anne Catherick itself determines what follows.

> What had I done? Assisted the victim of the most horrible of all false imprisonments to escape; or cast loose on the wide world of London an unfortunate creature, whose actions it was my duty, and every man's duty, mercifully to control? I turned sick at heart when the

question occurred to me, and when I felt self-reproachfully that it
was asked too late.

(p. 55)

Walter's rather hysterical pronouncements about the consequences
of his action suggest that it is being loaded with a significance that
cannot be found within the event itself. Thus, the establishment of
this moment as the primal event might be seen as a screen narrative
for the more questionable act of falling in love with Laura Fairlie,
which simply becomes one more of the events somehow set in
motion by his inability to respond adequately to this encounter. His
sense of having acted 'too late' in questioning his behaviour might
also apply to his belated guilt about falling in love with Laura. In
this instance, and in the affectively charged scenes that follow,
Walter seeks to locate the significance of events not just in their relation to a larger temporal sequence but in their dramatic sensational
force. Physical sensations that threaten to overwhelm the perceiver
must be transformed into mysteries to be explained. But if this is a
primal event, it is one produced as an origin through the mechanism
Freud describes as deferred action;[7] sensation is not in itself meaningful except when it has been endowed with meaning after the fact
of its occurrence. Thus, one of the meanings of Walter's response to
Anne Catherick has to do not with the woman herself, but with
how she is tied to his subsequent response to Laura.

Among the more immediate after-effects of Walter's encounter with
the woman in white is the way it heightens the striking force of his
visual first impressions of Marian and Laura Fairlie. The memory of
Anne Catherick is mingled with his anticipation of the other
women. 'What shall I see in my dreams tonight? ... the woman in
white? or the unknown inhabitants of this Cumberland mansion?'
(p. 57). Marian Halcombe, the sight of whose ugly and masculine
face provides the shocking conclusion to Walter's scrutiny of her
figure, confirms the idea that the female body and the male perception of it are legible indicators of sexual attraction. Fresh from his
ambivalence about Anne Catherick and his response to her, Walter
finds in Marian a woman whose body provokes immediate physical
repulsion, and in Laura the exact opposite.

Suspense builds for Walter's first encounter with Laura, which is
delayed by his meetings with other members of the household, and
his enlistment of Marian's help to investigate the woman in white's

references to Limmeridge House and the Fairlies. Primed by previous events, Walter begins to 'wonder ... whether [his] introduction to Miss Fairlie would disappoint the expectations that [he] had been forming of her' (p. 74). Although he accounts for his attraction as a case of love at first sight, it is difficult not to see it as a function of a series of expectations and prior events. When the moment finally arrives, he interrupts his narrative to alert us to his difficulties in describing the immediate effects of his experience because the event must be mediated by his language about it and by the history in which it is installed.

> How can I describe her? How can I separate her from my own sensations, and from all that has happened in the later time? How can I see her again as she looked when my eyes first rested on her – as she should look, now, to the eyes that are about to see her in these pages?
>
> (p. 74)

The burden of Walter's narrative is to explain his love for Laura as the unavoidable effect of her appearance. His alibi for social transgression is his helpless susceptibility to the physical sensation produced by her body. 'I let the charm of her presence lure me from the recollection of myself and my position' (p. 78). Describing Laura as the 'first woman who quickened [his] pulses', he attempts to chronicle the 'sensations that crowded on [him], when [his] eyes first looked upon her' (p.76). In order to recreate this experience for the reader, he must convert his text into an image in order that the eyes that read it become 'eyes that are about to see her'.

However, there is very little that is immediate about Walter's account of the event. He uses a drawing he has made in order to recall her freshly to mind, as though her body is an image or as though what he is really recalling is his perception of her rather than the woman herself. Furthermore, he ascribes the power of Laura's appearance to her body's status as the material instantiation of linguistic figures and mental ideas. She is the lyric love poem come to life; her eyes, for example, are 'of that soft, limpid, turquoise blue, so often sung by the poets, so seldom seen in real life' and convey 'the light of a purer and a better world' (p. 75). Invoking a Platonic metaphysics, Walter describes Laura as the embodiment of ideal form:

> Does my poor portrait of her, my fond, patient labour of long and happy days, show me these things? Ah, how few of them are in the

dim mechanical drawing, and how many in the mind with which I regard it! A fair, delicate girl, ... that is all the drawing can say; all, perhaps, that even the deeper reach of thought and pen can say in their language, either. The woman who first gives life, light, and form to our shadowy conceptions of beauty, fills a void in our spiritual nature that has remained unknown to us till she appeared. Sympathies that lie too deep for words, too deep almost for thoughts, are touched, at such times, by other charms than those which the senses feel and which the resources of expression can realise. The mystery which underlies the beauty of women is never raised above the reach of all expression until it has claimed kindred with the deeper mystery in our own souls. Then, and then only, has it passed beyond the narrow region on which light falls, in this world, from the pencil and the pen.

(pp. 75–6)

Rather than being a body, Laura is a physical representation of Walter's spiritual life, the entity that 'fills a void' and 'gives form' to 'shadowy conceptions'. Although this idealist rhetoric seems oddly out of context in a sensation novel, it aptly describes many of its sensational moments, which derive their force from the 'mystery' of a prediction or an expectation becoming a reality. Thus, we could read Laura's embodiment of his 'shadowy conceptions' as the fulfilment of a dream already firmly in place. Like his response to Anne Catherick, the immediacy of Walter's sensations is not in itself significant, for those sensations are always mediated and in part produced by a textual understanding of the event. Furthermore, by describing his pen and his language as incapable of rendering 'the mystery which underlies the beauty of women', Walter poses as the insoluble mystery of the novel Laura's physical attractiveness. I will have more to say about this mystery as a form of mystification that turns the woman's body into a fetish object in both the Freudian and the Marxist senses.

Walter's declaration that his response to Laura is immediate and instantaneous also seems suspicious because his first impressions of her are inhabited by his memory of Anne Catherick, even though he is at this point unaware of how substantial the link between the two women is. Some mystery in addition to the 'mystery' of the soul is created by her appearance:

Mingling with the vivid impression produced by the charm of her fair face and head ... was another impression, which, in a shadowy way, suggested to me the idea of something wanting. At one time it

> seemed like something wanting in her: at another, like something
> wanting in myself, which hindered me from understanding her as I
> ought. ... Something wanting, something wanting – and where it
> was, and what it was, I could not say.
>
> (pp. 76–7)

Although he does not yet recognise the 'something wanting' as her
resemblance to Anne, Walter's perception of Laura as the complete
embodiment of his desire seems to depend on her disturbing lack.
His first encounter with her, freighted with significance as the
moment at which his love originates, will turn out to have the
'shadow' of a prior event and of another woman cast over it. It is
possible to read the locution 'something wanting' as a description
of Walter's own desire, and his 'sense of an incompleteness' as an
attempt to find the lack in 'the harmony and charm of her face' that
suggests she requires his love to be truly whole. Laura's body would
thus again become a symbol for his mental state. However, the solution to the mystery of 'something wanting', that Walter has forgotten that Laura resembles Anne, complicates this relation
between body and psyche, since it suggests that Laura's body exerts
its sensational attraction only because it serves as the sign of something other than itself. She becomes attractive when her body ceases
to be merely a body and becomes a sign or text.

Walter's identification of the 'something missing' occurs when
Marian reads her mother's letter, in which she explains her acquaintance with Anne Catherick. Walter's narrative alternates sus-
pensefully between the text of the letter and the image of Laura; as
in the earlier encounters with both Anne Catherick and Laura
Fairlie, a woman's body arrives to fill the void created by narrative
expectation. Walter is like a voyeur aroused simultaneously by an
image and a text, and carried to a greater pitch of excitement by his
ability to project Marian's text onto Laura's body. As Marian asks
him about the woman in white, Laura flits at a distance across his
field of vision: 'My eyes fixed upon the white gleam of her muslin
gown and head-dress in the moonlight, and a sensation, for which I
can find no name – a sensation that quickened my pulse, and raised
a fluttering at my heart – began to steal over me' (p. 85). Walter re-
experiences the same sensation, a quickening of the pulses, he felt
when falling in love with Laura. Her figure provides a locus to
which he can assign the name of his unrepresentable sensation, the
locus that allows him to 'fix' his eyes while his mind wanders in a

combination of aimlessness and excitement, much like the pleasure of sexuality. He is both voyeur and fetishist here, taking pleasure in the view of Laura at a distance, and seeking to locate in her clothing the source of his pleasure.[8] As when he encountered Anne Catherick, his state of suspended tension begins to narrow to a single focus: 'All my attention was concentrated on the white gleam of Miss Fairlie's muslin dress' (p. 85). Even as Marian announces the 'extraordinary caprices of accidental resemblance', Walter comes to the same realisation through the repetition of an earlier sensation. It is not clear whether his memory is triggered by Laura's resemblance to Anne or by the recurrence of his own feeling.

> A thrill of the same feeling which ran through me when the touch was laid upon my shoulder on the lonely high-road chilled me again.
> There stood Miss Fairlie, a white figure, alone in the moonlight; in her attitude, in the turn of her head, in her complexion, in the shape of her face, the living image, at that distance and under those circumstances, of the woman in white! The doubt which had troubled my mind for hours and hours past flashed into conviction in an instant. That 'something wanting' was my own recognition of the ominous likeness between the fugitive from the asylum and my pupil at Limmeridge House.
>
> (p. 86)

The 'something wanting' is not a thing but a relation. As Neil Hertz suggests, what is uncanny is not the content of what is repeated but the fact of repetition.[9] Although this moment would seem to be startling because it repeats Walter's encounter with Anne Catherick, as he experiences 'a thrill of the same feeling', it would have to be more precisely described as a moment of deferred action. He constructs his encounter with Anne Catherick as meaningful because she resembles Laura, a significance only made possible by his acquaintance with Laura after the fact of his encounter with Anne. That original event acquires significance because of its relation to subsequent events, even though Walter has attempted to describe it as shocking in and of itself. Two primal moments with these women merge in this one, as Walter relives his encounter with Anne and recovers the solution to his sense of 'something wanting' in Laura.

If the fact of repetition is more important than the content of repetition, we have reason to be wary of how Walter gives that content a dark significance, reading the relation between the women as an 'ominous likeness' rather than merely an 'accidental resemblance'.

His response to the shock of repetition is to turn it into a meaningful harbinger of the future: 'To associate that forlorn, friendless, lost woman, even by an accidental likeness only, with Miss Fairlie, seems like casting a shadow on the future of the bright creature who stands looking at us now' (p. 86). This reaction bears out Freud's suggestion that the uncanny sensations produced by 'involuntary repetition ... [force] upon us the idea of something fateful and inescapable when otherwise we should have spoken only of "chance"'.[10] The hidden forces that Walter senses at work will ultimately appear manifest when the image Laura presents becomes a reality. This confirmation of 'the idea of something fateful and inescapable' finally seems to supersede the shock produced by the events themselves. Having discovered the connection between Laura and the woman in white, Walter is reassured against the confusion he has experienced: his 'doubt' 'flashes into conviction in an instant'. He regains control by being able to attribute his feelings to the supernatural coincidence of uncanny resemblance, and any possibility of his 'thrill' having a sexual content is dispelled. He has produced a mystery or secret that displaces or replaces the secret of his own love for Laura. The easing of anxiety produced by his 'conviction' suggests that the production of mystery, rather than simply producing further affect, also manages it.

For at the same time as Walter discovers the mystery of the relation between Anne and Laura, he also confesses his love for Laura: 'The poor weak words, which have failed to describe Miss Fairlie, have succeeded in betraying the sensations she awakened in me' (p. 88). He depicts himself as the victim of sensations which affect him in spite of himself ('my hardly-earned self-control was as completely lost to me as if I had never possessed it' [pp. 89–90]), implying that love is beyond considerations of social class. He confesses that which must remain a secret, although he doesn't manage to escape Marian's scrutiny, and her announcement that she has 'discovered [his] secret' leads to his departure from his position.

We might read Walter's subsequent detective work as a form of paranoid projection; he discovers the secrets that the other men who threaten his position possess in order to ward off discovery of his own secret. He disposes of Sir Percival and Count Fosco not simply by uncovering their plot to substitute Laura Fairlie for Anne Catherick but by threatening to expose their personal ghosts in the closet, secrets so threatening to their reputations that Walter can use his knowledge to blackmail these rivals into silence. He becomes a trader in secrets, using his discovery of Sir Percival's illegitimate birth and Count Fosco's membership in the Brotherhood in exchange for making public Laura Fairlie's hidden identity and his love for her. For both men, a single fact about their past dominates their entire identity and fate, and these secrets are represented by a single all-telling mark or text. Of Fosco's membership in the Italian secret society, Pesca tells Walter, 'We are identified with the Brotherhood by a secret mark, which we all bear, which lasts while our lives last' (p. 596).

Similarly, the secret of Sir Percival's illegitimacy is revealed by the absence of any notation of his birth in the second copy of the church registry. According to Walter, 'That space told the whole story!' (p. 529). With melodramatic excess, he ascribes to this fact explanatory power over all of Sir Percival's actions:

> Who could wonder now at the brute-restlessness of the wretch's life – at his desperate alternations between abject duplicity and reckless violence – at the madness of guilty distrust which had made him imprison Anne Catherick in the Asylum, and had given him over to the vile conspiracy against his wife, on the bare suspicion that the one and the other knew his terrible secret?
>
> (p. 530)

The novel derives its sensational force from casting events as the result of a single hidden cause. Furthermore, to know or to reveal a secret is to wield an enormous power, since Walter's discovery of the registry gives him access to property that is the equivalent of all that Sir Percival owns: 'This was the Secret, and it was mine! A word from me, and house, lands, baronetcy, were gone from him for ever' (p. 530). Because secrets render discourse powerful enough to strip a man of his possessions and his identity, Walter can rise in social position by acquiring knowledge. The sensational force of uncovering secrets obscures their function as a means to social mobility.

Walter's success depends not only on unmasking secrets but also on producing them. Faced with the painful impossibility of his love for Laura, he invents a mystery that allows him to believe that his feelings are more than just the result of a broken heart: 'Poignant as it was, the sense of suffering caused by the miserable end of my brief, presumptuous love seemed to be blunted and deadened by the still stronger sense of something obscurely impending, something invisibly threatening, that Time was holding over our heads' (p. 101). The production of anxiety acts as a way of diffusing and managing another anxiety. Given Walter's own secret and the desire for social mobility that it represents, it is not surprising that he should be so eager to believe Anne Catherick's claim that Sir Percival has a 'Secret', a word that he writes with a capital letter in order to increase its ominous power. His one hope for the success of his romance is that some dramatic turn of events will alter the outcome that social convention would normally dictate. He cannot rely on his own desires or actions, but must instead count on chance events or the working of a larger fate to rescue him. Thus, long before he has any reasonable evidence for Sir Percival's or Count Fosco's criminal behaviour, Walter is susceptible to the possibility that secrets exist and that some hidden fact will alter his fortunes. The 'delusions' he feels compelled to construct from 'common chances' and 'common coincidences', such as Anne and Laura's resemblance, are perhaps not quite so irrational as he might like to think (p. 101). Forced to leave Limmeridge House because of his own secret and because of Laura's commitment to Sir Percival, he can only hope that the future will hold dreadful consequences. The overshadowing of his 'sense of suffering' by the 'still stronger sense of something obscurely impending' suggests that 'Time' will rescue him from his misery (p. 101). It is to Walter's psychic, and, ultimately, economic and social benefit to believe in forces of determination that will bring about apocalyptic events and to believe that he cannot predict their outcome. Belief in chance allows him to hope that it will accrue to his good fortune. As Derrida says, 'To believe in chance can just as well indicate that one believes in the existence of chance as that one does *not*, above all, believe in chance, since one looks for and finds a hidden meaning at all costs.'[11]

The language of fate and chance events, which leads Walter to pursue Sir Percival and count Fosco, is first generated by the bodily resemblance of Anne Catherick and Laura Fairlie, and we might wonder how this mysterious coincidence is connected to those other secrets that determine the relations between men. We can note first of all that their resemblance is the product of yet another male secret, their father's sexual indiscretion, which produces the illegitimate Anne. Their blood relation further strengthens the social reading of their difference; they share a common parentage, but because Anne is illegitimate she is destined for the life that makes her body bear the marks of suffering. Furthermore, Walter's assumption of the family property is rendered morally secure by the fact that the father's crime ensures the instability of his transmission of property. Had there been no Anne Catherick, Laura's fortune might have been safe from the plots of Count Fosco and Sir Percival, and because she embodies the secret of her father's sexual promiscuity, Walter can finally reconsolidate the family line by replacing him:

> But for the fatal resemblance between the two daughters of one father, the conspiracy of which Anne had been the innocent instrument and Laura the innocent victim could never have been planned. With what unerring and terrible directness the long chain of circumstances led down from the thoughtless wrong committed by the father to the heartless injury inflicted on the child!
>
> (p. 575)

Walter seeks to locate a direct link between the father's 'thoughtless wrong' and subsequent events, again invoking the metaphor of the 'chain' that connects past and present. Causality is given an emotional valence, as he speaks of the 'unerring and terrible directness' of this teleology. But where exactly did the crime occur, given that the effects of the 'fatal resemblance' exceed its origin? The father's indiscretion provides no guarantee that a conspiracy will take place. The lineage of heredity somehow becomes responsible for determining all further events, but the causality here is not as necessary as the language suggests. The resemblance between Anne and Laura becomes a literalisation of the law that the 'sins of the father are visited upon the children', but that literal reality must be acted upon before 'heartless injury' makes 'accidental resemblance' a 'fatal resemblance'. The crime of the father gets written on the bodies of the two women, which bear the traces of his secret in an immediately visible form. Their 'resemblance' is striking in part because it renders concrete, literally embodies, the hidden causality that connects them.

Yet the compelling affect produced by both Anne's and Laura's appearance also seems related to Walter's sexual attraction. Once again, though, sexuality has to be read as a conduit for material and social forces. Walter's glorification of Laura's physical appearance can be seen as a version of commodity fetishism, which is described by Marx as a process of sensationalising objects, or creating a mystery that substitutes for a recognition of the true source of their power: 'The mysterious character of the commodity-form consists therefore simply in the fact that the commodity reflects the social characteristics of men's own labour as objective characteristics of the products of labour themselves, as the socionatural properties of these things.'[12] Walter makes the mistake of reading social relations as inhering in an object when he attributes Laura's attractiveness to her physical beauty. This is made evident by the fact that the only difference between her and Anne Catherick is their social class, and this can be the only explanation for why Walter loves Laura rather than Anne. If Laura's body is not naturally possessed of the characteristics that make her desirable, then the fascination she exerts must be explained by appeal to a theory of how objects become cathected, which is one way of describing Marx's notion of commodity fetishism. He explains commodity fetishism in specifically visual terms, a suggestive analogy in so far as Walter's relation to Anne and Laura is so insistently visual:

> Through this substitution, the products of labour become commodities, sensuous things which are at the same time suprasensible or social. In the same way, the impression made by a thing on the optic nerve is perceived not as a subjective excitation of that nerve but as the objective form of a thing outside the eye. In the act of seeing, of course, light is really transmitted from one thing, the external object, to another thing, the eye. It is a physical relation between physical things. As against this, the commodity-form, and the value-relation of the products of labour within which it appears, have absolutely no connection with the physical nature of the commodity and the material ... relations arising out of this. It is nothing but the definite social relation between men themselves which assumes here, for them, the fantastic form of a relation between things.[13]

Just as the commodity fetishist takes the evidence of sight as confirmation of the commodity's objective and intrinsic value, so Walter Hartright uses the immediacy of sight in order to locate the source of his desire in Laura's body rather than in social relations. And indeed Laura is a kind of commodity, the acquisition of which guarantees to its possessor social property. However, because her status as a site of property or position is mediated by the sexual attractiveness of her body, her power can be simultaneously mystified and naturalised. The sexualising or sensationalising of her body is the mechanism for romance, which is then the means to social mobility, and the steps in this process are collapsed when her body itself is seen as the source of her appeal. Furthermore, the 'definite social relation' that might explain the difference and similarity between Laura and Anne assumes in this sensational text 'the fantastic form of a relation between things'. The substitution of Laura for Anne seems to work two ways, both establishing and denying the importance of the body as a marker of identity and social position. On the one hand, if Laura can be sequestered away as Anne Catherick, and actually come to look like her, it would suggest that identity is contingent, that the body is not a guarantee of individuality, but can be moulded or propped upon to create another identity. On the other hand, Walter and Marian's discovery of Laura in the asylum works to suggest that she really is Laura and not Anne. Their instant recognition of her, even when she is disguised, implies that they see, beyond the trappings of society and the machinations of Fosco, the essential Laura. Of course, this real Laura is finally no more than body, since she is reduced to a state of childlike dependency once her memory and identity are stripped away by trauma. However, this is the only Laura who is necessary and desirable for Walter's purposes because he can then act as her parent and bring her back to life, while still being sure of her utter dependency on him and her conformity to his ideal of femininity.

The mystery that is created by Laura's and Anne's bodies can be connected to Marx's description of commodity fetishism as the production of a secret: 'Value, therefore, does not have its description branded on its forehead; it rather transforms every product of labour into a social hieroglyphic. Later on, men try to decipher the hieroglyphic, to get behind the secret of their own social product.'[14] We might understand from this passage how to read the sensation novel's interest in secrets, its fascination with uncovering the mystery of the object. The reference to value branded on the forehead conjures up the fantasy enabled by Fosco's brand, the possibility that a secret could be as easy to discover as a mark on the body. Similarly, Laura and Anne represent the possibility of a body that is meaningful in and of itself, while also showing how this objectification creates female desirability as a cover for social desirability. The difference between the two women is broached but then mystified as the product of fate or chance. Thus the sensation novel provides a narrative for social determination but obscures it by rendering it in the form of fatal determination. Furthermore, the fetishisation of the woman's body takes on a sexual quality, and both is and is not the real object that represents social relations.

It is difficult to say whether Anne and Laura are fascinating because they are bodies or because they are signs. Walter melodramatically concludes from the likeness between the two: 'If ever sorrow and suffering set their profaning marks on the youth and beauty of Miss Fairlie's face, then, and then only, Anne Catherick and she would be the twin-sisters of chance resemblance, the living reflections of one another' (p. 120). When this prediction is fulfilled, this sentence is repeated almost verbatim, suggesting that textual repetition is as important as bodily repetition. 'The sorrow and suffering ... *had* set their profaning marks on the youth and beauty of her face; and the fatal resemblance which I had once seen and shuddered at seeing, in idea only, was now a real and living resemblance' (pp. 454–5). What is being effaced here by the emphasis on repetition are the social circumstances that make this repetition possible. The difference between Laura and Anne could be read as the difference between a rich woman, safely ensconced in domestic comfort, and a poor woman confined to an asylum. Their resemblance is a reminder that identity is a product not of intrinsic qualities but of social determinations which mark the body sufficiently that identical women can have different appearances. This fact is revealed even more clearly by the fact that Laura can come to look like Anne. However, the text is structured so as to make this event seem to be the mysterious product of 'chance' or 'fate'. Our attention is focused on the blurring of the distinction between text and reality, as the 'idea' of resemblance becomes 'real and living'. Once again, Laura is not a body but an image. Similarly, when she becomes Anne revivified, and as her body enacts the drama narrated in the letter, she appears as a 'white figure' and a 'living image' rather than a real body. We are reminded by this language of the fact that Laura, even as a body, is a figure for something else. This in fact is the implication of Marx's description of the commodity; if correctly perceived it stands as a sign of social relations, and is perhaps the only way they are made tangible or visible. However, those social relations are always liable to be misrecognised if their power is located in the object's natural properties rather than in what it represents.

The Woman in White thus encodes within itself the process which it encourages the reader to enact. It provides the vehicle for a relation between a physical sensation and a text, attaching bodily responses to lurid tales. It thus fulfils the desire to make what the body fears meaningful, translating ordinary events into the effect of extraordinary tales. At one point in the narrative, we catch a glimpse of a different origin for sensation, prompted by the changes brought about by urban development. During one of his journeys to inquire about Sir Percival, Walter describes in gothic tones the scene that he comes upon, a very different landscape from that in which he encountered Anne Catherick:

> Is there any wilderness of sand in the deserts of Arabia, is there any prospect of desolation among the ruins of Palestine, which can rival the repelling effect on the eye, and the depressing influence on the mind, of an English country town in the first stage of its existence, and in the transition state of its prosperity? I asked myself that question as I passed through the clean desolation, the neat ugliness, the prim torpor of the streets of Welmingham. And the tradesmen who stared after me from their lonely shops – the trees that drooped helpless in their arid exile of unfinished crescents and squares – the dead house-carcasses that waited in vain for the vivifying human element to animate them with the breath of life – every creature that I saw, every object that I passed, seemed to answer with one accord: The deserts of Arabia are innocent of our civilised desolation – the ruins of Palestine are incapable of our modern gloom!
>
> (p. 503)

Walter transfers onto the landscape the hidden narrative of his own accession to power, observing with horror the waste and desolation that may be its byproducts.[15] He reacts by being 'repelled' and 'depressed'; here are the emotions and sensations of the individual subject, who, faced with a rapidly modernising capitalist society, reaches for a novel to escape. Progress in England, which should mean a move away from the primitive state of the 'deserts of Arabia' and the 'ruins of Palestine', seems only to bring a new form of anxiety rather than a new form of happiness. The commodity is suddenly unfetishised, no longer animated with the life of the labour that makes it; instead there are 'dead house-carcasses' standing in 'arid exile'. Yet the objects that lack 'the vivifying human element' still seem able to speak the words that the human subject cannot articulate. Walter anthropomorphises the products of capitalist accumulation even as he pronounces them dead, and they declare 'with one accord' that one of the products of urban advancement is a new affect, 'modern gloom'.

The Woman in White demonstrates how affect can be made melodramatic in order to enable male accession to power, while repressing or mystifying (both in the sense of obscuring and in the sense of making mysterious or sensational) the mechanisms by which this is made possible. Walter's sensational attraction to Laura Fairlie depends on both the mystification of the way, as a marriageable woman, she represents his means to social success, and the mystification of her body as significant in itself rather than as the marker of social relations. Her resemblance to Anne Catherick both reveals the nature of those social relations, and reconceals them by enabling a story about determination in the form of fate. This form of determination allows Walter to believe that his accession to power is not the result of his own transgressive ambition or desire, but is somehow in the cards. Furthermore, in so far as the resemblance is a function of chance, a realisation made possible by his accidental encounter, he can also believe that social determination does not prevent his rise in power, that accidents can happen and can be significant enough to change the course of events. This continues to be one of the social functions of sensation; it encourages the belief that all events are extraordinary and thus that change occurs miraculously rather than through more mundane or painstaking processes. Both fate and chance, while seemingly opposed, are invoked to obscure the nature of social determination, and are used to describe the relation between Anne and Laura. Walter's psychic fascination with the two women is the product of the fantasy that it might be possible to make social relations visible in single cataclysmic events.

If the passage about 'modern gloom' quoted above were read as the key to The Woman in White's affective power, it would suggest that the sensation novel merely transfers affect from one site to another. Walter's sensationalising of Laura and of secrets would represent a displacement of the affect generated by his own social mobility and the transitions created by capitalism, a displacement that transforms that affect from anxiety to magical fascination. But The Woman in White is also about the production of affect, not just about its transfer from one cathected site to another, demonstrating how Walter's fascination with the two women enables his accession to power. The mystery of the woman in white reveals why sensation might continue to exert its thrill, even when demystified by Marxist analysis, for Marx's own notion of the commodity implies that, if correctly seen, objects have the capacity to render social relations visible or concrete. If the woman in white and her double are affectively powerful because they are signs, and not just bodies, this is no less true for the reader of culture than it is for the fortune-hunter.

From *Novel*, 23 (1989), 24–43.

NOTES

[A different version of this essay later appeared in Cvetkovich's book, *Mixed Feelings: Feminism, Mass Culture and Victorian Sensationalism* (New Brunswick, NJ, 1992). This book focuses on 'the representation of social problems as affective dilemmas' in certain kinds of writing of the 1860s and 1870s in which 'a discourse about "sensationalism" became the vehicle for a politics of affect' (p. 2). In this Foucauldian study Cvetkovich is particularly interested in demonstrating how mass culture enables the regulation of subjectivity through the management and containment of emotion and affect. Cvetkovich's exploration of the ideology of narrative form in this essay links the economy of detection of *The Woman in White* to its economy of sensation, and reads both in terms of an interpretative economy of suspicion in which 'every fact that excites a sensation merits investigation' (p. 110). She looks particularly closely at the discrepancy between Walter Hartright's rhetoric of narration and what is narrated, and suggests that his foregrounding of objectivity and rationality, and his suppression of sensation is at the centre of a network of displacement strategies by means of which bodily sensations and emotional/psychological responses are substituted for and mask social and political realities. Ed.]

1. Wilkie Collins, *The Woman in White* (Harmondsworth, 1974), p. 33. All further citations are included in the text and refer to this edition.

2. [H. L. Mansel] 'Sensation Novels', *The Quarterly Review*, 113 (April 1863), 482. For the most comprehensive description of the genre and the critical controversy it provoked, see Winifred Hughes, *The Maniac in the Cellar: Sensation Novels of the 1860s* (Princeton, NJ, 1980).

3. Wilkie Collins, *The Woman in White*, ed. Harvey Peter Sucksmith (Oxford, 1975), p. xx.

4. See D. A. Miller, 'From *roman policier* to *roman-police*: Wilkie Collin's *The Moonstone*', *Novel*, 13 (Winter, 1980), 153–70 [see pp. 197–220 below – Ed.] for a discussion of how detection or surveillance operates through the form of multiple narration rather than through the overt intervention or representation of the police or even, finally, a detective. He argues that the novel aims to align ordinary experience with detection.

5. D. A. Miller, '*Cages aux folles*: Sensation and Gender in Wilkie Collins's *The Woman in White*', *Representations*, 14 (Spring 1986),

109. Although I agree with much of what Miller says, especially his argument that the sensation novel has to be read in terms of its production of bodily sensation, my reading departs from his in so far as he sees the somatic experience of sensation as a threat to be defended against, whereas I am arguing that it serves as a welcome screen and conduit for Walter Hartright's accession to power. Rather than having to secure himself against the feminising, and hence debilitating, effects of sensation, Walter is able to acquire power because of his sensitivity to affect. I would also argue that the somatic nature of sensation has to be read in relation to its projection onto a text, and thus would not separate thematic sensation and bodily sensation as readily as Miller does.

6. Perhaps the most conclusive instance of this phenomenon is one critic's discovery that, despite Collins's elaborate plotting, the scheme to substitute Laura for Anne was in fact technically impossible according to the dates established in the narrative. Collins corrected this error in subsequent editions, but the critic admits that the irrelevance of the supposedly all-important facts to the reader's enjoyment of the novel is testimony to the author's power. 'A plot that is worked out of impossibilities, like that of robbing the almanack of a fortnight, may not be treated as a jest; but we vote three cheers for the author who is able to practise such a jest with impunity. He will not have a reader the less, and all who read will be deceived and delighted' ('Appendix A', *The Woman in White*, ed. Sucksmith, p. 586). That Collins could make such an error suggests that the affect produced by his mystery is more important than the solution to it.

7. My understanding of Freud's notion of deferred action is derived from his case study of the Wolfman. Of the retroactive projection of meaning onto a primal event, which may itself only be a construction of the imagination, he says, for example: 'Scenes from early infancy, such as are brought up by an exhaustive analysis of neuroses ... are not reproductions of real occurrences, to which it is possible to ascribe an influence over the course of the patient's later life and over the formation of his symptoms. [The interpretation] considers them rather as products of the imagination, which find their instigation in mature life, which are intended to serve as some kind of symbolic representation of real wishes and interests, and which owe their origin to a regressive tendency, to an aversion from the problems of the present.' Sigmund Freud, 'From the History of an Infantile Neurosis' (1918), in *Three Case Histories*, ed. Philip Rieff (New York, 1963), pp. 236–7.

8. Freud describes fetishism as the cathexis on an object that substitutes for the penis the mother lacks. The fetish object both represents the threat of castration and provides reassurance against it: 'He [the fetishist] retains this belief [that the mother has a penis] but he also gives it up; during the conflict between the dead weight of the unwelcome perception and the force of the opposite wish, a compromise is

constructed such as is only possible in the realm of unconscious modes of thought – by the primary processes ... It [the fetish] remains a token of triumph over the threat of castration and a safeguard against it; it also saves the fetishist from being a homosexual by endowing women with the attribute which makes them acceptable as sexual objects.' Sigmund Freud, 'Fetishism' (1927) in *Sexuality and the Psychology of Love*, ed. Philip Rieff (New York, 1963), p. 216.

Walter reassures himself against the threat posed by the woman in white (and the threat of feminisation posed by his susceptibility to sensation) by finding pleasure in Laura's image. However, I don't want to read this moment simply as the sign of Walter's mastery of the shock he receives from Anne Catherick, as though that were the primal moment whose threat requires some form of reassurance. The earlier moment is not more primary than this one.

9. Neil Hertz, 'Freud and the Sandman', *The End of the Line* (New York, 1985), pp. 97–121.

10. Sigmund Freud, 'The "Uncanny"' (1919), in *The Standard Edition of the Complete Psychological Works of Sigmund Freud*, ed. James Strachey (London, 1953, 17:237).

11. Jacques Derrida, 'My Chances/*Mes Chances*: A Rendezvous with some Epicurean Stereophonies', in *Taking Chances: Derrida, Psychoanalysis, and Literature*, ed. Joseph H. Smith and William Kerrigan (Baltimore, MD, 1984), p. 4.

12. Karl Marx, *Capital*, Vol. I, intro. Ernest Mandel, trans. Ben Fowkes (New York, 1977), pp. 164–5.

13. Ibid., p. 165.

14. Ibid., p. 167.

15. I am indebted to Sabrina Barton for this observation.

6

Rewriting the Male Plot in Wilkie Collins's *No Name*

DEIRDRE DAVID

Whether Wilkie Collins was a feminist, deployed popular literature for feminist ideology, or even liked women is not the subject of this essay. My interest is in something less explicit, perhaps not fully intentional, to be discovered in his fiction: an informing link between restlessness with dominant modes of literary form and fictional critique of dominant modes of gender politics. In what follows, I aim to show how the narrative shape of one of Collins's most baroquely plotted, narratively complex novels is inextricably enmeshed with its thematic material. I refer to *No Name*, a novel whose subversion of fictional omniscience suggests Collins's radical literary practice and whose sympathy for a rebellious heroine in search of subjectivity suggests his liberal sexual politics.[1] To be sure, there are other Collins novels as narratively self-reflexive as *No Name*, *The Moonstone*, for one; and *Man and Wife*, for example, mounts a strong attack on misogynistic subjection of women (particularly when exercised by heroes of the Muscular Christian variety). But no Collins novel, in my view, so interestingly conflates resistance to dominant aesthetic and sexual ideologies as *No Name*, even as it ultimately displays its appropriation by the authority that both enables its existence and fuels its resistance.

Challenging authoritarian, patriarchal-sited power in his interrogation of form and theme, Collins collapses a binary opposition between the two, a separation assumed in Victorian criticism of the novel and still, perhaps, possessing a lingering appeal in these deconstructive times. The intense dialogism, the insistent relativism, of *No Name* makes it impossible to align in one column what is represented and in another the *ways* in which representation takes place. Neither is it possible to construct a neat alignment of fictionality and representation, to say that at this moment the novel performs self-reflexive cartwheels and that at another we are in the realm of strict mimesis. Mimesis, one might say, is always simultaneous with semiosis in *No Name*, so much so, in fact, that representation, say, of a character obsessed with the record keeping which is the means of his social survival, becomes a field for self-reflexive fictionality; and, to a lesser extent, fictionality is sometimes the ground on which Collins maps his persuasively realistic narrative.[2] Collapsing the neat polarities of literary analysis, upsetting the conventions of omniscient narrative, showing a woman's struggle for survival as she is both exiled from and enclosed within patriarchal structures – all this is the business of *No Name*, in my view an exemplary novel for 'naming' Collins's disruptive place in the tradition of Victorian fiction.

The original publication of Collins's novels covers some forty years, from *Antonina* in 1850 to *Blind Love*, left unfinished at his death in 1889, and his career encompasses two distinct periods in the history of Victorian fiction: At the beginning we are in the age of Dickens and Thackeray; at the end we enter a new generation composed of Hardy, Stevenson, Moore, Gissing, and Kipling.[3] With *Antonina*, a historical romance set in fifth-century Rome and owing much to Gibbon and Bulwer-Lytton, Collins established himself as a powerful storyteller with a commendable eye for detail, and by the time of his fifth novel, *The Woman in White*, he emerged as a master of diegesis with a narrative something for everyone: omniscience, free indirect discourse, autobiography, diary, letter, newspaper story, ledger book, memoranda. *No Name* appeared during the 1860s (Collins's stellar decade of literary production) between his two best-known novels, *The Woman in White* and *The Moonstone*, and was first published in Dickens's weekly magazine *All the Year Round* from March 1862 to January 1863 and published in three volumes at the end of 1862. Divided into eight dramatic 'scenes', punctuated by groups of letters which are, in turn, interpolated with newspaper stories and journal entries, *No Name* was phenomenally successful. Collins received 3000 pounds for the first edition, sold nearly 4000 copies on the day of publication, netted 1500 pounds for American serial rights, and obtained

5000 guineas from Smith Elder for his next novel before having written a word.[4]

Unlike most Collins novels, however, *No Name* discloses no secrets, rattles no nerves with sensational excitement; rather, as he observes in his preface, 'all the main events of the story are purposely foreshadowed, before they take place – my present design being to rouse the reader's interest in following the train of circumstances by which these foreseen events are brought about'.[5] For some critics, the absence of suspense seriously impairs *No Name*'s success. Jerome Meckier, in particular, finds 'the biggest mistake' to be 'procedural' and believes Collins 'sadly misjudges his own strengths' in forgoing surprise. From another perspective, however, one can argue that even before it begins *No Name*, a story about an unconventional female response to legal disinheritance, seeks to demystify the power of conventional, one might say inherited, Victorian narrative discourse. Rather than demanding from the reader acquiescence in a controlled revelation of plot, the narrator collaboratively offers a chance to see how plot comes into being, an opportunity to experience plot-in-process, so to speak, rather than plot-as-product. What's more, as several contemporary critics perceived, in forgoing narrative suspense for readerly collaboration, Collins situates his narrative practice in contention with the sort of instructive discourse perfected by George Eliot, whose *Adam Bede* and *The Mill on the Floss*, with their exemplary narrative discursions into questions of social responsibility, artistic representation, and cultural change preceded *No Name* by several years.[6]

As it is difficult to discuss any Collins novel without summarising what happens, I shall do that briefly before showing how *No Name* disrupts conventional narrative discourse in the process of interrogating Victorian gender politics. On the death of their father Andrew Vanstone, eighteen-year-old Magdalen and her older sister Norah are unable to inherit his considerable fortune. As a young officer in Canada, he married impetuously, repented quickly, and returned to England, where he met the mother-to-be of Magdalen and Norah, a woman courageous enough to live with him. In the opening chapter, Vanstone and his forty-four-year-old pregnant not-wife learn of the death of his legal wife and quickly go off to London to marry. But a few days later Vanstone is killed in a railway accident, and the now legal second wife rapidly declines into death after childbirth, leaving her orphan daughters to discover that, although they are now legitimate, they are disinherited because Vanstone made his will before marrying their mother. They are named 'Nobody's children', and their inheritance goes to a mean-spirited uncle who quickly departs the novel – leaving his puny son Noel immensely rich and vulnerable to Magdalen's considerable attractions. A born actress, she undertakes numerous disguises with the assistance of one Captain Horatio Wragge (a scoundrel who achieves respectability by the end of the novel), marries Noel under an assumed name, is unmasked by her husband's craftily intelligent housekeeper, falls desperately ill after the death of Noel, and is dramatically rescued by the son of a friend of her father, a Captain Kirke – whom she marries in a symbolic reconciliation with the father figure who left her legitimate yet disinherited at the beginning of the novel. Exiled from patriarchal protection in the opening chapters, she is enfolded within patriarchy's embrace by the end. And to complete this story of return to one's heritage, her sister marries the man who inherits the estate from Noel Vanstone.

No Name is notable for Collins's bold delineation of a heroine who sells her sexuality to regain her rightful fortune. An outraged Mrs Oliphant (always good for a scandalised response) declared in 1863 that Magdalen engages in 'a career of vulgar and aimless trickery and wickedness, with which it is impossible to have a shadow of sympathy', that she is tainted by 'the pollutions of ... endless deceptions and horrible marriage'.[7] The 'horrible marriage' part distressed almost all reviewers, and even now, in our far less prudish time, it is difficult not to be troubled, even embarrassed, by Collins's sexual frankness. He describes a young woman bursting with 'exuberant vitality', possessed of 'a figure instinct with such a seductive, serpentine suppleness, so lightly and playfully graceful, that its movements suggested, not unnaturally, the movements of a young cat ... so perfectly developed already that no one who saw her could have supposed that she was only eighteen', undergoing 'the revolting ordeal of marriage' to a frail little man with a miserable moustache, the complexion of a delicate girl, an appalling habit of screwing up his pale eyes, and a forehead that is always crumpling 'into a nest of wicked little wrinkles' (pp. 6, 357, 205). But the chilling picture of sexual bargain between vibrant young woman and sickly older man, undisguised as it is by the cosmetic of Victorian piety, serves its political purpose: Collins makes us see that disinherited middle-class women, deprived of paternal protection, assume an identity that is both inscribed and concealed by the gender politics of their social class – that of sexual object. We also see how the literal incarceration of women to be found in Collins's earlier novel *The Woman in White* becomes, in *No Name*, an incarceration formed of rigid laws, of patriarchal injunctions.

In his focus upon the 'sensational' aspects of *The Woman in White*, the ways that this novel (and others in the 'sensation' genre) elaborates 'a fantasmatics of sensation', D. A. Miller observes that Laura Fairlie 'follows a common itinerary of the liberal subject in nineteenth-century fiction: she takes a nightmarish detour through the carceral ghetto on her way *home*, to the domestic haven where she is always felt to belong'.[8] In *No Name*, Magdalen Vanstone also makes that journey. But whereas Laura is essentially passive, the quintessentially pale and quivering victim, Magdalen is aggressive, robustly in rebellion against the law that confines her to impecunious humiliation. What's more, Magdalen's awesomely vibrant performances (first in legitimate roles as Julia and Lucy in an amateur production of *The Rivals* at the beginning of the novel, then in illegitimate impersonations of her former governess and a parlourmaid) constitute energetic difference from the passivity of women in *The Woman in White* (excluding, needless to say, that fascinating pioneer woman detective, Marion Halcombe).

Magdalen possesses a frightening ability to lose her own self in the assumption of other identities,[9] and her first strategy for survival when she finds herself 'Nobody's' daughter is to leave home and seek out the manager of the amateur theatricals, who, amazed by her talent for mimicry, had given her his card and declared her a 'born actress'. Unable to find him, she is befriended (or, rather, appropriated) by Captain Wragge: He will turn her into a professional and will be compensated when Magdalen recovers her rightful fortune. Wragge's recounting (in one of his numerous Chronicles, which I shall discuss in a moment) of her first appearance in an 'At Home' (a performance featuring one actor assuming a series of extraordinarily different characters) indicates some of the larger meanings of gender politics in the novel. Wragge devises 'the Entertainment', manages 'all the business', writes two anonymous letters to the lawyer authorised to find her, fortifies her with sal volatile as antidote to unhappy memories of her family, and sends her on stage:

> We strung her up in no time, to concert pitch; set her eyes in a blaze; and made her out-blush her own rouge. The curtain rose when we

had got her at red heat. She dashed at it ... rushed full gallop through her changes of character, her songs, and her dialogue; making mistakes by the dozen, and never stopping to set them right; carrying the people along with her in a perfect whirlwind, and never waiting for the applause.

(p. 175)

Endowed with a natural vitality which is 'managed', disciplined, and shaped by Wragge, Magdalen during the actual performance reasserts her naturally vital, rebellious female self in 'out-blushing' her own rouge, thereby suggesting how the novel, in general, addresses the way woman's 'natural' talent is shaped by patriarchal culture, society, and the law. If Wragge, then, as stage manager operates as an omnipotent string puller, let us see how his other activities strongly suggest the omnipotence associated with narrative omniscience. Wragge may be seen as parodic emblem, as Collins's embodied and symbolic critique of prevailing literary form in the Victorian period.

Omniscience, according to J. Hillis Miller, finds its authority and its origin in the unsettling of established religious beliefs: 'The development of Victorian fiction is a movement from the assumption that society and the self are founded on some superhuman power outside them, to a putting in question of this assumption, to a discovery that society now appears to be self-creating and self-supporting, resting on nothing outside itself.'[10] As remedy for the profound unease occasioned by such a discovery, society turns to/authorises the fictionally omniscient/omnipotent narrator to fill the void, retard slippage from belief to scepticism. Through his unrelenting insistence on diegetic relativism, which is expressed in the multiple narrative perspectives we encounter in almost all his fiction, Collins refuses to perform the consolatory functions Miller identifies. Very much like Thackeray in *Vanity Fair*, who interrogates all forms of authority and wants us to examine the unthinking ways we accept fictions of various sorts, how, especially, we believe in a novelist's total knowledge of the world, Collins insists that we see the subjective, arbitrary nature of fictional representation, the hubristic nature of novelistic omnipotence.

Defining himself as a 'moral agriculturalist; a man who cultivates the field of human sympathy', Wragge scoffs at being labelled a 'Swindler': 'What of that? The same low tone of mind assails men in other professions in a similar manner – calls great writers, scribblers – great generals, butchers – and so on' (p. 153). Identifying

himself with 'great writers' who cultivate 'the field of human sympathy', he becomes, of course, both like and unlike Wilkie Collins,
the Victorian inheritor and reviser of conventional narrative discourse. But this is not all; Wragge's deft talent for inventing characters and identities also associates him with the creation of fiction.
For example, one of the books in his 'commercial library' (a repository of reference works in roguery and deception) is entitled 'Skins
to Jump Into'. Concocting plausible identities for himself, Mrs
Wragge, and Magdalen in the plot to attract and snare Noel
Vanstone, he selects the 'skins' of a Mr Bygrave, Mrs Bygrave, and
niece Susan and instructs Magdalen as follows:

> My worthy brother was established twenty years ago, in the ma-
> hogany and logwood trade at Belize, Honduras. He died in that
> place; and is buried on the south-west side of the local cemetery, with
> a neat monument of native wood carved by a self-taught negro artist.
> Nineteen months afterwards, his widow died of apoplexy at a board-
> ing-house in Cheltenham. She was supposed to be the most corpulent
> woman in England; and was accommodated on the ground floor of
> the house in consequence of the difficulty of getting her up and down
> stairs. You are her only child; you have been under my care since the
> sad event at Cheltenham; you are twenty-one years old on the second
> of August next; and, corpulence excepted, you are the living image of
> your mother.
>
> (pp. 235–6)

His imperative omniscience, his persuasive attention to detail, his
energetic keeping up of numerous journals and ledgers that record
assumable identities, characteristics of different 'districts', narratives of successful and unsuccessful swindles – all affirm his status
in No Name as parodic narrator, as emblem of convention, order,
and legitimacy (despite and because of his vagabond status).

Insisting 'he must have everything down in black and white', an-
nouncing that 'All untidiness, all want of system and regularity,
causes me the acutest irritation' (p. 147) in a manner worthy of
Conrad's accountant in Heart of Darkness, he writes his narratives
of deception in precise pages of neat handwriting, obsessively aligns
rows of figures, and permits no blots, stains, or erasures. To complete this empire of fiction making, of fabrication of identity, he
has, quite literally, authorised himself; everything, he proudly declares, is verified by 'my testimonials to my own worth and integrity'. In sum, Wragge performs a kind of burlesque of Victorian

narrative discourse, of the sovereign omniscience that dominates the period – and this, of course, is the mode of arbitrary narrative from which Wilkie Collins implicitly disinherited himself in his persistent interpolation of omniscience with the relativism of diary, letter, journalistic fragment, and so on. Bakhtin's observation that the novel form 'is the expression of a Galilean perception of language, one that denies the absolutism of a single and unitary language', is richly borne out by the dialogism of *No Name*.[11]

If Captain Horatio Wragge serves as vehicle for Collins's restlessness with dominant modes of literary form, then it is his wife, Matilda Wragge, who, absolutely unconsciously, expresses Collins's critique of dominant modes of gender politics. *No Name*, thick with the inherited themes of Victorian fiction – marriage, family, money, wills, female desire, male governance – contains an irregular, disruptive episode that functions as an important signifier for Collins's indictment of patriarchal law. Mrs Wragge is the alarming centre of this episode, an illegitimate, irregular, symbolically political action that molests the attempts at omnipotence practised by her husband. She is affiliated more with modes of signification, with interrogations of fictionality, than with the events of the signified, with what is being represented. I'm going to name this episode 'Captain Wragge Orders an Omelette'. And to explain what I mean by this, let me take you to the scene where Magdalen meets Matilda for the first time.

Characterised by her husband as 'constitutionally torpid' and declared by Lewis Carroll to be an uncanny anticipation of his White Queen,[12] Mrs Wragge is a physical marvel. A gigantic six feet, three inches, she has an enormous, smooth, moonlike face, 'dimly irradiated by eyes of mild and faded blue, which looked straightforward into vacancy' (p. 146), and complains constantly of a 'Buzzing' in her head. This buzzing is not helped by her husband's compulsion to bark orders like a sergeant major: Confiding to Magdalen that he is a 'martyr' to his own sense of order, Wragge shouts, 'Sit straight at the table. More to the left, more still – that will do' (p. 151), and 'Pull it up at heel, Mrs Wragge – pull it up at heel!' – this occasioned by the sight of her worn slippers. The buzzing, she explains, began before she married the Captain and was working as a waitress in Darch's Dining Rooms in London: 'The gentlemen all came together; the gentlemen were all hungry together; the gentlemen all gave their orders together' (p. 148). Years later she is still trying to get the gentlemen's orders sorted out; becoming 'violently excited' by Magdalen's sympathetic questioning, she begins to repeat the orders retained in her muddled mind:

> Boiled pork and greens and peas-pudding for Number One. Stewed beef and carrots and gooseberry tart, for Number Two. Cut of mutton, and quick about it, well done, and plenty of fat, for Number Three. Codfish and parsnips, two chops to follow, hot-and-hot, or I'll be the death of you, for Number Four. Five, six, seven, eight, nine, ten. Carrots and gooseberry tart – peas pudding and plenty of fat – pork and beef and mutton, and cut 'em all, and quick about it – stout for one, and ale for t'other – and stale bread here, and new bread there – and this gentleman likes cheese, and that gentleman doesn't – Matilda, Tilda, Tilda, Tilda, fifty times over, till I don't know my own name.

> (p. 148)

In this City chophouse, eerily suggestive of Harold Pinter's *Dumb-Waiter* where two hit men attempt to fill orders for steak and chips, jam tarts, and so on, Matilda, disoriented by the barrage of gentlemen's orders, does not know her own name, feels herself deprived of identity by the incessant discipline of male directions; she becomes, in a sense, somewhat like Magdalen, a woman deprived of her identity as inheriting daughter and disciplined by laws that legislate legitimacy and correct irregularity.

It is at Darch's Dining Rooms that Mrs Wragge meets the Captain, 'the hungriest and the loudest' of the lot. Once married, her servant duties are transferred from a multitude of hungry and demanding gentlemen to one: She shaves him, does his hair, cuts his nails, presses his trousers, trims his nails, and, misery of miseries, cooks his meals. This latter duty requires constant recourse to a 'tattered' cookery book, and when Magdalen meets her, she is attempting to master the directions for making an omelette (ordered by the Captain for breakfast the next day). As I'm going to suggest, this is an omelette with many fillings.

Here's how she interprets the recipe to Magdalen:

> 'Omelette with Herbs. Beat up two eggs with a little water or milk, salt, pepper, chives, and parsley. Mince small' There! mince small! How am I to mince small, when it's all mixed up and running? 'Put a piece of butter the size of your thumb into the frying pan.' – Look at my thumb, and look at yours! whose size does she mean? 'Boil, but not brown.' – If it mustn't be brown, what colour must it be? ...

'Allow it to set, raise it round the edge; when done, turn it over to double it ... Keep it soft; put the dish on the frying-pan, and turn it over.' Which am I to turn over ... the dish or the frying-pan? ... It sounds like poetry, don't it?

(p. 150)

Probably not, I think is our response, but Mrs Wragge's innocent deconstruction of a recipe generates a kind of narrative poetics and gender politics for *No Name*. On the level of narrative, her contention with the cookery book implies female subversion of male-authorised texts or laws (the cookery book written by a woman for the instruction of other women in filling male orders); on the level of story, her resistance to accepted interpretation intimates the larger battle in this novel between legitimacy and illegitimacy, between male governance and female revenge. And she doesn't let up. Grandiosely introducing Magdalen to the Wragge way of life, the Captain offers 'A pauper's meal, my dear girl – seasoned with a gentleman's welcome'; his wife begins to mutter, 'Seasoned with salt, pepper, chives, and parsley'. Negotiating terms with Magdalen for her dramatic training, the Captain begs her 'not to mince the matter on your side – and depend on me not to mince it on mine'; his wife (of course) mutters that one should always try to 'mince small'. Her 'torpid' yet disruptive presence not only prefigures Lewis Carroll's White Queen but also anticipates the interrogation of arbitrary systems of signification that we find in *Alice in Wonderland*. If her husband's attitudes, despite his raffish demeanour and picaresque career, represent conformity and conservatism, then Mrs Wragge's attitudes represent resistance and interrogation.

And what of Mrs Wragge's omelette? Well, she makes it, but, as she says, 'It isn't nice. We had some accidents with it. It's been under the grate. It's been spilt on the stairs. It's scalded the landlady's youngest boy – he went and sat on it' (p. 161) Her interpretation of male orders results in something not 'nice', and certainly illegitimate as an omelette. And what of Captain Wragge? Abandoning 'moral agriculture' for 'medical agriculture', he goes in for the manufacture and sale of laxatives. Turning his talent for narrative to the production of stories about 'The Pill', his skill in creating identities to the fabrication of testimonials about its dramatic effects, he becomes very rich. Meeting Magdalen at the end of the novel, 'the copious flow of language pouring smoothly from his lips', he declares, 'I merely understand the age I live in' (p. 529). It seems as if his attitudes no longer *represent* conformity and acceptance (as I suggested earlier); speaking the dominant sociolect of 'the age', which will never be understood by his wife, he ceases to function as parody or burlesque and becomes the thing itself. In other words, he goes legit. And instead of shouting at his wife, he appropriates her astonishing physical presence for the narrative that makes him rich: She is, he says, 'the celebrated woman whom I have cured of indescribable agonies from every complaint under the sun. Her portrait is engraved on all the wrappers, with the following inscription beneath it: – "Before she took the Pill, you might have blown this patient away with a feather. Look at her now!"' (p. 526). Just as Magdalen's story of return to legitimate social identity in marriage assumes conventional narrative form, so Mrs Wragge's story of respectable celebrity puts an end to her disruption of parodic omnipotence. No longer the resisting reader of a recipe, like the Captain she becomes the thing itself and is read by others, engraved and inscribed as she is on all the wrappers for 'The Pill'. Mrs Wragge is in custody, just as, one might venture, Collins's interrogations of narrative form, patriarchal law, misogynistic sexual politics are (must be) eventually placed in the demanding custody of his serialised novel. They are disciplined by the contingent demands of his career, by the male-dominated directives of his culture. In sum, the subversiveness of *No Name* must ultimately be contained by the structure that enables its existence. Shall we say real life as opposed to fiction? But perhaps we should remember Noel Vanstone's astonished response to the revelation of Magdalen's plot for revenge: 'It's like a scene in a novel – it's like nothing in real life' (p. 403) In deconstructing Collins's literary practice and gender politics in *No Name*, we should not try to break the dialectical bond between theme and form, life and novel.

From *Out of Bounds: Male Writers and Gender Criticism*, ed. Laura Claridge and E. Langton (Massachusetts, 1990), pp. 186–96.

NOTES

[This deconstructive reading of *No Name* investigates the relationship of gender politics and fictional form. It explores what its author argues is a significant link between Collins's impatience with the dominant codes of literary representation and his critique of dominant forms of gender politics. In the case of the complexly plotted *No Name*, the crucial link, it is argued, is that between the novel's sympathy for its rebellious heroine and her search for subjectivity, and the subversion of narratorial omniscience implied in the dialogism and relativism of Collins's form with its range of narrating voices and texts. The absence of a particular mode of representation is seen as having as much significance as the presence of other modes. Thus the absence of suspense (to which Collins draws the reader's attention in his Preface) is seen as a subversive break with tradition, and a means by which the reader is involved collaboratively in an experience of plot-as-process rather than as plot-as-product. Ed.]

I am grateful to Gerhard Joseph for pointing out to me that Mrs Wragge 'goes into custody'.

1. Comparing *No Name* with *Great Expectations* (which followed it in Dickens's periodical *All the Year Round*), Jerome Meckier finds Collins's novel inferior. Meckier's interest is in the way these two novels address barriers to 'social progress', their meaning as 'serious, philosophical critique of shortcomings traceable to the very nature of things'. Meckier's tendency to focus exclusively on informing connections between the private plight of Pip and public disorder blinds him, I think, to the very real social difficulties experienced by women in Collins's novel. Jerome Meckier, *Hidden Rivalries in Victorian Fiction: Dickens, Realism, and Reevaluation* (Lexington, KY, 1987), p. 129.

2. For stimulating discussion of relationships between mimesis and semiosis, I am indebted to Michael Riffaterre's lecture series at the University of Pennsylvania, February 1988.

3. Norman Page (ed.), *Wilkie Collins: The Critical Heritage* (London, 1974), pp. i–xvi.

4. Ibid., 169.

5. Wilkie Collins, *No Name* (1864; rpt. Oxford, 1986); preface pages are not numbered [subsequent page references in the text are to this edition – Ed.].

6. An unsigned review in *Dublin University Magazine* in February 1861 observes that 'a writer like George Eliot may look down from a very far height on such a dweller in the plains as he who wrote *The Woman in White*'. For this critic, Collins's novel is infected by 'the spirit of modern realism'. In 1863, Alexander Smith in the *North British Review* more neutrally noted that Collins was 'a writer of quite a different stamp from George Eliot' (Page, *Wilkie Collins*, pp. 104, 140).

7. Page, *Wilkie Collins*, p. 143.

8. D. A. Miller, *The Novel and the Police* (Berkeley, CA and Los Angeles, 1988), p. 172.

9. Jonathan Loesberg makes the interesting point that 'sensation novels evoke their most typical moments of sensation response from images of a loss of class identity. And this common image links up with a fear of general loss of social identity as a result of the merging of the classes – a fear that was commonly expressed in the debate over social and parliamentary reform in the late 1850s and 1860s.' Part of the implicit threat to established gender and class politics posed by Magdalen's protean ability to switch roles may be ascribed to such a fear. Jonathan Loesberg, 'The Ideology of Narrative Form in Sensation Fiction', *Representations*, 13 (Winter, 1986), 117.

10. J. Hillis Miller, *The Form of Victorian Fiction: Thackeray, Dickens, Trollope, George Eliot, Meredith, and Hardy* (Notre Dame, IN, 1968), p. 30.

11. Mikhail Bakhtin, *The Dialogic Imagination*, trans. Caryl Emerson and Michael Holquist, ed. Michael Holquist (Austin, TX, 1981), p. 366.

12. Page, *Wilkie Collins*, p. 245.

7

Armadale: The Sensitive Subject as Palimpsest

JENNY BOURNE TAYLOR

> The Mind is not a passive recipient of external impulses but an active co-operant ... it is a variable mechanism which has a *history*. What the senses inscribe on it are not merely changes in the external world, but these characters are co-mingled with characters of preceding inscriptions. The sensitive subject is no *tabula rasa* but a *palimpsest*.
>
> (G. H. Lewes, *Foundations of a Creed*)[1]

In the Prologue of *Armadale*, Allan Armadale II (Senior), father of Allan Armadale II (Junior), alias Ozias Midwinter, warns his son in his deathbed confession of the possible consequences of his name-sake's murder:

> Guiltless minds may see nothing thus far but the result of a series of events which could lead no other way. I ... with my crime unpunished and unatoned, see what no guiltless minds can discern. I see danger in the future, begotten of the danger in the past ... I look into the Book which all Christendom venerates; and the Book tells me that the sins of the father shall be visited on the child. I look out into the world; and I see the living witnesses round me to that terrible truth. I see the vices that have contaminated the father, descending and contaminating the child; I see the shame which has disgraced the father's name descending and disgracing the child. I look in on myself – and I see My Crime, ripening again for the future in the self-same circumstance which first sowed the seeds of it in the past; and descending in inherited contamination of Evil, from me to my son. ...
>
> My son! The only hope I have left for you, hangs on a Great Doubt – the doubt whether we are, or are not, the masters of our own destinies.[2]

Armadale opens with a confession, a complicated narrative of a guilty past involving doubling, pursuit, and retribution. But the confession does not form a reconstruction and reassessment of that past which will lead to atonement and reassimilation. It turns it into a force that will determine the future progress of the story, but not in a straightforward way. The confession is the novel's opening assertion, setting up a framework of expectation wherein the language of scriptual judgement merges with moral transmission. *Armadale*'s son, the receiver of the confession, is placed in a similar position to Robert Mannion in *Basil* (1852) as the threefold 'look' of the father – into the 'Book', into the world, into himself – becomes his own social and psychic inheritance. That destiny is thus simultaneously resisted and fulfilled by the progress of the narrative. It is internalised by the hypochondriacal obsessions of the son, the sensitive subject who indirectly transmits the tensions and mysteries of the story, and the subject of a psychological investigation of the way that a monomania can work its own fulfilment. He is the victim, too, of a plot to steal the name and identity that are the subject of so much complication and confusion, a plot that depends for its sensation on fulfilling the very expectations that have been rendered problematic.

Armadale is a fascinating and elusive novel which combines, in a bizarrely kaleidoscopic way, many of the narrative elements and psychological methods in Collins's fiction. The narratives of *The Woman in White* and *No Name* hinged on one of the basic conventions of sensation fiction: gaining a name and an identity by assuming another false one. In *Armadale* there are plots, and plots within plots, which in turn become the breeding ground for further plots, all proliferating around the name 'Allan Armadale' – a name without an identity, not, as in *No Name*, an identity that has been rendered problematic by the loss of name. It is a blank space standing for a property that has no real owner, a stage on which various psychological propensities and dispositions are acted out, though the replications and inversions take on different meanings in different contexts. The confessional narrative of the Prologue – the letter addressed to the son – sets up the basic conflict around the inheritance of name, property, and morbid traits that works in two directions, between self and other, and father and son, and it shapes the presuppositions that both determine and undermine the story. The fathers, the two Allan Armadales of the Prologue, are set in opposition by directly replicating the other's transgression in a way that presents the excess of power itself as morbid, as a form of moral insanity. The conflict is given the apparently exotic setting of Barbados, but the colony primarily gains its 'wild' connotations from its position as the site of unlicensed *domestic* feudal power, an imaginary reversion to an earlier historical epoch. The confessing Armadale, née Wrentmore, inherited the Armadale name and estates in both England and Barbados in the place of the Armadale who had 'disgraced himself beyond redemption', though Wrentmore's own youth had echoed this absence of restraint:

> My mother was blindly fond of me ... she let me live as I pleased. My boyhood and youth were passed in idleness and self-indulgence, among people – slaves and half-castes mostly – to whom my will was law ... I doubt if there was ever a young man in this world whose passions were left so entirely without control of any kind.
>
> (pp. 39–40)

Both echo Pritchard's case of

> an only son of a weak and indulgent mother [who] gave himself up habitually to the gratification of every caprice and passion of which an untamed and violent temper was susceptible. ... The money with which he was lavishly supplied removed every obstacle to the indulgence of his wild desires.[3]

But Wrentmore is then displaced himself by the original Armadale, who takes on another assumed name to steal back his inheritance and to marry an English heiress and gain an English estate; in revenge Wrentmore drowns him by locking him in a sinking ship; when dying himself of a degenerative (implicitly venereal) disease, he confesses this to his son.

There are no stable oppositions between self and other, reality and imposture here, and this process of displacement of significance is taken further in that there is nothing but displacement; even the desire to (re)claim a name becomes another form of imposture. The story itself re-enacts the 'gaining a name and identity through dissemblance' plot through two counterveiling registers, which follow the way in which the projected narrative that is the father's legacy is resisted and fulfilled. The first revolves round the relationship between the two Armadales, focusing on the morbid self-consciousness of Wrentmore's son, discovered as an outcast under the bizarre name of 'Ozias Midwinter', a name now assumed to avoid inheriting the property and the prophecy. The junior Armadales deconstruct the discourses through which their fathers are set up while at the same time upsetting the very expectations generated by their own opposition. They are respectively dark and fair, burdened with anxiety and harmlessly irresponsible, yet this involves a complex notion of the splitting, shadowing, or doubling of the self, which emerges most clearly in the premonitory dream which foreshadows the future and which 'belongs' to both of them. The second focuses on the one surviving figure from the Prologue, the extraordinary villainess, the red-haired Lydia Gwilt, who conspires to acquire the English inheritance by assuming the Armadale name through marriage, not to Armadale, but to his replica Midwinter, under his 'real' name. The 'fatal' force of the father's prophecy and projected threat now turns out to be the power of manipulative female sexuality.

So *Armadale* juggles with the concept of transmission, scrutinising the way in which a legacy of the past is reproduced by the next generation, becomes internalised within the consciousness, and then is again transmitted through various 'psychic' phenomena – most notably the dream in which one morbid state is transposed into the subjectivity of another. It uses the devices of doubling and substitution of names and identity and exploits the links between names and inherited property to question the stable boundaries of the self, as well as to explore its social construction. It draws on contradictory psychological conventions and assumptions in building up and breaking down outcast and deviant figures, figures who are either shown to be threatening and anomalous because of others' fears and preconceptions, or who make use of those projections and fears to build up Collins's most ambitious villainess in a way that can never be assimilated, as it is in *The Woman in White*, within the overall framework of moral management. *The Woman in White* explored how identity could be built up and broken down by manipulating a consistent rhetoric that simultaneously covered and disclosed its interests, with the asylum as the pivot. A secluded asylum for nervous patients also makes an appearance in *Armadale*, but as an 'overwrought' melodramatic device at the climax of the story.

This replicates the contrast in the way the novels operate, for *Armadale* draws on a set of psychological processes that suggest opposing interpretations. By continually replaying a plot with modifications the novel elicits distinct interpretations which succeed and overlap with one another, and which form a set of interlocking but dissonant frameworks. In this respect, *Armadale* generates a sense of mystery by continually undermining the terms on which its own cognitive assumptions are founded while allowing them, on another register, to remain intact. Towards the beginning of the novel the naïve and boorish Allan Armadale I (Junior) tells his surrogate father, Decimus Brock, a joke about 'three Bedouin brothers at a show':

> Ali will take a lighted torch, and jump down the throat of his brother Muli – Muli will take a lighted torch, and jump down the throat of his brother Hassan – and Hassan, taking a third lighted torch, will jump down his own throat, and leaving the spectators in total darkness.
>
> (p. 54)

Armadale is a story which 'jumps down its own throat', and unlike *The Moonstone* and *The Woman in White*, there are no sympathetic detectives, only victims and conspirators. There is no reconstruction which proceeds through distinct narrative frameworks as part of a process of detection, yet neither is there an overall omniscient narrative authority as there is in *No Name*.

Armadale works as a sensation novel as the conventions of the mode are pushed to their limits, and Collins took as many explicit aesthetic and moral risks with this novel as he had done with *Basil*. But he wrote *Armadale* when his economic security and position as a popular writer seemed most assured. Smith, Elder had lured him from *All the Year Round*, following the serialisation of *No Name* as the result of the phenomenal success of *The Woman in White*. He serialised *Armadale* in the well-established middle-class, middlebrow *Cornhill Magazine*, paying Collins no less than £5000 for the publishing rights.[4] Again the Preface offers defence and justification:

> Readers in particular will, I have some reason to suppose, be here and there disturbed – perhaps even offended – by finding that *Armadale* oversteps, in more than one direction, the narrow limits within which they are disposed to limit the development of modern fiction – if they can.[5]

Armadale certainly was condemned by critics as an exaggerated sensation novel, Miss Gwilt – 'a portrait drawn with masterly art, but one from which every rightly constituted mind turns with loathing' – being singled out for their special detestation.[6] But although the novel was attacked for both aesthetic and moral distortion, on the one hand winding up the narrative to such a pitch as to render the characters 'puppets', on the other producing dangerously attractive and realistic criminals, it was also accorded a grudging admiration. The *Athenaeum* complained:

> Those who make plot their first consideration and humanity the second – those, again, who represent the decencies of life as so often too many hypocrisies – have placed themselves in a groove which goes, and must go, in a downward direction, whether as regards fiction or morals. We are in a period of diseased invention, and the coming phase of it may be palsy.[7]

But the *Saturday Review* was more ambivalent, acknowledging Collins's

> strange capacity for weaving extraordinary plots; *Armadale*, from first to last, is a lurid labyrinth of improbabilities. It produces upon the reader the effect of a literary nightmare. ... If it were the object of art to make one's audience feel uncomfortable without letting them know why, Mr Wilkie Collins would be beyond doubt a consummate artist. ... As a whole the effect is clever, powerful, and striking, though grotesque, monotonous, and to use a French word, *bizarre*.[8]

Though the review is finally dismissive it points to the real complexities of the way the novel works – that it produces the same effect that Marian had on Hartright, 'a sensation oddly akin to the helpless discomfort familiar to us all in sleep, when we recognise yet cannot recognise the anomalies and contradictions of a dream'.[9] And here the dream itself and the way that it is offered up to distinct kinds of interpretation are both the fulcrum of the plot and a direct analogue of a more generalised process whereby meaning is rendered problematic in the novel. Collins wrote an Appendix to *Armadale* where he made it clear that he left the meaning of the dream deliberately opaque:

> My readers will perceive that I have purposely left them, with reference to the Dream in this story, in the position that they would occupy in the case of a dream in real life – they are free to interpret it by the natural or the supernatural theory as the bent of their own minds may incline them.[10]

This means that overlapping forms of 'double consciousness' are at work in the novel: firstly, the 'double consciousness' of contemporary dream theory that is put to work in the text; secondly, the ambiguous possible interpretations of the dream focused through the consciousness of individuals; and thirdly, the way in which the text works as a dream through mingling its own past and present. *Armadale* works in a way that is analogous to Elliotson's analysis of dreams in *Human Physiology*: he reiterates that dreams are marked by loss of control over the thoughts, but goes on to argue that the mind can, in fact, 'perceive the grossest incongruities and impossibilities ... thoughts riot on in confusion ... more like the cross reading of a newspaper. ... A dream sometimes continues rational or consistent till near the end, when suddenly it becomes absurd.'[11] The novel 'jumps down its own throat' through its juxtaposition of these different modes, without signalling that anything peculiar is happening. The effect is to collapse the natural into the supernatural, but in ways which never move beyond the devices of the manipulation of sensation and perception. It thus extends the dream theory of physiological psychology, even as it points to its limitation of explaining psychical realities as morbid phenomena by investigating the social construction of a morbid consciousness in the figure of the 'sensitive subject' of Ozias Midwinter. To analyse how this works it is necessary to look at the dream, its own immediate relationship to contemporary dream theory, and the way both are manipulated by the workings of the narrative and the shaping of identities that this involves.

Armadale's dream, which takes the form of a series of static tableaux which then 'work their own fulfilment' in the later narrative through strategies that are open to contrasting interpretation, is itself subjected to two contrasting analyses immediately the dreamer wakes, which straightaway puts it on a different footing from the dreams that have emerged so far in Collins's novels.[12] In *Basil* and *The Woman in White* (with the exception of Marian's trance) unexplainable forebodings were discussed by the partial view of sceptical but naïve narrators who were sensitive to the 'influences' around them, but unable to perceive the hidden connections that the dream or 'other' state represented. They therefore interpreted monition as a monomania but in a way that could then be reworked (by Basil in delirium, by Hartright by gaining self- and narrative control) as part of a process of transformation or reassimilation. In *Armadale* there is also a split between superstition and rationality, but it is given a different emphasis and serves a different narrative function. The dream is given a superstitious 'supernatural' reading by Midwinter, reworked in the framework of expectation that he is set within as 'sensitive subject'; yet also given a materialist interpretation by the local doctor, Hawbury, who serves no other function than as the voice of medical authority. This sets up a direct correlation between the dream's narrative function, enabling the bizarre juxtaposing of anomalous elements, and the use of dream theory to explain it. This means that Hawbury's theory should be credible in external terms in order for it to be effectively qualified and developed in the narrative itself.

Hawbury's explanation of Armadale's dream corresponds closely to the dream analysis of MacNish, Abercrombie, Symonds, and other contemporaries in the medical profession, but it does so selectively. Like his non-fictional counterparts, Hawbury is more concerned to offer a causal explanation of the dream's different elements than a reading of its meaning, and like them, too, he offers a purely physiological explanation with an account of how the dream selects and combines past traces, working 'as the shuffling of a deranged kaleidoscope'.[13] Hawbury opines:

> We don't believe that a reasonable man is justified in attaching a supernatural explanation to any phenomenon which comes within the range of his senses, until he has certainly ascertained that there is no such thing as a natural explanation of it to be found in the first instance. ...
> There is nothing at all extraordinary in my theory of dreams: it is the theory accepted by the great mass of my profession. A Dream is the reproduction, in the sleeping state of the brain, of images and impressions produced on it in the waking state; and this reproduction is more or less involved, imperfect or contradictory, as the action of certain faculties of the dreamer is controlled more or less completely, by the influence of sleep.
>
> (pp. 136,137)

Hawbury, Armadale, and Midwinter then attempt to 'trace [their] way back to these impressions', speculating on how they will be transformed in the dream, which is 'like guessing a riddle' (p. 141). This process directly corresponds with Abercrombie's outline of the different processes at work in dreaming, where he notes that 'one of the most curious objects of investigation is to trace the manner, in which the particular visions or series of images arise'.[14] The process of tracing back in the dream analysis of *Armadale* correlates with Abercrombie's identification of 'Recent events and recent mental emotions, mingled up into one continuous series';[15] Allan combines the image of the landscape of a recent trip with a scene he has been reading about, and condenses this with other memories and suggestions: 'And behold the dream, Mr Midwinter, mixing up separate waking impressions just as usual!' (p. 142).[16]

But Hawbury's analysis only gives a partial account of the theory outlined by Abercrombie. It focuses on the recent past, while Abercrombie stressed 'Recent events ... mingled up ... with old events', and 'Dreams consisting in the revival of past associations, respecting things which had entirely passed out of mind, and which seem to have been forgotten', as well as those in which 'a strong mental emotion is embodied in a dream and is fulfilled'.[17] The text suggests a more complex understanding of the dreaming process, corresponding to the concept of 'double consciousness' current in contemporary theory which was developed by associationist analysis and mesmerism, and was a starting-point for E. S. Dallas's *The Gay Science* (1866).

'In dreams each man's character is disintegrated, so that he may see the elements of which it is composed.'[18] Frank Seafield's summary of methods of dream interpretation is taken literally in *Armadale*. On hearing that a bad dream has been had, the doctor immediately assumes that Midwinter has had it: 'with your constitution, you ought to be well used to dreaming by this time' (p. 133). By giving Allan the dream which reproduces Midwinter's anxieties, the novel directly makes use of one the tenets of mesmerism – that impressions can be directly transmitted – as well as the claim that clairvoyance offers a method of prediction which is not 'contrary to nature': 'Say, now, what can be concealed from us, present and future?' Elliotson asks, 'the soul of magnetiser and the magnetised can be mingled, and afterwards separated again.'[19] This further blurs the boundary between natural and supernatural explanation as well as between Midwinter's and Armadale's identities. But the novel mixes this with less obviously transcendental processes in both the text of the dream itself and its narrative setting.

Allan's dream is presented as an embedded narrative carefully itemised and noted by Midwinter:

> 1. The first event of which I was conscious, was the appearance of my father. He took me silently by the hand, and we found ourselves in the cabin of a ship.
> 2. Water slowly rose over us in the cabin; and I and my father sank through the water together.

> 3. An interval of oblivion followed; and then the sense came to me of being left alone in the darkness.
> 4. I waited.
> 5. The darkness opened and showed me the vision – as in a picture – of a broad, lonely pool, surrounded by open ground ...
> 6. On the near margin of the pool, there stood the Shadow of a Woman.
>
> (pp. 134–5)

Like Basil's early dream (in *Basil*) it takes the form of a set of static tableaux, which have an allegorical, already interpreted quality about them, but which are themselves embedded in the narrative as the dreamer sinks into the other world of double consciousness, and he and the father sink beneath the water in a state which is neither past nor future. This use of the language of sinking and drowning is closer to Basil's delirium and Hartright's fear (in *The Woman in White*): 'my mind sinks in darkness and confusion when I think of it', making literal use of the metaphors of unconscious activity to describe the process within the dream itself.[20] The use of metaphors or currents or tides to conceptualise unconscious processes within the self, either as a force linking the individual to the surrounding world or as a set of currents forming channels within the mind that could be developed, blocked, or controlled, was developed in different contexts within physiological psychology.[21] But Dallas in particular conceptualised the unconscious as a sea or expanse of water containing a range of different currents or tides that both frame the perimeters of the self and exist within or beneath it.

> When one is most struck with the grandeur of the tides and currents of thought that belong to each of us, and yet all beyond our consciousness, one is apt to conceive of it as a vast outer sea or space that belts our conscious existence. ...
>
> In the dark recesses of memory, in unbidden suggestions, in trains of thought unwittingly pursued, in multiplied waves and currents all at once flashing and rushing, in dreams that cannot be laid ... we have glimpses of a great tide of life ebbing and flowing, rippling and rolling and beating about where we cannot see it. ... Our conscious existence is a little spot of light, rounded or begirt with a haze of slumber.[22]

Thus the device of sinking beneath the waters with the father to produce the 'visions' of the preternatural state of consciousness simultaneously moderates and disrupts the distinction between alternative states of consciousness within the dream. And this corresponds with Dallas's sense that

> this unconscious part of the mind is so dark and yet so full of activity; so like the conscious intelligence and yet so divided from it by a veil of mystery, that it is not much of a hyperbole to speak of the human soul as double, or at least leading a double life.

But a double life in which there is a secret 'constant traffic' between conscious and unconscious existence, and where each is necessary to the other.[23]

It also directly echoes the patterns at work in creating the immediate conditions of dreaming and disrupts the linear sequence of time. The 'sinking beneath the waters with the father' sequence mixes Allan's 'unconscious past' (the drowning of the father in the ship) with the immediate one (the two Armadales finding themselves stranded on the wreck of the same ship) here coincidence perversely reproduces the patterns of the intractable past. But it also seeps into the language describing the waking present, and suffuses the terms of reference of the novel as a whole. Allan Armadale's lack of discipline in early life evaporates harmlessly but it means that he becomes a principle of free association in the novel, flitting from one idea to the other, but never being anchored to any meaning. His passion for sailing and the sea both underpins this and is made explicit when the narrator comments on his confusion about the dreams: 'In both senses of the word his mind was at sea already'; a disruption of the distinction between the metaphorical and the literal reinforced by the way that Midwinter, the more obvious outcast, is continually described as being 'cast adrift' (p. 137). And this comes to permeate the language of the narrative itself. As the story moves into the sequence of the fulfilment of the dream with the trip to the Norfolk Broads and the first encounter with the fatal Lydia the landscape becomes increasingly dreamlike – not, as in *Basil*, through the dramatic Fuseli-like imagery of cliffs and chasms, but in the way that the flat monotony of the Norfolk Broads is built up by the juxtaposing of unexpected elements, presented by a dissociated narrative consciousness that does not know how to make sense of it.

> All the strange and startling anomalies presented by an island agricultural district, isolated from other districts by its intricate surrounding network of pools and streams – holding its communication

and carrying its produce by water instead of land – began to present themselves in closer and closer succession. Nets appeared on cottage palings; little flat-bottomed boats lay strangely at rest among the flowers in cottage gardens; farmer's men passed to and fro clad in the composite costume of the coast and the field, in sailor's hats and fisherman's boots and ploughman's smocks, – and even yet the low-lying labyrinth of waters, embosomed in its mystery and its solitude, was a hidden labyrinth still.

(p. 236)

Armadale also turns into a bizarre or dreamlike text as processes of psychical transmission are explored through a narrative which continually displaces any stable authority. Yet this displacement is still aligned in a social framework where the meaning of identity is overdetermined by the expectations and perceptions of others, which can compound or undermine the legacy of the past. There is neither a clear shift between narrators nor an identifiable moralised narrative rhetoric in *Armadale*. It modulates between different kinds of narrative moods which can correspond to different modes of remembering the past. For example, the most clearly identifiable benign authority is Armadale's substitute father, the rector Decimus Brock. The Epilogue of the novel closes with the posthumous re-reading of his letter, which states his belief in rational religion, autonomy, and moral management, and which finally cancels out the opening of the scriptual denunciation of the absent father in the Prologue. The opening of the Story is focused through Brock's memory and presents his immediate response to Midwinter. It takes place *after* the two Armadales have met and after some of Midwinter's past is known, but *before* Brock has read the confessional letter of the Prologue.

The reader thus has a latent knowledge of the past which qualifies the way that the opening events of the story are transmitted through the retrospective analysis of the rector. Brock recalls Armadale's early life, his mother's self-imposed exile, and the mysterious appearance of Midwinter as a vagabond through a process of 'natural or philosophical association', which, following Abercrombie, takes place 'when a fact or statement, on which the attention is fixed, is, by a mental process, associated with some subject which it is calculated to illustrate'.[24]

> One by one the events of those years – all connected with the same little group of characters, and all more or less answerable for the

anxiety which was now intruding itself between the clergyman and his night's rest rose, in progressive series, on Mr Brock's memory.

(p. 44)

So narrative mood and the modes of focus and recall are bound up with the control of narrative time, which is itself built up as a palimpsest of distinct kinds of memory. As the novel progresses suspense is heightened as knowledge of the past turns into anticipation of the future via the dream, and this involves a shift from 'natural' to 'fictional' forms of association in Abercrombie's term. This process coincides with a shift in the use of narrative voice as well as focus. The main body of the story takes the form of continuous narration into which other texts – the dream, letters – are embedded. But as the plot thickens the significance of the embedding shifts; as Lydia Gwilt gains power over Midwinter her diary substitutes itself for continuous narration. She becomes in both senses the author of the plot, while remaining a shadow within it – in both capacities the fatal force of the past.

The dream disrupts the coherent order of the narrative and is the means by which the past, in another register, exerts a pressure on the future, and is also the means by which the 'double consciousness' of Armadale and Midwinter becomes a means of resisting and replaying the drama of the past. The junior Armadales, I have suggested, overturn the expectations by their fathers' and their own opposition, and they add a twist to Collins's methods of doubling and replicating identity and exploring patterns of exclusion through the means by which the unitary self is disintegrated in the dream. Midwinter at first seems to represent Allan's 'unconscious', as repository of the guilty knowledge of the past, describing himself as 'an ill-conditioned brat, with my mother's negro blood in my face and my murdering father's passions in my heart, inheritor of their secret, in spite of them', and is the source of the dream (p. 81). But it is as Allan's conscience as much as his submerged consciousness that Midwinter compounds as well as resists his 'destiny' – turning an over-anxious gaze back on himself. The figure of Midwinter represents Collins's most sophisticated treatment of the ways in which 'sensitive' subjectivity is perceived as pathological and becomes morbid without being constructed by the narrative as pathological itself. He represents a complex overlapping of psychological codes, not only in the mingling of contrasting sets of expectations through which he makes sense, but in the way that these implied terms themselves are rendered problematic and provisional, and resist any coherent set of correspondences between identity and physical sign.

Midwinter is burdened by a social and a psychic inheritance, but he is developed in a way that goes against the grain of Spencer's development of the organic paradigm to discuss psychical inheritance: 'Hereditary transmission ... applies not only to physical but psychical peculiarities ... modified nervous tendencies ... are also bequeathed.'[25] He is built up as a palimpsest in a way that corresponds more closely with the way Lewes developed the metaphor to emphasise the 'double root, the double history' of development, which 'passes quite out of the range of animal life, and no explanation of mental phenomena can be valid which does not allow for this extension of range', an extension which here includes the traces of others' projections and the force of memory.[26] The narrative voice shifts between indirect narration focused through others' views of Midwinter, his own consciousness, and his own embedded confessional accounts of his past. In the first place this takes the form of an interrogation of even the more liberal assumptions of moral management. Midwinter is introduced through Brock's perspective as a mixed-race outcast and the precise method of narrative focus used emphasises Brock's pathologising response as much as its object:

> Ozias Midwinter, on recovering from brain-fever, was a startling object to contemplate on first view of him. His shaven head, tied up in an old yellow silk handkerchief; his tawny, haggard cheeks; his bright brown eyes, preternaturally large and wild; his rough black beard, his long supple, sinewy fingers, wasted by suffering till they looked like claws – all tended to discompose the rector at the outset of the interview. When the first feeling of surprise had worn off, the impression that followed it was not an agreeable one. Mr Brock could not conceal from himself that the stranger's manner was against him. The general opinion has settled that if a man is honest, he is bound to assert it by looking straight at his fellow-creatures when he speaks to them. If this man was honest, his eyes showed a singular perversity in looking away and denying it. Possibly they were affected in some degree by a nervous restlessness in his organisation which appeared to pervade every fibre of his lean, lithe body. The rector's healthy Anglo-Saxon skin crept responsively at every casual movement of the usher's supple brown fingers, and every passing distortion of the usher's haggard yellow face. 'God forgive me!' thought Mr Brock, with his mind musing on Allan and Allan's mother, 'I wish I could see my way to turning Ozias Midwinter adrift in the world again.'
>
> (pp. 55–6)

This manifestation of the figure through the shifting response to it moves through a succession of interpretative modes and calls each of them into question. The first two sentences, concentrating on him as a 'startling object' who surprised the rector's habitual perception, present him simply as a collection of disembodied objects. Here there are no clear boundaries of the body: head, handkerchief, cheeks, eyes, beard, claw-like fingers, both discompose the rector and are presented as the product of a process of suffering which itself only makes sense within a particular analytical framework. This is taken further in the rector's response to Midwinter's 'shiftiness', which in turn distances Brock's unquestioning appropriation of 'the general opinion's' use of a set of vaguely defined physiognomic codes. Midwinter's shiftiness and twitchiness are both cultural – the particular interpretation of a set of physical responses – and physiological, but it is a physiology that has no meaning beyond its cultural reception. Thus the initial impression is gradually qualified as his history of social isolation and rejection is revealed, Brock's perception being replaced by a distanced and anonymous stranger:

> The fatal reserve which he had been in a fair way of conquering some minutes since possessed itself of him once more. Again his eyes wandered, again his voice sunk in tone. A stranger who had heard his story, and who saw him now, would have said: 'his look is lurking, his manner is bad, he is, every inch of him, his father's son'.
>
> (p. 93)

'Nerves' are a key term in defining Midwinter. But the particular class and gender connotations that the rhetoric of 'nervous sensibility' had absorbed through Basil's hypochondriacal fancies or Laura's vulnerability, are here transformed by being applied to a physically resilent, racially ambiguous, male vagabond even as the rhetoric itself is developed to suggest Midwinter's sensitive subjectivity. It is a sensitivity, however, that is put forward in gender terms rather than class ones: his 'sensitive feminine organisation' coexists with resilience while remaining the sign of vulnerability; anxiety continually hovers on the brink of *hysteria* – not hypochondria – as he struggles for control over his own nervous fancies and associative processes. This not only gives his sensations feminine connotations, but also shifts the emphasis from the delusion itself to the subject's immediate response to it in a way that exposes the limitations of a moral management that simply takes the form of an exhortation to pull oneself together. For Midwinter's hysteria arises from his struggles to suppress his nervous fancies, not from giving in to them; from his attempts to enact an exaggerated cheerful sociability, not from his customary melancholy. Thus 'the hysterical passion rose, and conquered him' as he describes his history to Brock, but the passion is the strength of his gratitude to Armadale (p. 95). The chapter in which he attempts to build an acceptable persona is headed 'Midwinter in disguise' and here he presents a face which takes the form of throwing off reserve, which was 'no new side of Midwinter's character … it was only a new aspect of the ever-recurring struggle of Midwinter's life'. This leads to his most morbid and bizarre behaviour, loss of control and hysterical breakdown.

> His artificial spirits, lasted continuously into higher and higher effervescence since the morning, were now mounting hysterically beyond his own control. He looked and spoke with that terrible freedom of licence which is the necessary consequence, when a diffident man has thrown off his reserve, of the very effort by which he has broken loose from his own restraints. … He looked backwards and forwards from Miss Milroy to Allan and declared jocosely that he understood now why his friend's morning walks were always taken in the same direction. He asked her questions about her mother, and cut short the answers she gave by remarks on the weather. …
>
> There are limits even to the licence of laughter; and these limits were ere long so outrageously overstepped by one of the party as to have the effect of almost instantly silencing the other two. The fever of Midwinter's false spirits flamed out into sheer delirium as the performance of puppets came to an end. His paroxysms of laughter followed one another with such convulsive violence, that Miss Milroy started back in alarm.
>
> (pp. 213–17)

The dream is the most explicit example of how the narrative both analyses the basis of Midwinter's morbid delusions and makes his superstitious reading of it work while scrutinising the effects of his ability to resist its implications. Hawbury's explanation of the dream, and his subsequent interpretation of its elements as having a limited significance, provide a framework for Midwinter's 'prophetic' response to it. This interpretation continues to operate even as Midwinter's interpretation itself qualifies it. This in turn reinforces the sense of fatality in the text itself, as he is caught in the spell of the dream. In sinking under it, he hastens the very end that he is seeking to evade while struggling to control the delusion and reassert the claims of moral management. Yet in attempting to control his associations Midwinter enacts the prescriptions set up by Abercrombie and Conolly in their outline of 'the qualities and acquirements which constitute a well-regulated mind'. He does so by reworking the associations and impressions of the dream into different contexts, and this becomes a process of self-analysis.[27] For example, he is able to dispel the superstitious connotations of Armadale's mother's old room, not by shutting it away and turning it into a site of repressed associations but by opening it up and transforming those past accretions:

> Here, more strangely still, he looked on a change in the household arrangements, due in the first instance entirely to himself. His own lips had revealed the discovery that he had made on the first morning in the new home; his own voluntary act had induced the son to establish himself in his mother's room.

This turns into a more sustained analysis:

> It was only after he had unreservedly acknowledged the impulse under which he had left Allan at the Mere, that he had taken credit to himself for the new point of view from which he would now look at the Dream. Then, and not till then, he had spoken of the fulfilment of the first vision, as the doctor on the Isle of Man might have spoken of it – he had asked, as the doctor might have asked, where was the wonder of their seeing a pool at sunset, when they had a whole network of pools within a few hours drive of them? And what was there extraordinary in discovering a woman at the Mere, when there were roads that led to it, and villages in its neighbourhood, and boats employed on it, and pleasure parties visiting it? So again, he had waited to vindicate the firmer resolution with which he looked to the future, until he had first revealed all that he now saw himself of the errors of the past. ... The glaring self-contradictions betrayed in accepting the Dream as the revelation of a fatality, and in attempting to escape that fatality by an exertion of free will – in toiling to store up knowledge of the steward's duties for the future, and in shrinking from letting the future find him in Allan's home – were, in their turn, unsparingly exposed.
>
> (p. 284)

Yet here, too, the very effort that Midwinter makes to shake off the past reinforces the sense of the strength of its hold; the weighty,

convoluted sentences themselves all build up the sense of its in-
tractability while working through the processes by which it has
gained its power.

But the legacy of the past is most decisively enacted in the future
by the plots of the *femme fatale*, Lydia Gwilt. She is the figure of
all-embracing, disarming, and suffocating female power – in whom
fear of the father and his legacy of male violence becomes transformed into the threat of the castrating woman. She is everything
that men desire in the feminine and everything they fear, a villainess
who comes to control the narrative and who is never overpowered
by successful detection, though her past is revealed by it; she only
finally overpowers herself through the retribution of suicide. As
most critics realised, Miss Gwilt's villainy makes her the most force-
ful character in *Armadale*, and one aspect of her dangerous attraction is the initial absence of shame with which, like Fosco in *The
Woman in White*, she perpetuates her conspiracies. But this takes
on a completely different set of meanings: firstly, her villainy is
mediated through her femininity and secondly, her diary plays an
important role in compounding and undermining this villainy as
she experiences contrition and attempts to reform herself.

'Gwilt' is emblematically set up as a study of 'guilt' in the dual
sense of both wickedness and conscience; but she also operates as a
study of the limitations of conventions of feminine transgression
and remorse – the repentant fallen woman – and she enacts the
narrator's remark that

> a man entering on a course of reformation ought, if virtue is its own
> reward, to be a man engaged in an essentially inspiring pursuit. But
> virtue is not always its own reward, and the way to reformation is
> remarkably ill-lighted for so respectable a thoroughfare.
>
> (p. 218)

She is first seen as the embodiment of the shadow in the dream,
as a shadow, and is built up through the juxtaposing of her appearance manifested as shadow with the self that manipulates that appearance as a means of gaining power. But while with Midwinter
the delusions are dispelled through his gaining self-control, Lydia's
lack of shame and ability to control her appearance can only be interpreted as moral insanity. Pedgift, the lawyer, compares her to
other female criminals: 'All had a secret self-possession which
nothing could shake' (p. 357).

This means that Lydia gains power when she is not what she appears to be, and loses it when she becomes subjected to her own desire for Midwinter, when she wants to fill the role that she had been able to manipulate as a masquerade. She first puts herself in the position of being able to seduce both Armadale and Midwinter by becoming the neighbour's governess. She acts the role of governess the more successfully by seeming to be too attractive and too self-possessed to be one: 'The sudden revelation of her beauty, as she smiled and looked at him inquiringly, suspended the movements of his limbs and the words on his lips. A vague doubt beset him whether it was the governess after all' (p. 258). She seduces through simulating the apparent passivity of the *femme fatale*, while in reality actively conspiring:

> Perfectly modest in her manner, possessed to perfection of the graceful refinements of a lady, she had all the allurements that feast the eye, all the Siren-invitations that seduce the sense – a subtle suggestiveness in her silence and a sexual sorcery in her smile.
>
> (p. 373)

She plays the role of repentant fallen woman as a means of concealing her real history (which remains concealed from the reader for most of the story) and uses the conventions of melodrama to persuade Midwinter of the 'truth' of her past: 'There was nothing new in what I told him: it was the commonplace rubbish of the circulating libraries. A dead father, a lost fortune, vagabond brothers whom I dread ever seeing again' (p. 480). And the 'repentant fallen woman' story is further dismantled when Armadale thinks he has discovered Lydia's past. Here an intrusive narrator switches from sensation-novel conventions to a pastiche of melodrama:

> One conclusion, and one only ... forced itself into his mind. A miserable, fallen woman, who had abandoned herself in her extremity to the help of wretches skilled in criminal concealment – who had stolen her way back into decent society and a reputable employment, by means of a false character – and whose position now imposed on her the dreadful necessity of perpetual secrecy and perpetual deceit in relation to her past life – such was the aspect in which the beautiful governess at Thorpe-Ambrose now stood revealed to Allan's eyes!
>
> Falsely revealed or truly revealed? Had she stolen her way back into decent society and a reputable employment by means of a false character? She had. Did her position impose upon her the dreadful necessity of perpetual deceit in relation to her past life? It did. Was

she some such pitiable victim to the treachery of a man unknown as Allan had supposed? *She was no such pitiable victim.* The true story of the house in Pimlico – a house rightly described as filled with wicked secrets, and people rightly represented as perpetually in danger of feeling the grasp of the law – was a story which coming events were yet to disclose: a story infinitely less revolting, yet infinitely more terrible, than Allan or Allan's companion had either of them supposed.

(p. 334)

Lydia Gwilt's attempted reform, as she falls for Midwinter and attempts to fill subjectively the role that was previously an imposture, is negotiated and shown to be impossible in the terms of her own self-defining identity, in the shifting confessional function of her diary. The diary is the means by which Miss Gwilt both mediates the tensions of the plot – where she meditates on the significance of coincidence – and is 'haunted' by the resemblance of names and by herself:

My nerves must be a little shaken, I think, I was startled just now by a shadow on the wall. It was only after a moment or two that I mustered sense enough to notice where the candle was, and to see that the shadow was my own. ... Here is my own handwriting startling me now! ... The similarity of names never struck me in this light before.

(pp. 428–9)

It is also the place where her 'wicked' self speaks and where she incubates the plot against the Armadale property, and a means of self-control (as it was for Marian in *The Woman in White*):

Would it help me to shake off these impressions, I wonder, if I made the effort of writing them down? There would be no danger, in that case, of my forgetting anything important, and perhaps, after all, it may be the fear of something I ought to remember, this story of Midwinter weighing as it does on my mind.

(p. 412)

But while with Marian the gradual loss of this self-control is the sign of defeat by forces beyond it, with Lydia a split gradually arises in the function of the diary between the conspiring and controlling self, and the 'guilty' self as she becomes 'reformed'. Thus the movement of penitence is marked by the merging of narrative time and story time as Lydia renounces her diary and herself, and loses self-possession: 'Six o'clock ... How is it that he alters me so that I hardly know myself again? ... I felt a dreadful hysterical choking in the throat when he entreated me not to reveal my troubles' (p. 479). '*Sunday August 10th* The eve of my wedding-day! I close and lock this book, never to write in it, never to open it again. I have won the great victory; I have trampled my own wickedness underfoot. I am innocent' (p. 504).

But as she finds the sheer boredom of domesticity and wifely dependence to be the falsest role of all, she comes to depend on her diary as much as her 'drops' of laudanum: 'My misery is a woman's misery and it *will* speak here rather than nowhere; to my second self, in this book, if I have no-one else to hear me' (p. 532). The diary is the only place where she achieves a sympathetic subjectivity, but self-imposed moral management and reform involve that loss of self-possession, a contradiction which in the end can only be expressed by suicide.

The climax of *Armadale* and of the Gwilt conspiracy is when Lydia, with the accomplice Dr Downward, now transformed into the sinister Dr le Doux, lures Armadale and Midwinter into le Doux's newly built model 'Sanitorium' for nervous patients; Gwilt uses one of the asylum's boasted non-restraint methods as a means to attempt to poison Armadale by 'drowning' or suffocating him in poisoned air – a method she finally applies to herself. While the non-restraint asylum was the means of Laura's transformation in its very acceptability in *The Woman in White*, here the image of the sanitorium winds up the elements that are disturbing for their realism in the earlier novel, and draws on the 'older' image of the asylum as a melodramatic force of evil, a means of sensational conspiracy and horror. But it does this, as in Charles Reade's *Hard Cash* (1863), by blowing up moral management itself as a sinister force and transforming seclusion and repose into literal sources of suffocation – firstly of the hero, finally of the repentant villainess – and thus creates a sensational framework to achieve the 'fatal' end that is a pastiche of the very means by which it is resisted.

The sanatorium is an explicit parody of a private asylum for nervous patients directly based on those aspects of Conolly's *The Treatment of the Insane Without Mechanical Restraints* that stress suppression and seclusion rather than self-control, and it turns the image of the theatre round to parody those presuppositions. It is a theatre of its own techniques, open to public inspection and offering a welcome relief to the visitors from the propriety of their private lives while replicating its essential forms:

> In the miserable monotony of the lives led by a large section of the middle classes of England, anything is welcome to the women which offers them any sort of harmless refuge from the established tyranny of the principle that all human happiness begins and ends at home.
>
> (pp. 621–2)

Doctor le Doux has graduated to the proprietorship of the sanatorium from an earlier position as 'ladies' medical man': 'One of those carefully constructed physicians ... he had the necessary bald head, the necessary double eyeglass, the necessary black clothes and the necessary blandness of manner, all complete' (p. 336). His description of the asylum is a direct echo of Conolly's argument. Conolly wrote in *The Treatment of the Insane*:

> Many English superintendents speak of seclusion as something worse than mechanical restraint; seeming to forget that it is as much adapted to secure an irritable brain from causes of increased irritability as a quiet chamber and the exclusion of glare ... is adapted to the same state of brain in a fever. The patient needs repose, and every object, or every person seen, irritates him. ... It is often seen that the mere moving of the cover of the inspection-plate in the door of a patient's room if not cautiously done, rouses the patient from tranquility and causes him to start up and rush violently to the door. Seclusion gives him the benefit of continued tranquility, by removing at once every cause of excitement.[28]

Le Doux extends this to cover all forms of nervous disorders of modern life:

> Literally a word, on nervous derangement first ... I throw up impregnable moral entrenchments between Worry and You ... I assert the medical treatment of nervous suffering to be entirely subsidiary to the moral treatment of it. That moral treatment of it, you find here ... [The patient's mind] is one mass of nervous fancies and caprices, which his friends (with the best possible intentions) have been ignorantly irritating at home ... I pull a handle when he is snug in his bed, and the window noiselessly closes in a moment. Nothing to irritate him, ladies and gentlemen, nothing to irritate him!
>
> (pp. 625–7)

The two doctors, Hawbury and le Doux, thus form two poles in the use of psychological discourse – dream theory and moral management – around which the plot revolves; but they do so by having contradictory fictional functions; the function of le Doux (to transform perception through transforming moral management into a bizarre and uncanny device) undermines Hawbury's role as realigning the trains of association.

Armadale has two endings as well as two beginnings: the end of the Story with Lydia's suicide and the Conclusion, 'Midwinter', where Midwinter himself finally reaches a satisfactory interpretation of the dream, and a means of explaining coincidence, and reversing the terms of his father's letter: 'I have learnt to view the purpose of the Dream with a new mind. ... In that faith I can look back without murmuring at the years that are past, and can look on without doubting to the years that are to come' (p. 661). Brock's rational Christianity is the final means of closing the novel. But it is in seeking out the resolution and generating the mystery that the cognitive complexity of *Armadale* is created; and it is never finally able to emerge from its involuted heuristic structure and either reach a final interpretation of the dream, or offer a stable interpretation of itself to the reader. *Armadale* seems to be set up as a struggle between fate and chance, destiny and autonomy, but it quickly turns into a novel about the different ways the present and present identity are over-determined by the forces of the past, emerging in coincidence as much as conspiracy. Finally the great doubt – 'the doubt whether we are, or are not, masters of our own destiny' – of the father remains unresolved, but in the process the meaning of destiny has splintered through the process of working out what that process of working out might mean. And as a palimpsest of traces of the past, *Armadale* – both the name and the title – anticipates Collins's most ambitious attempt to investigate that process of investigation, set within a psychological context that incorporates an analysis of the unconscious – *The Moonstone*.

From J. B. Taylor, *In the Secret Theatre of Home: Wilkie Collins, Sensation Narrative and Nineteenth-Century Psychology* (London, 1988), pp. 151–73.

NOTES

[Jenny Taylor's *In The Secret Theatre of Home*, from which this extract is taken, is a comprehensive study of Collins's engagement with nineteenth-century theories of subjectivity and issues of identity. The study is informed by feminist cultural history and theory, and also by Michel Foucault's work on the history of sexuality and on the history of the construction and treatment of madness. However, it seeks to avoid the monolithic nature of much of Foucault's work by exploring Collins's fiction in relation to the contradictions in the conceptualisation and management of psychological 'deviance' in a very specific historical period.

Taylor reads Collins's fiction in the context of nineteenth-century literary, medical and psychological theories of sensation, and focuses particularly closely on contemporary theories of psychology and the management of psychological 'deviance' or 'moral insanity'. Her book focuses on the distinction made in late-eighteenth- and nineteenth-century theories of madness between intellectual and moral insanity, the former being associated with irrationality, and the latter with perversion (see Taylor, *Secret Theatre*, pp. 47–8). One of the main methods of treating insanity (and especially moral insanity) was 'moral management', a form of social training and self-regulation according to dominant 'values, codes of conduct, and proper living' (Taylor, *Secret Theatre*, p. 31). Taylor traces the development of ideas about moral insanity and moral management during the nineteenth century, and argues that the contradictory concept of identity on which they were posited and which they reproduced 'provides the overarching ideological framework for Collins's fiction' (ibid). Ed.]

1. G. H. Lewes, *The Foundations of a Creed*, 2 vols (London, 1874), I, 162.

2. Wilkie Collins, *Armadale* [1866] 2 vols (London, 1908) [subsequent page references in the text are to this edition – Ed.]

3. James Cowles Pritchard, *A Treatise on Insanity* (London, 1835), p. 14.

4. J. A. Sutherland, *Victorian Novelists and Publishers* (London, 1976), p. 105. As Sutherland points out, George Smith was an aggressive publisher who actively solicited his authors. He had made Collins the offer in 1861, but the writing of *Armadale* was delayed both by an attack of gout and by the sheer intricacy of its structure. See Sue Lonoff, *Wilkie Collins and his Victorian Readers: A Study in the Rhetoric of Authorship* (New York, 1982), pp. 33–7, for Collins's working methods on *Armadale*.

5. *Armadale*, Preface. The Preface concludes: 'Estimated by the claptrap morality of the present day, this may be a very daring book. Judged by the Christian morality which is of all time, it is only a book that is daring enough to speak the truth.' For an excellent discussion of Collins's tone in his prefaces in relation to the critical establishment, see Lonoff, *Wilkie Collins and his Victorian Readers*, pp. 55–66. Dickens's remarks to Collins on *Armadale* are interesting:

> The plot is extraordinarily got together; its compactness is quite amazing ... but insuperable and ineradicable from the whole piece is – *Danger*. Almost every situation in it is dangerous. I do not think any English audience would accept the scene in which Miss Gwilt in

that widow's dress renounces Midwinter. And if you had got so far you would never have got to the last act in the Sanatorium. You would only carry those situations on a real hard wooden stage ... and ... *by the help of interest in some innocent person who they placed in peril, and that person a young woman.* (Letter to Collins, 9 July 1866, *The Letters of Charles Dickens to Wilkie Collins*, selected by Georgina Hogarth, ed. Laurence Hutton [1892], p. 146.)

The initial stage adaptation of *Armadale*, written in collaboration with Regnier, was produced in England; the final version, *Miss Gwilt*, was produced at the Globe Theatre in 1876.

6. *London Quarterly Review* (October 1866), pp. 107–9. In Norman Page (ed.), *Wilkie Collins: The Critical Heritage* (London, 1974), p. 156.

7. H. F. Chorley (a critic particularly hostile to Collins), *Athenaeum*, 2 June 1866, pp. 732–3.

8. *Saturday Review*, 16 June 1866, p. 726.

9. *The Woman in White*, ed. Harvey Peter Sucksmith (Oxford, 1873), p. 25.

10. *Armadale*, Appendix. This is followed, however, by another story of a bizarre coincidence concerning the name of the novel.

11. John Elliotson, *Human Physiology* (London, 1840), p. 726.

12. J. A. Symonds, *Sleep and Dreams* (London, 1851), p. 78.

13. Frank Seafield, *The Literature and Curiosities of Dreams*, 2 vols (London, 1865), I, p. 61.

14. John Abercrombie, *Inquiries Concerning the Intellectual Powers and the Investigation of Truth* (Edinburgh, 1830), p. 267.

15. Ibid.

16. Hawbury also explains the intervals of oblivion between the visions in strictly physiological terms:

    It means, in plain English, the momentary reassertion of the brain's intellectual action, while a deeper wave of sleep flows over it, just as the sense of being alone in the darkness, which follows, indicates the renewal of that action, previous to the reproduction of another set of impressions.

17. Abercrombie, *Intellectual Powers*, pp. 274, 280.

18. Seafield, *Literature and Curiosities of Dreams*, I, 272.

19. Elliotson, *Human Physiology*, p. 676.

20. *The Woman in White*, p. 378.

21. For example, G. H. Lewes, *The Physiology of Common Life* (London, 1859–60), pp. 55–8, developed the concept of channels formed by culture directing and determining the flow of energy. See Sally Shuttleworth, 'Fairy tale or science? Physiological psychology in Silas Marner', in Ludmilla Jordanova (ed.), *Languages of Nature: Essays on Science and Literature* (London, 1986), p. 277.

22. E. S. Dallas, *The Gay Science*, 2 vols (London 1866), I, 249, 250–1.

23. Ibid., I, 200, 207.

24. Abercrombie, *Intellectual Powers*, p. 107.

25. Herbert Spencer, *Principles of Psychology* (London, 1855), p. 526.

26. Lewes, *The Foundations of a Creed*, I, 125.

27. Abercrombie, *Intellectual Powers*, p. 421. Also Seafield:

> If our prevalent state and disposition of mind ... determine and shape the complexions of our dreams it follows that those evil dreams are not innocent ... Our success in our efforts after self-government may be estimated partly by our dream correctness. (*Literature and Curiosities of Dreams*, I, 71)

28. John Conolly, *The Treatment of the Insane Without Mechanical Restraints* (London, 1856), p. 43.

8

Dreams, Transformations and Literature: The Implications of Detective Fiction

A. D. HUTTER

I

Detective fiction involves the transformation of a fragmented and incomplete set of events into a more ordered and complete understanding. As such it seems to bridge a private psychological experience, like dreaming, and literary experience in general. And like a psychoanalysis, the detective story reorders our perception of the past through language. Although psychoanalysis and detective fiction are so different in conscious design and intent, they share a significant structural relationship, just as they share a close historical relationship: *The Moonstone* (1868) was the first full-length English detective novel, and it preceded Freud's first work on hysteria by less than twenty-five years.

The Moonstone is the prototypical detective novel. It combines a narrative structure that is thoroughly subjective and unreliable with the characteristic action of all detective fiction: the restatement and restructuring in the present of a past event. Thus the detective stories of Edgar Allan Poe and Arthur Conan Doyle begin with the recent impact of a crime and work backward to restructure the incomplete fragments of present knowledge into a more intelligible whole and consequently to explain the past. A total reliance on intellectual restatement fostered, in the early part of this century, a series of sterile sub-genres, like the stories of pure puzzle or the tales from the badly misnamed 'Golden Age of Detection'. What saves Poe and Conan Doyle from sterility is not that, like Collins, they came first, but that the relentlessly logical process of ratiocination is thrown into question by a deeper irrationality. Dupin seeks the dominance of pure intellect, but, as with Holmes, there is always the presence of some profound personal disturbance which impinges on the apparently objective vision of the detective; Dupin, 'enamoured of the Night for her own sake',[1] loathe to interact with others except at a distance and through a distancing mind, anticipates Holmes and his need for seclusion, his addictions and depressions.

Not only are the objective and the rational called into question by the subjective and intuitive vision of the detective, but they are made to appear as two faces of the same coin. This duality is essential in Poe's 'Purloined Letter': the ingenuity of the police blocks their discovery of the truth, whereas Dupin provides instead a combination of poetic imagination and 'mathematical' reasoning. Stories of pure puzzle fail to sustain a tension in the reader between mystery and solution. When we read such stories we are driven to anticipate the plot and deduce, in advance, the solution to the crime; but if we succeed, the work is a failure. In Poe, the essential interest is not so much in solution as it is in recognition, testing the limits of rational deduction in a world of subjectivity and deceit, a world ultimately irrational. Just as the reader is meant to identify with the relentless logic of Dupin, he is also forced to recognise another part of his own personality which is uncivilised and instinctual, like the ape of the Rue Morgue.[2] Collins connected the elements of rational detection with subjective distortion in *The Moonstone's* narrative structure itself, forcing us to build a rational solution from the distorted and fragmented visions of his individual narrators. The novel begins with the tale of a priceless Indian diamond, 'passed … from one lawless … hand to another',[3] and the possession of the diamond leads again to theft and murder when it is taken by Colonel John Herncastle at the siege of Seringapatam. The colonel maliciously wills the gem to his niece, Rachel Verinder, on her eighteenth birthday, knowing that it carries a curse with it, a curse materially aided by three ruthless Brahmans who have devoted their lives to returning the diamond, at any cost, to their moon-god. Rachel's cousin, Franklin Blake, brings her the moonstone and then, it seems, steals it during the night of her birthday celebration. Rachel, we learn much later, has seen him do so and is even more outraged by Franklin's hypocritical attempt to catch the thief, for it is Franklin who thinks to call in Inspector Cuff from London. Several romances are twisted into these events: Rachel and Franklin fall in love with each other; Rosanna Spearman, a misshapen servant girl with a criminal past, falls hopelessly in love with Franklin and behaves mysteriously in what seems to be an effort to help him cover his crime; Godfrey Ablewhite, a too-charming philanthropist, pursues the reluctant Rachel and almost succeeds in the aftermath of her disappointment in Franklin. The Hindus appear and disappear, along with servants, clairvoyants, pawnbrokers, lady philanthropists, and lawyers, in a setting that ranges from India through London to the Brontë-like Yorkshire coast where Rosanna kills herself. Collins makes use of his own intimate knowledge of opium to provide a suitable final twist. A local doctor, Ezra Jennings, helps Franklin to reconstruct the crime. He discovers that Franklin did indeed take the stone, unknowingly, out of his anxiety over its safety and while under the influence of opium. He reproduces Franklin's original state on the night of the theft and succeeds in solving part of the mystery. With the discovery of a murdered Ablewhite, the real thief who had seen Franklin pick up the stone and had relieved Franklin of it while he slept, the solution is completed. The novel ends where it began, in India, with the stone restored to its rightful place.

This intricate tale is further complicated by a prologue that describes the theft of the jewel at the seige of Seringapatam, a three-part epilogue that traces the jewel back from England to India where it is restored, and the nine-part narration itself, in which each narrator tells his tale for different reasons and with different information – or misinformation. Old Betteredge, the Verinder family steward, contributes twice to the narrative, as does Franklin Blake: Betteredge because he is asked, Franklin because he wants to clarify further his own innocence and to bring together all the threads of the story. Miss Clack, a family retainer, writes because she is paid to do so, and others – like Dr Candy – contribute unknowingly. Collins achieves verisimilitude by this method, and he is legitimately able to withhold important information from the reader, delaying the solution while increasing the story's suspense. But the most important function of this complex narration is its involvement of the reader in a wealth – or morass – of contradictory detail. We must experience the confusion of observation and of report until we can decipher the language of the text, probe its ambiguities and contradictions and symbolism in order fully to understand the crime itself. Detective fiction is the peculiarly modern distillation of a general literary experience that makes central the subtle interaction with, and interpretation of, language.

Detective fiction is generally conceived of as an offshoot of the gothic or some combination of gothic romance and the detailed realism associated with the rise of the novel. But this purely literary genealogy ignores the historical rise of the detective police and their relationship to a form of fiction that is essentially urban. England needed the New Police only when the older forms of self-policing in a rural or restricted urban area were obviously inadequate. City slums provided a safe warren for what eventually became a popular and elaborately organised system of lower-class employment – as Mayhew eloquently testifies – and the middle classes required protection to deal with the increasingly puzzling and anonymous face of crime as it rapidly evolved into that 'organised crime' which now reflects the modern corporate state. Crime, like the Victorian city, was growing, diffuse, confusing, materialistic, and violent largely in proportion to material deprivation and exclusion. The first function of the new detective police was the preservation of property and the protection of the middle-class consumer; the police were needed to 'read' a city which had grown far beyond the easy knowledge of its inhabitants. They were part of that elaborately constructed social system which developed in response to a bewildering jump in technology, and it is no accident that railway timetables and telegraphic communication were almost instantly absorbed into the fictional representation of detection.

The first fictional detectives were amateur scientists. They were also first-rate actors (Dupin's bluffing the minister, Holmes's impersonations, Bucket's disguises). The ability to impersonate, to identify with, and to reproduce the idiosyncratic behaviour of the criminal, characterises the way in which Dickens portrayed Bucket's original, Inspector Field. Like Bucket, Field uses his knowledge to pierce to the very heart of a labyrinthine city and identify that larger disease which affects all levels of society.[4] Detectives are thus inevitably concerned with the problem of knowledge, a problem only intensified by the urban upheaval of the world in which they move, by the disorder, the multiplicity of detail, the constant impinging presence of other people, other accounts, other viewpoints.

A confusion of subjective and objective knowledge is present everywhere in *The Moonstone*. It shows itself, for example, as the central conflict in the hero's personality, epitomised by his foreign education:

> ... he had come back with so many different sides to his character, all more or less jarring with each other, that he seemed to pass his life in a state of perpetual contradiction with himself. ... He had his French side, and his German side, and his Italian side – the original English foundation showing through, every now and then ...
>
> (first period, ch. 6)

When Franklin is left with time to himself, 'it let out all the foreign sides of his character, one on the top of another, like rats out of a bag' (first period, ch. 22). And Franklin, in despair over Rachel's treatment of him, mocks his own confusion as he argues that Rachel is not really Rachel but someone else:

> Now, being in a state of nervous excitement, how are we to expect that she should behave as she might otherwise have behaved to any of the people about her? Arguing in this way, from within-outwards, what do we reach? We reach the Subjective view. I defy you to controvert the Subjective view. Very well then – what follows? Good Heavens! the Objective-Subjective explanation follows, of course! Rachel, properly speaking, is *not* Rachel, but Somebody Else. Do I mind being cruelly treated by Somebody Else? You are unreasonable enough, Betteredge; but you can hardly accuse me of that. Then how does it end? It ends, in spite of your confounded English narrowness and prejudice, in my being perfectly happy and comfortable. Where's the sherry?
>
> (first period, ch. 22)

Here, the comedy reminds us that it is the very failure of the characters to know not only the motivation of others, but even their own minds, which has led to the central crime of the novel: Franklin's 'theft', itself an unconscious act. The more we learn about the mystery, the more we are ourselves confused, in much the same way that Betteredge is confused by Franklin's sophistry: 'My head was by this time in such a condition, that I was not quite sure whether it was my own head, or Mr Franklin's' (first period, ch. 22). Rachel cannot decide on the basic moral nature of the hero or the villain, and her confusion adds to our own. Rosanna Spearman also deceives us, and so, in his way, does Cuff, who suspects Rachel. Even

Miss Clack, if she can still amuse a modern audience, does so because of her perverse refusal to understand anyone's real motives, especially her own.

Collins contributes significantly to a changing fictional aesthetic: verisimilitude is combined with intentional contradiction and subjective inconsistency; opposing viewpoints are the very basis for *The Moonstone*'s artistic integration. Collins had already experimented with multiple narration, and he was undoubtedly influenced by the double narrative of Dickens's *Bleak House*, which was also directly linked to *The Moonstone* because it was the first British novel to introduce a detective. But *The Moonstone*, and the rise of detective fiction generally, signal a more pervasive literary change. William Marshall writes that in *The Moonstone* 'in the dramatic and ironic manipulation of character, in the exploration of the reality of the self lying beneath the personality, Collins reflected some of the serious intellectual concerns of his age' (Marshall, *Wilkie Collins*, p. 82). In 1868 Robert Browning wrote *The Ring and the Book*, and like Collins, Browning builds carefully from fact, the true gold of the ring,[5] which is then shaped by a variety of subjective truths that add further meaning to the factual surface. Browning was more deliberate and self-conscious in his intentions than Collins, and art in his poem 'shows the truth twice in that it shows the physical facts and the metaphysical meaning behind them'; art plays off detailed observation against imagination (Langbaum, *Poetry of Experience*, p. 110).

The broader cultural shift which led to changes in narrative fiction reflects the nineteenth-century Englishman's fundamentally new perspective of himself, both politically and psychologically.[6] Collin's sensitivity to British colonial exploitation is apparent in the political moral of *The Moonstone*, which closes when the gem is restored to its proper and original shrine. In Collins's narrative everyone suffers who possesses the moonstone's wealth without a full right to such possession. As Dickens was to do two years later in *The Mystery of Edwin Drood*, Collins also exploits the racial prejudice of his characters – and readers. He creates a false solution to the mystery and attributes the crime to the Indians; Jennings is at first discredited by his strange appearance and 'his complexion ... of a gypsy darkness' (second period, ch. 4); even Ablewhite's final disguise, with black hair and a 'swarthy' complexion, encourages our misperception and prejudice until the very end of the tale. And the mystery, fear, and prejudice associated with the Indians is built into the very structure of a novel, which is itself founded on prejudicial testimony, misunderstanding, and exploitation. The conflicting motives of disinterestedness and greed, love and exploitation, are made to coexist in the way the characters see themselves and, until the final solution, in the way the reader must regard the characters, as he regards them in virtually every detective story – with suspicion. The novel does end with a solution; but the reader's experience throughout *The Moonstone* is weighted the other way: it encourages us to distrust closure. This particular mystery may be solved, but the mystery of the characters and the shadowy space between their actions, their observations, and their intentions are meant to puzzle. The novelist himself has come to distrust his own fictional world.

New psychological theories, like the changing political attitudes of the mid-nineteenth century, are significant in Collins's solution to *The Moonstone*. Collins relies particularly on two medical authorities, Dr William Benjamin Carpenter and Dr John Elliotson, to introduce into his dialogue descriptions of preconscious thought, memory, and the related effects of drugs and hypnosis that authenticate 'the physiological experiment which occupies a prominent place in the closing scenes of *The Moonstone*':

> Having first ascertained not only from books, but from living authorities as well, what the result of that experiment would really have been, I have declined to avail myself of the novelist's privilege of supposing something which might have happened, and have so shaped the story as to make it grow out of what actually would have happened – which, I beg to inform my readers, is also what actually does happen in these pages.
>
> (Preface)

An admirable piece of reasoning, in which the final proof of the reality of an event is fictional. What Collins never reveals – although it is something his original readers would have known – is that Elliotson, in spite of a number of valuable contributions to physiology, had been regarded by many as a quack. He was eccentric in his dress and appearance, had an early reputation for prescribing large quantities of dangerous drugs, was founder and first president of the Phrenological Society, and was forced to resign his

professorship at University College, London, because of his es-
pousal of mesmerism. Carpenter, on the other hand, with a reputation for a careful and conservative approach to new scientific
claims, was an eminent biologist and physiologist very much a part
of the medical and scientific establishment, and a strong critic of
mesmerism and phrenology. The basis for Collins's apparently
factual authority is itself, then, contradictory – like the testimony of
his characters or the confused evidence of the crime. Ezra Jennings
resembles Elliotson not only in his intelligence and imagination,
but also in his role as outcast and quack. Bruff, for example, finds
his experiment 'like a piece of trickery, akin to the trickery of
mesmerism, clairvoyance, and the like' (second period, fourth narrative). Like Cuff, he is an eccentric. It was as important for Collins
to introduce the element of quackery in the method of the novel's
solution as it was first to assert, in the prologue, the scientific basis
of the solution: he deepens, simultaneously, our belief and our
distrust.

Historically, the line between scientific investigation of the mind
and the rash claims of the mesmerists or phrenologists was blurred;
modern psychoanalysis owes its origins to an interest in the same
phenomena of hypnotic trance, free association, and sleep-walking
described by Collins, and so important to nineteenth-century
studies of the occult. Clairvoyance is described as the highest state
of mesmerism: it connects the forgotten past and even the unknown
future with the present; it overcomes space and time.[27] And in *The
Moonstone* we are confronted with apparent clairvoyance in the
performance of the Hindu's medium, the English boy who looks at
the ink they pour onto his hand, goes into a trance, and foretells the
future. Murthwaite assures the reader that this is nonsense, 'simply
a development of the romantic side of the Indian character'. He
connects such behaviour to the child's being 'a sensitive subject to
the mesmeric influence' (second period, ch. 3) and assures us it is
simply a trick of the imagination – all of which seems to be quite
true. There is a great deal the Indians do not know, and
Murthwaite analyses the issue of clairvoyance with admirable
scientific rationality. But the action of the novel, and in particular
Jennings's solution, will prove him wrong, as, for example, when
Murthwaite asserts that 'we have nothing whatever to do with
clairvoyance, or with mesmerism, or with anything else that is hard
of belief to a practical man, in the inquiry that we are now pursu-
ing. My object ... is to trace results back, by rational means, to
natural causes' (second period, ch. 3). Here again we have that

tension between rational deduction and the presence of the irrational which is so crucial to this novel and to detective fiction generally. Such contradictions cannot be overcome by pure logic but require the force of the imagination.

The very title of the novel recalls Coleridge's Romantic concept of the imagination, which gives new shape to familiar landscapes by accidents of light or shade, moonlight or sunset.[8] Betteredge discovers 'under the light of the moon' (first period, ch. 8) the inky substance used in the boy's palm reading; Herncastle, who steals the diamond, was the only one among the British who had had the imagination to believe the tales of the precious stone and to seek it – his 'love of the marvellous induced him to believe', writes Collins (prologue, pt. III). And Cuff lectures Seegrave for failure of imagination, using an example that must remind us of the clairvoyant boy 'reading' ink: 'I made a private inquiry last week. ... At one end of the inquiry there was a murder, and at the other end there was a spot of ink on a tablecloth that nobody could account for. In all my experience along the dirtiest ways of this dirty little world, I have never met with such a thing as a trifle yet' (first period, ch. 12). He anticipates Sherlock Holmes's famous dictum from 'A Study in Scarlet': 'From a drop of water, a logician could infer the possibility of an Atlantic or a Niagara.' However, we require Poe's particular kind of logician, combining imagination and reason; even Cuff is unable to reconstruct the crime because it exceeds the range of his imagination.

Ezra Jennings is the ultimate detective of the novel who succeeds precisely because he is able to see both the significance of the most trivial details and to allow his mind to wander past the boundaries of rational thought. Even more than Cuff, he is able to adopt the perspective of others and thus use their subjective experience. When he discovers, for example, the significance of Dr Candy's fevered ravings, he has hit upon the quintessential method of the modern detective and also on something which sounds remarkably like psychoanalytic free-association:

> I reproduced my short-hand notes in the ordinary form of writing – leaving large spaces between the broken phrases, and even the single words, as they had fallen disconnectedly from Mr Candy's lips. I then treated the result thus obtained, on something like the principle which one adopts in putting together a child's 'puzzle'. It is all confusion to begin with; but it may be all brought into order and shape. ... I filled in each blank space on the paper, with what the words or phrases on either side of it suggested to me as the speaker's meaning;

altering over and over again, until my additions followed naturally on the spoken words which came before them. ... I found the superior faculty of thinking going on, more or less connectedly, in my patient's mind, while the inferior faculty of expression was in a state of almost complete incapacity and confusion.

(second period, ch. 9)

Here is the reconstructive core of detective fiction, that restatement of the past in the language of the present which transforms the shape of a personal or collective history, which provides it with new meaning and coherence. The reconstructive act is essential to both form and content in detective stories, and it is most gripping when it is in opposition to an equally powerful sense of mystery – not merely the mystery of the crime, but of human experience more generally. Psychoanalysis undertakes a similar and broader reconstruction, and it, too, attempts to shape a personal history into its most complete and most convincing form. Reductionism occurs, as it occurs in the sterile forms of detective fiction, with an insistence on total explanation.

There have been several psychoanalytic readings of both *The Moonstone* and detective fiction; but all of these articles suffer from the limitations of an earlier and reductive model of wish-fulfilment.[9] Sexual symbolism is unquestionably important in any full reading of *The Moonstone*, and the title image, like all gems, may be linked with women and sexuality (beauty, great value); the association to the moon further identifies the diamond with women. Collins's description of 'a defect, in the shape of a flaw, in the very heart of the stone' (first period, ch. 6) even suggests some of the sexual prejudice so strongly attached to women in the nineteenth century. And these sexual symbols help to integrate the various love stories with the theft of the jewel; they also explain some of those elements of the story which still puzzle its critics.

What is stolen from Rachel is both the actual gem and her symbolic virginity. Rachel finds herself attracted to Franklin as she is coming of age. She is in the process of deciding between suitors and sorting out, as well, the nature of her own desire. Franklin's questionable conduct on the Continent ('some imprudence ... with a woman or a debt at the bottom of it' [first period, ch. 8], thinks Betteredge) greatly disturbs her, and she in turn persuades Franklin to give up cigars. As a result, Franklin is thrown into a state of nervous tension until he enters Rachel's room in the middle of the night and steals her most valued possession. If we see the taking of the jewel only in its most literal meaning, then we cannot understand Rachel's behaviour. The *Spectator's* review in 1868, for example, describes her as 'an impulsive girl, generally slanging somebody, whose single speciality seems to be that, believing her lover had stolen her diamond, she hates him and loves him both at once, but neither taxes him with the offence nor pardons him for committing it'.[10] And Rachel does seem to behave in a most irrational way: she watches Franklin take the jewel but makes no attempt to stop him. Later she will claim that she continued to hope for some explanation, although all of her actions contradict such a hope. In fact, her behaviour is so ambiguous and so incriminating that Sergeant Cuff finds *her* guilty of the crime. She is unable to confront Franklin, unable to forgive him, unable to help in finding another solution, and unable not to love him after what he has done (she does later find the strength to call him a 'mean, miserable, heartless coward!') (second period, ch. 7). Her sudden reversal, in response to the theory of an unknown doctor, is equally puzzling: 'She tells me', writes Jennings, 'in the prettiest manner, that my letter has satisfied her of Mr Blake's innocence, without the slightest need (so far as she is concerned) of putting my assertion to the proof' (second period, fourth narrative).

All of these contradictions are resolved when we regard Franklin's action both as a literal theft and as a symbolic seduction which leads to confusion, ambivalence, and finally, to marriage and a child. Seduction is implicit in the very clues, like his stained nightshirt, which help connect Franklin to the first taking of the stone. And Rosanna Spearman does, in fact, see one link between the paint-smeared nightshirt and the supposed seduction of Rachel by Franklin:

> I saw the stain of the paint from Miss Rachel's door!
> I was so startled by the discovery that I ran out, with the nightgown in my hand, and made for the back stairs and locked myself into my own room, to look at it in a place where nobody could intrude and interrupt me.
> As soon as I got my breath again, I called to mind my talk with Penelope, and I said to myself, 'Here's the proof that he was in Miss Rachel's sitting-room between twelve last night, and three this morning!'
> I shall not tell you in plain words what was the first suspicion that crossed my mind, when I had made that discovery. You would only be angry –
>
> (second period, ch. 4)

However, Rosanna is regarded by the other characters as either criminal or lunatic, and Collins encourages the reader to dismiss her thinking because she is blinded by her own passion – another example of the way in which we must learn to accept and use the distorted visions of individual characters if we are to arrive at the fullest comprehension of the novel's action. Rosanna's suspicion of Franklin and Rachel is both a false clue to the solution of the mystery and a correct reading of the sexual implications of their relationship.

To some extent Collins used his wit to stretch the accepted limits of sexual discussion in the Victorian novel. Betteredge amuses the very proper Lady Verinder with his unintended double entendres and a naïve linking of women and money: 'I have been turning Selina Goby over in my mind ... and I think, my lady, it will be cheaper to marry her than to keep her' (first period, ch. 13); and Ablewhite is urbanely described as 'a man of pleasure, with a villa in the suburbs which was not taken in his own name, and with a lady in the villa, who was not taken in his own name, either' (second period, sixth narrative). Within the conventions of melo-drama, Collins could also allude to a sordid past (and, at the same time, connect theft and sexual exploitation): 'I was put in the prison', writes Rosanna Spearman, 'because I was a thief. I was a thief, because my mother went on the streets when I was quite a little girl' (second period, ch. 4). Collins, however, could not make this connection between his hero and heroine. Instead, he adopts, consciously or intuitively, the device so common to the Victorian novel of splitting hero and villain and giving one the crime and pun-ishment so that the other may be free to enjoy his rewards without guilt. Dickens, for example, linked his heroes with a convenient and ultimately expendable alter ego, like Steerforth or Uriah Heep in *David Copperfield* or Orlick in *Great Expectations*. Thus, Franklin steals the jewel and appears to be guilty and despised by the heroine; but, conveniently, Ablewhite will finally be exposed as the true thief just as he is exposed as a consummate betrayer of women. The sexual implications of the theft make a clearer connection between the stealing of the jewel and the various love stories of the novel while they also explain some of the apparent contradictions of the text.

Most psychoanalytic studies, however, identify a more deeply buried content in *The Moonstone* and in all detective fiction, and they reduce adult conflicts to their presumed sources in infancy.

Oedipus, like the inevitable butler, always proves to be the true villain, the original perpetrator of the crime:

> ... for all the diversity, only a few repressed wish phantasy types are the force behind all art. The sexual force is responsible for much of the wish phantasy that accounts for art. The usual expression of the sexual wish fulfilment phantasy is through some form of the Oedipus situation, the sexual desire of the child for his parent of the opposite sex.
>
> Now, to return to *The Moonstone*, what do the characters symbolise to their creator?
>
> (Lawson, 'Collins and *The Moonstone*', p. 72)

With such a limited and relentlessly one-directional set of assumptions, the question hardly requires an answer. The wish-fulfilment model commits us to oversimplification and distortion. And the larger the subject the more sweeping the distortion:

> Mystery fans ... are, criminologically speaking, harmless people with an unsolved unconscious hysteric-passive tension, stemming in man from the 'negative' Oedipus complex, in women, from the 'positive' Oedipus. These people get temporary release of their tension vicariously.
>
> (Bergler, 'Mystery Fans', p. 317)

'Of course', we are quickly assured, 'the whole process is unconscious.' Even when it is not pushed so absurdly, such criticism invariably confuses affective and biographical issues: it moves too glibly from 'what do the characters symbolise for their author' to the unresolved Oedipal tensions of mystery readers. In the process, form is virtually ignored.

Another application of the wish-fulfilment model uses a specific early memory connected to the Oedipal complex. It reads detective fiction as an expression of primal scene fears and wishes, that is, as an expression of the conflicts of the child who witnesses parental intercourse. Charles Rycroft takes an earlier article by Pederson-Krag on 'Detective Stories and the Primal Scene' and applies it to *The Moonstone*.[11] Pederson-Krag's original assumption is badly oversimplified:

> The reader addicted to mystery stories tries actively to relive and master traumatic infantile experiences he once had to endure passively. Becoming the detective, he gratifies his infantile curiosity with

impunity, redressing completely the helpless inadequacy and anxious guilt unconsciously remembered from childhood.

(Pederson-Krag, p. 214)

Yet the specific application of this theory to *The Moonstone* may help our critical understanding of the novel because so much of the formal structure of the text is built around a visual tension – seeing and not seeing, the characters watching a crime committed in a bedroom at night, not understanding it, and suffering because they are forced into a new view of a loved object.

The fear of intercourse expressed by the primal scene is most strikingly presented in *The Moonstone* through the image of The Shivering Sand, 'the most horrible quicksand on the shores of Yorkshire' (first period, ch. 4). Like the title image, the sands are connected to the phases of the moon, here through the movement of the tide: 'At the turn of the tide, something goes on in the unknown deeps below, which sets the whole face of the quicksand shivering and trembling in a manner most remarkable to see' (first period, ch. 4). And the tide itself behaves like some grotesque co-quette: 'The broad brown face of it heaved slowly, and then dimpled and quivered all over' (first period, ch. 4). Several of the women in the novel are seen as strong-willed and hurtful, like Rachel; violent, like Limping Lucy; even deadly, like the symbolic tide or the moonstone itself. Rosanna Spearman is most clearly identified as a man-killer by her explicit last name, and she identifies herself in turn with the sands that suffocate hundreds of people, 'all sinking lower and lower in the dreadful deeps! Throw a stone in, Mr Betteredge! Throw a stone in, and let's see the sand suck it down!' (first period, ch. 4). She finally merges with the quicksand in death, strengthening the symbolic connection between the deadly sands and unrequited passion. When Franklin later probes the sands with a stick to find a chest left by Rosanna, the combination of sexual excitement and sexual fear seems to perme-ate Collins's language:

> In this position, my face was within a few feet of the surface of the quicksand. The sight of it so near me, still disturbed at intervals by its hideous shivering fit, shook my nerves for the moment. A horrible fancy that the dead woman might appear on the scene of her suicide, to assist my search – an unutterable dread of seeing her rise through the heavy surface of the sand, and point to the place – forced itself into my mind, and turned me cold in the warm sunlight. I own I

closed my eyes at the moment when the point of the stick first entered the quicksand.

The instant afterwards, before the stick could have been submerged more than a few inches, I was free from the hold of my own superstitious terror, and was throbbing with excitement from head to foot.

(second period, ch. 3)

Collins's images connect one 'superstitious terror' with another, and the implicit sexual fantasies of this passage intensify the excitement and terror of the mystery. We can see at once that this reading also tells us something of Collins's deeper fears and desires, and something as well about what a reader might be responding to as he is thrilled, or fearful, or even bored by *The Moonstone*. But an identification of the novel's hypothetical first cause, or an important component of a reader's response, unconscious or not, still does not 'explain' the novel; it cannot even offer a full psychological explanation without being placed in that larger structural context I have described.

Take, for example, Miss Clack. This frustrated spinster adopts the most sanctimonious tone and bludgeons her way through the world with religion. She is continually prying and eavesdropping, and when she spies on her beloved Godfrey Ablewhite, she transforms mere looking into a comically voyeuristic nightmare. Obviously jealous of Godfrey's attentions to Rachel, Miss Clack is also excited vicariously, although she tries to hide this by her religious fervour. Godfrey and Rachel think they have escaped Drusilla by retreating from library to drawing room, but she is there, 'inadvertently' secreted in a neighbouring closet: 'A martyrdom was before me. In justice to myself, I noiselessly arranged the curtains so that I could both see and hear. And then I met my martyrdom, with the spirit of a primitive Christian' (second period, ch. 5). It becomes more primitive than she knows as she suffers the extremes of 'a burning fever' and shivering cold very similar to Franklin 'turned ... cold in the warm sunlight' by the Shivering Sand. She watches Godfrey confess his love: 'Alas! the most rigid propriety could hardly have failed to discover that he was doing it now' (second period, ch. 5). Her prudery exaggerates every gesture. She tells us that Rachel sat

> without even making an effort to put his arms back where his arms ought to have been. As for me, my sense of propriety was completely bewildered. I was so painfully uncertain whether it was my first duty

to close my eyes, or to stop my ears, that I did neither. I attribute my being still able to hold the curtain in the right position for looking and listening, entirely to suppressed hysterics. In suppressed hysterics, it is admitted, even by the doctors, that one must hold something. ... He had another burst – a burst of unholy rapture this time. He drew her nearer and nearer to him till her face touched his; and then – No! I really cannot prevail upon myself to carry this shocking disclosure any farther. Let me only say, that I tried to close my eyes before it happened, and that I was just one moment too late. I had calculated, you see, on her resisting. She submitted. To every right-feeling person of my own sex, volumes could say no more.

(second period, ch. 5)

Miss Clack's account reproduces the most essential features of the primal scene: the vision of love-making which is both attractive and repellent to the viewer and which is accompanied by excitement and guilt particularly focused on looking and hearing. It connects a comic sub-plot with the fantasies generated by the central mystery. The parody of Drusilla also parodies that very hypocrisy which prevents a frank description of adult relationships and which Collins fought both in his fiction and in his personal life.[12] Drusilla comically provokes and tantalises the reader by seeing too much and telling too little, as Collins more subtly manipulates the reader through the puzzling theft of the moonstone, making him fear the worst while revealing only half-truths until the close. And partially perceived truth is most essential to Drusilla's account: her attempt to explain an action she cannot comprehend because of her own bias and the reader's need to combine her observation and her bias to arrive at the truth. Even her obsession with seeing and not seeing, hearing and not hearing, reproduces that 'detective fever' which has gripped us from Collins's time to our own. The content of Drusilla's thought seems to be sexual, but the form of her behaviour reproduces that larger process of looking, interpreting, and reinterpreting which goes on throughout the novel. Miss Clack, of course, cannot reinterpret, but she teaches the reader to distrust all eye-witness accounts until he can make from them his own more complete version of the truth. The specific early psychological configuration called 'primal scene' does *contribute* here to the novel's dominant concerns with looking and with the problem of knowledge; but it does not *determine* those concerns, nor is it the central focus of a full psychological reading of the text. Latent structure, not latent content, is the critical interpretive issue.

II

Dreaming and detective fiction are connected by a common latent structure; and in order to perceive that structure, we require that literary criticism – like current analytic dream interpretation – subordinate an earlier libido theory into a model of conflict resolution, a model no longer exclusively aimed at wish-fulfilment or the most primitive conflicts of childhood. Freud provides a clear final illustration for us in his most famous literary analysis, which first appeared in *The Interpretation of Dreams*:

> The action of the play consists in nothing other than the process of revealing, with cunning delays and ever-mounting excitement – a process that can be likened to the work of a psycho-analysis – that Oedipus himself is the murderer of Laius, but further that he is the son of the murdered man and of Jocasta. Appalled at the abomination which he has unwittingly perpetrated, Oedipus blinds himself and forsakes his home. The oracle has been fulfilled.[13]

Freud's full account stresses an 'Oedipal' subject matter as the essential ingredient of the play, whereas here the key seems to be the repeated word 'process' and the comparison of the play to the clinical technique of psychoanalysis. The process of *Oedipus Rex* is an insistent movement toward self-discovery by a reconstitution of the past through language. Oedipus's 'complex' is less central than his behaviour, that repeated, even obsessive, probing of his own history. He behaves as the dreamer does, or the good detective: confronted with a present conflict, he forms a series of new patterns, reordering the present and integrating into it wishes and conflicts from the past, always aiming toward the resolution of contradiction. The infantile sexual subject matter of *Oedipus Rex* is of unquestionable importance, and it must touch, in turn, the most archaic and universal conflicts of its audience. But the powerful unconscious fantasies the play stirs in us are brought into the service of process, of formal movement: past to present, conflict to resolution, ignorance or partial knowledge to a more integrated truth. Parricide and incest form part of a larger psychological structure, akin to the therapeutic pattern of psychoanalysis itself and to the broadest pattern of mythical thought which 'always progresses from the awareness of oppositions toward their resolution'.[14]

Detective fiction, as we have seen, sustains a tension between subjective mystery and objective solution. Although it often uses rational thought in the service of solution, it need not allow that rationality to dominate; instead, the intellect may destroy absolute predictability and determinism, as it does more generally in play: 'play only becomes possible, thinkable and understandable when an influx of *mind* breaks down the absolute determinism of the cosmos.'[15] Detective fiction intensifies a quality present in dreaming, in literary experience, and indeed in all those activities our culture defines as 'play' by taking as both its form and its subject a conflict between mystery and unifying solution. Put another way, the tension between mystery and solution is so essential to every detective story that it superimposes itself onto any subject matter or plot and thus becomes a second story. Tzvetan Todorov has claimed that there must always be two stories in a single detective tale – the story of the crime and the story of the investigation.[16] It is precisely because *Oedipus* is built around this same duality that it is most usefully compared to detective fiction:

> While many a hero finds himself, Oedipus is unique in being the only one who, when he finds himself, is looking for himself. In other words, this is the only play in which the finding of the self is the whole process, not a product of the action but the whole of it.[17]

The ultimate conflict of *The Moonstone* is not within the novel but within the reader who must distrust the story's various narratives in order to create his own more authentic story. The resolution of the mystery is never as important as the process itself of connecting and disconnecting, building a more complete account from an incomplete vision or fragment. And as in a dream, it is precisely this tension between the reordering imagination and the facts on which it works that formally defines the genre. The dream, like all fiction, projects into the shape of a story the changing responses to our own changing conflicts, the 'creative and aesthetic experiences that depict ... the present state of our connections and disconnections with the world about us'.[18] Literary process and dreaming share a pattern of conflict-resolution, and psychoanalytic textual analyses need to subordinate the search for infantile wish-fulfilling fantasies, and their defences, to such a pattern. This should bring us closer to an appreciation of the unique style of individual works because the literary work is in this sense identical with the dream: a freshly created attempt at integration and solution which becomes final only with the death of the dreamer.

From *Victorian Studies*, 19 (1975), 181–209.

NOTES

[I have omitted the first section of Hutter's essay in which he explores Freud's theories of dreaming and their subsequent revision by psychoanalysts and literary critics, and examines the implications of the revised theory for constructing a new model of literary criticism whose aim would be the transformation of the symbolic meanings of language and narrative structures 'within the context of both the individual psyche and the shared language of the culture' (Hutter, *Victorian Studies* [1975], 190). The discussion of *The Moonstone* reprinted here suggests that there are close structural and historical links between detective fiction and psychoanalysis. Both are cultural products of the latter half of the nineteenth century and both involve the solution of mysteries by means of the reordering of the past and a transformation of a fragmented and incomplete set of events into an apparently more ordered and complete understanding. Hutter not only uses post-Freudian psychoanalytic theories to develop a model of reading detection, but he also reads this novel (and particularly its supreme detective/psychoanalyst Ezra Jennings) in the context of specific nineteenth-century ideas of and about psychology and psychologists. Hutter also offers interesting psychoanalytic readings of the sexual symbolism and implications of the theft of Rachel's diamond, and of the narrative structure of *The Moonstone* as an enactment of primal scene wishes and fears. Ed.]

1. James A. Harrison, 'The Murders in the Rue Morgue', in *The Complete Works of Edgar Allan Poe*, ed. James A. Harrison (New York, 1902, III, 151).

2. Marie Bonaparte was one of the first to point to the connection between the orangutan and man's instinctual life: *The Life and Works of Edgar Allan Poe*, trans. John Rodker (London, 1949), p. 445. Also see: Richard Wilbur, 'The Poe Mystery Case', *The New York Review of Books*, 13 July 1967, p. 25; Daniel Hoffman, *Poe Poe Poe Poe Poe Poe Poe* (Garden City, NY, 1972), pp. 112–15; and David Halliburton, *Edgar Allan Poe: A Phenomenological View* (Princeton, NJ, 1973), pp. 237–45. For a more general study of the detective genre see A. E. Murch, *The Development of the Detective Novel* (London, 1958).

3. Wilkie Collins, *The Moonstone*, 3 vols (London, 1868), prologue, pt. III. All future references are to this edition. For an analysis of Collins and detective fiction see Dorothy Sayers's 'Introduction' to *The Moonstone* (London, 1944); J. I. M. Stewart's 'Introduction' to *The Moonstone* (Middlesex, 1966); and Robert P. Ashley, 'Wilkie Collins and the Detective Story', *Nineteenth-Century Fiction*, 6 (1951), 47–60. Ashley's article is a good summary of the detective elements in all of Collins's fiction, although I believe he misreads *The Moonstone* by insisting on its formulaic adherence to the sensation novel. The most complete and balanced current appraisal of Collins is William H. Marshall, *Wilkie Collins* (New York, 1970).

4. See particularly 'On Duty with Inspector Field', *The Nonesuch Dickens: Reprinted Pieces* (London, 1938), pp. 177–89. See also Elliot L. Gilbert, 'The Detective as Metaphor in the Nineteenth Century', in Francis M. Nevins (ed.), *The Mystery Writer's Art* (Bowling Green, OH, 1970), pp. 285–93.

5. Robert Langbaum, *The Poetry of Experience* (New York, 1963), p. 109.

6. Sir Leslie Stephen is most interesting here as a representative Victorian – self-conscious and conscience-stricken – and his attitude is a product of battles like Seringapatam. Initially, Seringapatam seemed indicative of England's total domination of India. One nineteenth-century historian describes the battle and its importance for English colonisation with obvious relish: 'Seringapatam was invested and reduced to extremities, and Tipoo Sahib was obliged to sign a peace, surrendering half his dominions to the allies, paying a sum of more than four millions sterling in compensation for the war, releasing all his prisoners of war, and giving up two of his three sons as hostages to the English.' (W. E. H. Lecky, *A History of England in the Eighteenth Century* [London, 1887], p. 210.) But before the end of the nineteenth century Seringapatam, which had been ceded to the British, was restored to Mysore. For a detailed account of other connections between English colonisation of India and *The Moonstone*, see John R. Reed, 'English Imperialism and the Unacknowledged Crime of *The Moonstone*', CLIO, 2 (1973), 281–90. Reed oversimplifies the novel in arguing that 'the Moonstone becomes the sign of England's imperial depredations – the symbol of a national rather than a personal crime' (p. 286), but he does convincingly connect Collins's novel with an English policy of exploitation.

7. John Elliotson, *Human Physiology*, 5th edn (London, 1835), pp. 662, 674. See also Robert Darnton, *Mesmerism* (New York, 1970).

8. Samuel Taylor Coleridge, *Biographia Literaria* (London, 1817), ch. 14.

9. See particularly Leopold Bellak, 'On the Psychology of Detective Stories and Related Problems', *Psychoanalytic Review*, 32 (1945),

403–7; Edmund Bergler, 'Mystery Fans and the Problems of "Potential Murderers"', *American Journal of Orthopsychiatry*, 15 (1945), 309–17; Geraldine Pedersen-Krag, 'Detective Stories and the Primal Scene', *Psychoanalytic Quarterly*, 18 (1949), 207–14; Charles Rycroft, 'A Detective Story: Psychoanalytic Observations', *Psychoanalytic Quarterly*, 26 (1957), 229–45; and Lewis A. Lawson, 'Wilkie Collins and *The Moonstone*', *American Imago*, 20 (1963), 61–79. It is also instructive to look at the clinical uses of detective fiction, particularly Edith Buxbaum, 'The Role of Detective Stories in a Child Analysis', *Psychoanalytic Quarterly*, 10 (1941), 373–81 and Rudolf Ekstein and Seymour W. Friedman, 'The Function of Acting Out, Play Action and Play Acting in the Psychotherapeutic Process', *Journal of the American Psychoanalytic Association*, 7 (1959), 581–629. Buxbaum sees only the neurotic use of detective stories in her young patient, and her case study is used in turn as further evidence for those psychoanalytic critics writing about adult detective fiction. Ekstein and Friedman perceive a very different function for an adolescent patient's fictionalised identifications with criminals and detectives: here the patient's fantasies allow him to break the repeated neurotic patterns of his earlier childhood, to adapt and change the detective fantasies are malleable and become, like literature, a vehicle for growth.

10. Reprinted in Norman Page (ed.), *Wilkie Collins: The Critical Heritage* (London, 1974), p. 172.

11. Rycroft, 'A Detective Story: Psychoanalytic Observations'. This article suffers from some of the same reductionist assumptions which Rycroft attacks in his recent articles for *The New York Review of Books*. However, he has provided the most sensitive psychoanalytic reading of *The Moonstone*, both because he includes a wider range of evidence from Collins's fiction and because he seems to recognise the clear formal limitations of his analysis.

12. Marshall describes Collins's contempt for 'the shams of the Victorian middle class' from *Basil* on (*Wilkie Collins*, p. 25). See also Kenneth Robinson, *Wilkie Collins: A Biography* (New York, 1952) and Nuel Pharr Davis, *The Life of Wilkie Collins* (Urbana, IL, 1956).

13. ['The Interpretation of Dreams (1900)', *The Standard Edition of the Complete Psychological Works of Sigmund Freud*, trans. and ed. James Strachey and others (London, 1953–64), IV, 261–2. Ed.]

14. Claude Lévi-Strauss, 'The Structural Study of Myth', in *European Literary Theory and Practice*, ed. Vernon W. Gras (New York, 1973), p. 307.

15. Johan Huizinga, *Homo Ludens: A Study of the Play Element in Culture* (Boston, 1955), p. 3.

16. Tzvetan Todorov, 'Typologie du roman policier', in *Poetique de la prose* (Paris, 1971), p. 57.

17. Alister Cameron, *The Identifying of Oedipus the King* (New York, 1968), p. 51.

18. Ullman, 'The Transformation Process in Dreams', *The Academy*, 19 (1975), 9.

9

From *roman policier* to *roman-police*: Wilkie Collins's *The Moonstone*

D. A. MILLER

I

The classical detective story disposes of an interestingly paradoxical economy, at once parsimonious and squandering. On one hand, the form is based on the hypothesis that *everything might count*: every character might be the culprit, and every action or speech might be belying its apparent banality or literalism by making surreptitious reference to an incriminating Truth. From the layout of the country house (frequently given in all the exactitude of a diagram) to the cigar ash found on the floor at the scene of the crime, no detail can be dismissed *a priori*. Yet if the criterion of total relevance is continually invoked by the text, it turns out to have a highly restricted applicability in the end. At the moment of truth, the text winnows grain from chaff, separating the relevant signifiers from the much larger number of irrelevant ones, which are now revealed to be as banal and trivial as we originally suspected they might *not* be. That quarrel overheard in the night, for example, between Mr and Mrs Smith is shown for an ordinary martial row. That cigar ash – say, pointing unambiguously to Colonel Asquith's brand – is proven to have been deposited on the floor *before* the crime took place. Of the elaborate house-plan, only this door or that window enters into the solution, and of the exhaustive description of the scene of the crime, only a few items count while the rest relapse into insignificance. It is hardly an accident that most readers of detective fiction can afterwards remember 'who-dunit?' but have totally forgotten the false clues and suspects that temporarily obscured his identity. For the detective's final summation offers not a maximal integration of parts into whole, but a minimal one: what is totalised is just – and no more than – what is needed to solve the crime. Everything and everybody else is returned to a blandly mute positivity.

This observation, of course, is meant to shift the emphasis from where it normally falls in discussions of the detective story: away from the mystery that it solves towards a recognition of the hypothetical significances that it finally dissolves. Though the detective story postulates a world in which everything might have a meaningful bearing on the solution of the crime, it concludes with an extensive repudiation of meanings that simply 'drop out'.[1] It is often argued that the detective story seeks to totalise its signifiers in a complete and all-encompassing order. On the contrary, it is concerned to restrict and localise the province of meaning: to guarantee large areas of irrelevance. One easily sees, moreover, what else is guaranteed in such a form. For as the fantasy of total relevance yields to the reality of a more selective meaningfulness, the universality of suspicion gives way to a highly specific guilt. Engaged in producing a social innocence, the detective story might well take for its motto 'The truth shall set you free'.

One might take a step further: the detective story is invariably the story of a power-play. The quasi-universal suspicion is only another way of putting a quasi-total investigation. When the sheer fact of meaningfulness incriminates and has a policing force, the limits of the detective's knowledge become the limits of his power as well: his astonishing explications double for a control exercised in the interests of law and order. Detective fiction is thus always implicitly punning on the detective's brilliant 'super-vision' and the police *supervision* that it embodies. His intervention marks an explicit putting-under-surveillance of the entire world of the novel. As such, it can be alarming. When Poe's Dupin reads his sidekick's mind in 'The Murders in the Rue Morgue'; when, after a half-hour's sniffing about the scene of *L'Affaire Lerouge*, Gaboriau's Père Tabaret announces how and when the murder was committed as well as offers a physical description of the murderer; when Sherlock Holmes deduces a man's moral and economic history from his hat in 'The Adventure of the Blue Carbuncle' – these events are greeted as prodigies, as though they opened up the fearful prospect of an absolute surveillance under which everything would be known, incriminated, policed.

Typically, the detective's super-vision is dramatised by being exercised on what would seem to resist it most: the ordinary, 'trivial' facts of everyday life. During the police investigation in *The Moonstone* (1868), for example, a smear is noticed on Rachel Verinder's newly varnished door. Superintendent Seegrave, an impressive-looking but incompetent local, dismisses the detail as a 'trifle'. Expert Sergeant Cuff, however, knows better: 'In all my experience along the dirtiest ways of this dirty little world, I have never met with such a thing as a trifle yet.'[2] He goes on to discover that the varnish dries after twelve hours; that it was applied at 3 p.m.; that it was still intact at midnight. Therefore, he concludes, the theft of the Moonstone was committed between midnight and 3 a.m. by someone whose dress – possibly a nightgown – is stained with varnish. The whole sequence makes a neat parable of the detective's work: to turn trifles into 'telling' details, telling – what else? – a story of dirty linen.

Yet, as we know, the investigation from which nothing seems safe is also subject to clear and strict limits, and so ultimately reassures the community that it initially frightens. In the first place, it restricts its scope to a socially approved enterprise: the identification and apprehension of a criminal who is by definition the 'other'; and it lasts no longer than the criminal goes uncaught. In the second place, it is characterised as a dramatic instance of intervention and, as such, it is marked with a high degree of visibility. In this sense, the detective's extraordinary power of vision can be seen in turn by the community he appears to investigate. And just as the community invariably perceives the detective's personality as 'eccentric', it views the sheer disruptiveness of his investigation (think of the hysterical housemaids in *The Moonstone*) as an anomaly, a dramatic exception to a routine social order in which police and surveillance play no part. Thus seen, the investigation is fixed in place: outside a social normativeness, which it finally leaves untouched, free to be itself once more.

The final localisation of culpability might thus be thought of as a single tactic in the wider and more important strategy of *localising the investigation*: limiting its scope (the apprehension of a single criminal), limiting its agency (a single eccentric detective), and fore-grounding its interventionary character (exceptional, out-of-the-ordinary). I said a moment ago that the detective story worked to

produce a social innocence – an innocence that we can now for-
mulate as substantially more than a mere freedom from guilt. For if
the community is not finally the object of detection, neither is it the
subject of detection: innocent of crime, it is – *a fortiori* – innocent
of criminology too. Its most radical innocence, then, derives from
its sheer ignorance of power, its incapacity to assume a machinery
of surveillance, control, and punishment. The crime and the failure
to solve it both testify to the community's naïve state of vulnerability. Taken charge of by an ec-centric outsider, the investigation pre-
serves such naïveté at the same time as it neutralises the
vulnerability attending it. If one were to speak of an ideology produced by the form of the detective story, here would be one of its
major sites: in the perception of everyday life as fundamentally
'outside' the network of policing power.

II

It is not difficult to recognise that *The Moonstone* begins by invoking and observing the norms of detective fiction. Rachel Verinder's
Indian diamond is mysteriously stolen, and her mother, Lady Julia,
has 'no alternative but to send for the police' (p. 116). The police
investigation quickly proves to require 'a cleverer head than
Superintendent Seegrave's' (p. 127), and the brilliant Sergeant Cuff
– of whom 'when it comes to unravelling a mystery, there isn't the
equal in England' (p. 32) – is called in to take charge. Cuff's powers
of penetration are anticipated in the description of his gaze: 'His
eyes, of a steely light grey, had a very disconcerting trick, when they
encountered your eyes, of looking as if they expected something
more from you than you were aware of yourself' (p. 133). And such
promise is soon made good in the impressive piece of reasoning
about the varnish-smear. In short order, the text organises itself as a
movement from mystery to solution supervised by an extraordinary
police detective. It comes somewhat as a puzzle, then, when the text
abandons the scenario it has so conscientiously set up. Cuff's investigation is broken off, suspended, and even its provisional conclusions are revealed to be erroneous. The detective disappears from
what remains a novel of detection, and although he reappears to
clear up some incidental matters at the end, the mystery is solved
without his doing. With Cuff's failure and departure, *The*

Moonstone stages a conspicuous modification of what had seemed to be its programme. We can begin to elaborate what is at stake in this modification by looking at what motivates it in the novel. For Cuff's failure and departure are precisely what the novelistic community *has wished for*. In the First Period of the novel, his sheer presence is a disgrace, and he bears the burden of a general dislike. Franklin Blake treats him 'haughtily' (p. 181); Lady Julia, who has an 'unaccountable objection' to him, is always 'eager' to be 'out of [his] society' (pp. 146, 147); and even as Gabriel Betteredge serves him with the best of everything, he 'shouldn't have been sorry if the best of everything had choked him' (p. 174). Part of what these characters are responding to is the obvious affront of police intervention. Cuff is considered largely responsible for the fact that, as Betteredge's daughter puts it, 'nothing is like what it used to be' (p. 176). The natural order of the Verinder estate is brutally democratised, in the sense that all members of its hierarchy stand equal before Cuff's inquiry and suspicion. In his search for the stained garment, he intends 'to examine the wardrobes of *everybody* – from her ladyship downwards' (p. 145), and he is capable of advancing an hypothesis that links in guilt a maidservant who is a former convict and a young lady who is the mistress's daughter. His, indeed, is 'an abominable justice that favoured nobody' (p. 206).

Cuff's investigation threatens the community in even more radical ways as well. Systematically, his 'roundabout' and 'underground' practices (pp. 155, 177) undertake to violate the common decencies and genteel forbearances on which daily social life is based. He trails Rosanna Spearman 'privately' on her walk (p. 155); he eavesdrops on Betteredge and Blake on a couple of occasions; and he sets a spy on the rumble of Rachel's carriage. Ordinary actions and encounters are no longer protected by the socially given obviousness that precludes scrutiny, or by the socially accepted conventions that prohibit it. The First Period of the novel is dominated by the community's shocked sense of violation. It has been invaded by an outsider, who not only watches what is not supposed to be watched, but also construes what he sees according to other rules than those by which this community is used to regulating itself.

It is just this 'heteronomous' reconstruction of its world that the community resists. Practically, resistance takes the form of a reluctance and even refusal to collaborate with Cuff. Rachel virtually declines to speak with him at all. Blake is determined to shield

Rosanna Spearman from him ('... I can't, and won't, help Sergeant Cuff to find the girl out' [p. 183]). And even Betteredge, whose fascination and compliance with Cuff registers his scruples all the more effectively, tries to conceal information about Rosanna from him (p. 152). In all cases, there stands behind such resistance a genteel code of honour and loyalty. A lady does not betray the gentleman she loves; a gentleman does not expose an unfortunate woman to suspicion; and a faithful retainer does not fail to imitate the code of his betters. It is already apparent that resistance is offered as well in an ideological mode, in the form of a socio-moral critique of Cuff's operations. When Blake infers that Cuff has listened in on his conversation with Betteredge, the latter knows that

> He had done worse than listen. ... He had remembered my telling him that the girl was in love with Mr Franklin; and he had calculated on that, when he appealed to Mr Franklin's interest in Rosanna – in Rosanna's hearing.
>
> (p. 183)

Cuff's interventions always strike the community as being unfair, and it is easy to see why. The very 'manners' whose traditional, taken-for-granted authority has maintained the self-identity of the community are now exploited to produce an alienated knowledge that rives it apart. Not the least of Cuff's sins in this perspective is that he is a liar, one who abuses the conventional stability of language and contexts of communication in order to mislead and deceive. Seeking information about Rosanna from her friends, the Yollands, Cuff tells Mrs Yolland that his purpose is to clear Rosanna 'from the unjust suspicions of her enemies in the house' (p. 164), even though he has done more than anyone to accumulate evidence for such suspicions. Betteredge's sense of outrage is qualified only by the comically literal terms in which it is cast:

> It might be all in the way of the Sergeant's business to mystify an honest woman by wrapping her round in a network of lies; but it was my duty to have remembered, as a good Protestant, that the father of lies is the Devil – and that mischief and the Devil are never far apart.
>
> (pp. 164–5)

If Cuff's methods are troubling, their findings are untenable. Superintendent Seegrave has already implied a willingness to suspect Betteredge's own daughter, and Cuff proves even more perverse in suspecting Rachel Verinder herself. 'I don't suspect', claims Cuff, moreover, 'I know' (p. 173). Unable rationally to extricate Rachel from Cuff's impressively taut weave of evidence, the community relies most simply on a strategy of disavowal. Listening to Cuff's persuasive case, Betteredge rejoices that he is 'constitutionally superior to reason' (p. 208). Yet even Betteredge, whose comical intuitions nonetheless embody community norms, is capable of refuting Cuff's 'knowledge' in less merely wilful ways:

> If Sergeant Cuff had been Solomon in all his glory, and had told me that my young lady had mixed herself up in a mean and guilty plot, I should have had but one answer for Solomon, wise as he was, 'You don't know her; and I do'.
>
> (p. 174)

With greater authority, Lady Julia makes the same point when Cuff confronts her with his 'truth'.

> ... I have to tell you, as Miss Verinder's mother, that she is *absolutely incapable* of doing what you suppose her to have done. Your knowledge of her character dates from a day or two since. My knowledge of her character dates from the beginning of her life. State your suspicion of her as strongly as you please – it is impossible that you can offend me by doing so. I am sure, beforehand, that (with all your experience) the circumstances have fatally misled you in this case. Mind! I am in possession of no private information. I am as absolutely shut out of my daughter's confidence as you are. My one reason for speaking positively, is the reason you have heard already. I know my child.
>
> (p. 205)

The nature of her and Betteredge's quarrel with Cuff is thus explicitly epistemological: at one extreme, an 'outside' knowledge constituted by an interventionary reconstruction of its object; at the other, an 'inside' knowledge consubstantial with what it comes to know. Lady Julia's knowledge is analogous to the 'old money' her estate represents: so gradually acquired that it becomes a 'natural' possession which never had to be actively possessed. Conversely, just as Cuff's status as a detective would have announced his upward mobility to a mid-Victorian readership, his knowledge too bears the mark of the 'nouveau', at once impressive and in bad taste, quickly assertive and asserting only monstrous propositions.

Now, before all else, Cuff's intervention is a sign that the community has failed to know itself. And if the results of his inquiry were verified, that failure of self-knowledge would become definitive. As it happens, however, Cuff is positively wrong. The diamond has been stolen not by Rachel or Rosanna (whose suspicious behaviour is only intended to screen Franklin Blake, the man they love and think has stolen it), but by Godfrey Ablewhite, who needs ready cash to pay off his debts. By producing a solution that contradicts Cuff's conclusions but is consonant with the community's intuitions, the text blatantly endorses the latter. At a moment in Cuff's investigation, he scolds Betteredge for doing some detection on his own: 'For the future, perhaps you will be so obliging as to do your detective business along with me' (p. 157). In fact, in a striking reversal of the pattern of detective fiction, it is rather the blinded Cuff who ought to have done his 'detective business' along with the community. And the main effect of Cuff's departure is to turn over the work of detection to prominent members of this community, like Matthew Bruff, its lawyer, and Franklin Blake, its *jeune premier*.

In a way, such a shift is bound to remind us of the typical displacements of detective fiction, where the function of detection passes either from a local to a national agent (from Seegrave to Cuff in the First Period of *The Moonstone*), from a police to a private detective (from Scotland Yard to Sherlock Holmes in 'The Naval Treaty'), or from a professional to an amateur (from Inspector G—— to Dupin in the Poe stories). Taken as a whole, *The Moonstone* obviously exemplifies the third type of displacement. Yet too many 'amateurs' are involved here for the term to be wholly adequate. It is not just Betteredge who contracts 'the detective fever'. Nor is it merely the obvious detective figures (Blake, Bruff, Ezra Jennings) who together with their helpers (Murthwaite, Gooseberry) prosecute the case to a successful conclusion. Necessary information is provided by Rachel (who confesses that she saw Blake take the diamond), Mr Candy (whose partially recovered memory helps bring his drugging of Blake to light), Limping Lucy (who delivers Rosanna's letter), and even Rosanna herself (whose letter puts Blake in possession of the missing nightgown). That none of these characters *intends* to assist the work of detection is irrelevant to the fact of their practical collaboration, without which the mystery would never be solved. In effect, the work of detection is carried forward by the novel's entire cast of characters, shifted not just from professional to amateur, but from an outsider to a whole community. Thus, the move to discredit and finally dismiss the *role of the detective* is at the same time a move to diffuse and disperse the *function of detection*.

It might of course be thought that the community simply represents an alternative agency of detection, just as unified and localisable as that embodied in Sergeant Cuff. At its most radical, however, the dissemination of the detective-function precludes the very possibility of identifying the agency in charge of it. For not only does the work of detection fail to correspond to any one character's design, it never even corresponds to an implicitly 'collective' intentionality. What integrates and consolidates the efforts of characters is a master-plan that no one governs or even anticipates. The community serves such a master-plan but is not its master. Significantly, the work of detection is prosecuted in large degree as a result of chance and coincidence. It would have been impossible to calculate on Mr Candy's recovery from amnesia, or on an Ezra Jennings turning up in the right place at the right time. Such happy chances, moreover, are produced only in the course of time, which is also invested with the detective-function. One recalls the following exchange from Dickens's *The Mystery of Edwin Drood* (1870):

> '[I]t seems a little hard to be so tied to a stake, and innocent; but I don't complain.'
> 'And you must expect no miracle to help you, Neville,' said Mr Crisparkle, compassionately.
> 'No, sir, I know that. The ordinary fulness of time and circumstance is all I have to trust to.'
> 'It will right you at last, Neville.'
> 'So I believe, and I hope I may live to know it.'[3]

Though Dickens's novel is unfinished, it seems obvious that it writes here a promissory note that any possible ending would have met. *The Moonstone* promotes a similar reliance on the 'ordinary fulness of time and circumstance', which, while it accommodates characters' efforts to speed its ripening process along, is not finally or fully identified with them. 'Let us trust to time', says Mr Bruff, 'time would show' (p. 452), and the text bears him out. In the course of time, Franklin Blake returns from abroad, Limping Lucy delivers Rosanna's letter, Rachel reveals what she has been hiding, Mr Candy makes a recovery, and Luker's term of deposit on the diamond expires. What needs to come out somehow does, and the work of detection advances, an intentionality without a subject, a design that no one is allowed to assume responsibility for forming.

Confronted with this phenomenon, critics like Ian Ousby have been tempted to invoke the familiar notion of Providence, which would enable us to ascribe the work of detection to an agency in control of it. Yet one should beware of using the notion of Providence to neutralise the ways in which the 'providential' is characterised in the novel. Contrary to Collins's practice, say, in *Armadale* (1866), the 'providential' here is divested of any explicit religious dimension. We are meant to respond with a very worldly smile when Betteredge speaks, like a good Protestant, of the Devil, and only in hypocrites like Miss Clack or Ablewhite do we find the traditional pious belief in divine will. Moreover, if such a will is at work in the novel, it functions only through the established logic of a thoroughly ordinary world. The providential effect of detection in *The Moonstone* does not depend on its proximate causes. These are individual psychologies, social institutions and scenarios, even onto-logical laws that operate in overwhelmingly conventional ways. Rather, it depends on the fact that detection, working exclusively through its agents' intentions, uncannily but benignly transcends them. Discreet and, in the last analysis, agentless, the detective-function is able to organise the text without raising the moral prob-lems posed by Cuff's interventionary police enquiry.

It is this 'discreet' detection, blandly and automatically attaching to the way things are, that our reading needs to foreground. We might begin by noticing that Cuff's morally unacceptable investiga-tion has its pre-condition in a prior investigation. In his clever de-duction regarding the door-smear, all Cuff really does is assemble and co-ordinate the information gathered and given to him by members of the community. Blake knows the drying-time of the varnish and when it was applied; Penelope has noticed that it was still intact at midnight. The door, as it were, was under a patchy and unconscious surveillance even before Cuff's arrival. What may seem a gratuitous observation becomes more significant when Cuff proceeds to find the stained article of dress.

> Before we begin, I should like, if convenient, to have the washing-book. The stained article of dress may be an article of linen. If the search leads to nothing, I want to be able to account next for all the linen in the house, and for all the linen sent to the wash. If there is an article missing, there will be at least a presumption that it has got the

paint-stain on it, and that it has been purposely made away with, yesterday or today, by the person owning it.

(pp. 146–7)

Suggestively, the washing-book belongs to a pre-established system for accounting for the linen. Cuff's hypothesis would verify itself by a means that already exists *as a means of verification*. And later, when he has traced Rosanna to a linendraper where she purchased 'enough [cloth] to make a nightgown' (p. 188), he explains:

> ... her nightgown must have brushed the wet paint on the door. ... [S]he couldn't safely destroy the nightgown without first providing another like it, to make the inventory of her linen complete.

(p. 189)

'To make the inventory of her linen complete': even as it tells us what Rosanna would have had to circumvent, the phrase glances as well at the extent to which the servants' lives are already administered and controlled. A preventive detection inheres in the very management of the estate. One might also recall how Rosanna's secret signs of interest in Franklin Blake are 'surprised' and 'surprised again' by Penelope (p. 79); or how, again by Penelope, the private meeting between Rachel and Godfrey Ablewhite is watched and overheard from 'behind the holly' (p. 98). In both cases, Penelope hastens to report to her father, who happens also to be head servant. Natural curiosity and common gossip double for an informal system of surveillance that is in force on the estate well before the Moonstone is stolen.

In a more diffuse way, the system is implied in the very 'knowledge' characters have of one another. Everyone's behaviour in this world is being continuously encoded according to shared norms of psychological and moral verisimilitude. Invariably, the points at which behaviour seems insufficiently 'motivated' by these norms are points of *suspicion*. As early as the First Period, one could make an accurate guess at the thief simply by ranking the main suspects (Rachel, Rosanna, Blake and Ablewhite) in the degree to which each stands outside the collective cognition whose spokesman is Betteredge. Like her mother, he has known Rachel from birth. He intuitively senses the goodwill of Rosanna, who in any case has been thoroughly watched both at the Reformatory and at the Verinder estate. He knew Blake as a boy, and though he is somewhat baffled by the man, he notes that the passing years have left 'the bright, straightforward look in his eyes' (p. 60). Blake's eccentricities (his moodiness, his frivolousness, his foreign 'sides') are soon accommodated as idiosyncrasies, not deviations. Only in the case of Ablewhite does Betteredge claim no more than an extrinsic knowledge, gathered from hearsay and as a spectator:

> I do suppose this was the most accomplished philanthropist (on a small independence) that England ever produced. As a speaker at charitable meetings the like of him for drawing your tears and your money was not easy to find. He was quite a public character. The last time I was in London, my mistress gave me two treats. She sent me to the theatre to see a dancing woman who was all the rage; and she sent me to Exeter Hall to hear Mr Godfrey. The lady did it, with a band of music. The gentleman did it, with a handkerchief and a glass of water. Crowds at the performance with the legs. Ditto at the performance with the tongue.
>
> (p. 89)

It ought to come as no surprise that Godfrey is leading a double life when even in Betteredge's apparent commendation, one can read a hollowness – an absence of the 'real' Godfrey. Significantly, Betteredge praises his *rhetoric*, traditionally the sign of an outward appearance whose correspondence with inward being is not to be taken for granted. By the time Godfrey is associated with Miss Clack, and it is known that he has asked to see Lady Julia's will, there is little to learn except the logistics of the theft and the details of the secret life motivating it. Indeed, one might say that the remaining actions in the novel – the discovery that Franklin Blake stole the diamond, its confirmation and disconfirmation – merely distract characters from the obvious epistemological gaps that identify Godfrey as the thief. In this sense, the revelation at the end is a fact that the community knew all along, but simply didn't know that it knew.

In effect, then, a policing power is inscribed in the ordinary practices and institutions of the world from the start. The full extent of this inscription can already be measured in the Prologue, where a cousin writing to relatives in England accuses Colonel John Herncastle of stealing the Moonstone from its Indian shrine. 'I declare, on my word of honour, that what I am now about to write is, strictly and literally, the truth' (p. 33). Beginning like a legal deposition, the cousin's manuscript proceeds to marshal the 'moral evidence' for his accusation, and concludes by submitting the case to the family's judgement. And the family network that detects and judges crime is also empowered to enforce its own sentence:

> [Herncastle] came back with a character that closed the doors of all his family against him. ... The mystery of the Colonel's life got in the Colonel's way, and outlawed him, as you may say, among his own people. The men wouldn't let him into their clubs; the women – more than one – whom he wanted to marry, refused him; friends and relations got too near-sighted to see him in the street.
>
> (pp. 63–4)

The quasi-legal status of the Prologue extends to the entire novel, as a 'record in writing' (p. 39) containing 'the attestations of witnesses who can speak to the facts' (p. 236). Each deposition is under the juridical restraint not to overstep the boundaries of the 'personal experience' (p. 40) of the deposer. Betteredge is only the first to remind us that he is forbidden to tell more in his narrative than he knew himself at the time: 'In this matter of the Moonstone the plan is, not to present reports, but to produce witnesses' (p. 233). According to the same plan, the narratives are being collected to provide a record of the facts to which those who come after [the protagonists] can appeal' (p. 39). Betteredge imagines 'a member of the family' reading his narrative fifty years later: 'Lord! what a compliment he will feel it, to be asked to take nothing on hearsay, and to be treated in all respects like a Judge on the bench' (p. 233). In the most active sense of the term, the community is concerned to 'justify' itself – *to make its own justice.* If this community can afford to dispense with the legal systems of surveillance, trial, and punishment, this is because its own organisation anticipates and contains them.

With one crucial difference: its policing apparatus is inscribed not just 'in' but 'as' the ordinary practices of the world. Everyday roles, motivations, scenarios *naturalise* this apparatus effortlessly. Herncastle's cousin swears not in the name of God, as he would in a court of law, but on his honour, as he would in ordinary intercourse among ladies and gentlemen. The institution of justice to which he appeals is also, on its most visible face, the institution of the Family. Herncastle is not so much 'punished' as he is 'snubbed' – the natural response of gentility to someone with a bad character. Penelope's spying is perceived as 'the natural curiosity of women' (p. 79), a young girl's innocent interest in the love-relationships of her mistress and her fellow-servants. She doesn't, moreover, go tattle to the head servant; she quite properly confides in her father. As for the washing-book, its function is presumably to make sure that nothing is lost. Even many of the deposition-like narratives that record the story are no more than everyday forms of writing (letters, journals, diaries), or are at least derived from them. In a similar pattern, detective figures such as Blake, Bruff and Jennings have no intrinsic interest in detection at all. Blake needs to clear up the mystery in order to gain Rachel's hand. A close family friend, Bruff is naturally concerned to protect the fatherless and soon altogether orphaned Rachel from adventurers, as well as to promote an obvious love-match between her and Blake. And Jennings gets involved because he feels sorry for Blake, whom he sees as a double of himself. Typically, characters become detectives in the exact degree that they remain what they already are. As an eminent lawyer, Bruff can easily find out who has asked to see his client's will; as a psychologist, Jennings is able to decipher Mr Candy's fragmentary utterances and to create the opium-experiment that exculpates Blake once for all. At the most basic, what assists the work of detection can be as 'natural' as one's physical constitution. Candy helps simply by recovering from his amnesia, and Blake merely by having the same somatic responses to his second dose of opium as to his first. In the end, moreover, even the most voluntaristic efforts of detection are sublated in a self-regulating moral ontology. For the thief of the Moonstone is identified and discovered only after he is dead – murdered by Indians who have recovered the jewel for their Hindu shrine. The text's suggestion is obvious: the nature of things is so arranged that Godfrey's crime inevitably designates and punishes itself. 'Questo è il fin di chi fa mal.'

In general, the effects of a police apparatus are secured as side-effects of their motivation *in another register*. They surface as incidental consequences of actions and institutions that have other, more obvious and 'natural' explanations for their being. Thus, without having to serve police functions in an *ex officio* way, gossip and domestic familiarity produce the effect of surveillance; letters and diaries, the effect of 'dossiers'; closed clubs and homes, the effect of punishment. The intention to detect is visible only at a 'microscopic' level, casually implied in self-evident moral imperatives (to love, to take care of, to feel sorry for), or at a 'macroscopic' level, inscribed in the fullness of time and in the moral–ontological law that compels guilt to confess itself. In either case, a direct assumption of policing power by the community is avoided. In a way, then, *The Moonstone* displaces the structures of detective fiction only to restage its ideology of everyday life in more ambitious ways. The detective story, I claimed, put policing power at the margins of everyday life, from which it made an occasional, anomalous incursion. More radically, *The Moonstone* dismisses the police altogether, and the mysterious crime is worked to a solution by a power that no one has charge of. The equivocal role of the 'providential' – immanent in the social world yet distinct from its intentionalities – is thus part of a strategy whose ideological implications should be plain. The exercise of policing power inheres in the logic of the world, but only as a discreet 'accident' of normative social practices and models of conduct. The community does not mobilise in a concerted scheme of police action, and yet things turn out as though it did. *The Moonstone* satisfies a double exigency: how to keep the everyday world entirely outside a network of police power and at the same time preserve the effects of such power within it. Indeed, the novel *increases* this power in the very act of arranging for it to 'disappear', absorbed into (as) the sheer positivity of being in the world. It cannot be decried as an intervention because it is already everywhere. It cannot be resisted for long since it exerts the permanent pressure of 'reality' itself. Finally, it cannot even be seen, for it is a power that never passes as such: therein lies its power.

III

Students of detective fiction commonly grow wistful when discussing its ancestors in the nineteenth-century novel. Such novels, it is usually lamented, approach the 'classical' detective story, but stop disappointingly short of realising its programme fully and point by point.[4] Yet if these novels are not detective stories, it is, as we say, because they do not wish to be. In the case of *The Moonstone*, this is a quite literal truth. The text, we have seen, invokes the norms of detective fiction precisely to rework and pass beyond them. It moves from a story of police action to a story of human relationships in less 'specialised' social contexts. Simultaneously, the move is a shift in genre: away from the detective novel to what can only be called the 'novel' *tout court*. In superseding detective fiction, the text might thus be taken to elaborate a certain 'genealogy of the

Novel'. The Novel, as it were, would be the form that results when the detective story is exploded and diffused. The genealogy, of course, is not a genesis. It would be absurd to claim that the novel emerged historically from the literature of crime and detection. Although examples of detective fiction were certainly available in the nineteenth century (Collins, for instance, knew the work of both Poe and Gaboriau), the genre did not really come into its own until the turn of the century and after, with Doyle, Christie, Leroux, et al. Generic labels here are simply a convenient way to foreground a double pattern of revision that the Novel typically enacts: the circumscription of professional offices of detection and punishment, and the reinscription of their functions in everyday life.

Traces of this pattern may be found throughout nineteenth-century fiction, where a police apparatus, legally charged with the detection of crime and the punishment of criminals, frequently stands on the periphery of the representation. Quarantined at the margins of the world, its status too seems 'marginal', its pertinence limited. At the same time as a legal police apparatus is thus restricted, however, its powers are extended by attaching to other, extrajudicial and fully ordinary agencies. Dickens's *Great Expectations* and *Bleak House* rewrite the concerns of a police apparatus into the logic of an individual psychology or a whole society. Similarly, the professional detective work in Balzac's *Père Goriot* merely presents in miniature the general social expertise that Rastignac needs to master; and Corentin, the government spy in *Les Chouans* and *Une Ténébreuse Affaire*, is only the official version of a surveillance that is carried out more informally elsewhere, in the *Scènes de la vie privée*. In Trollope's *The Eustace Diamonds*, Lizzie is brought to justice not by the law, but by the society that relegates her to an untouchable *bohème*. And in Zola's *Le Ventre de Paris*, the police who are finally called in to arrest Florent merely execute the sentence of an elaborate inquest that the community has already seen through. Even when the police are not actually involved, moreover, the pattern persists as a move from obvious agencies of detection and punishment to less salient, more insidious ones. The seminary that Julien Sorel attends in *Le Rouge et le Noir* fills manifest functions of incarceration and surveillance; but the same functions are served, less blatantly, at the Hôtel de la Mole ('Tout se sait, ici comme au seminaire!'). In George Eliot's *Middlemarch*, the public unmasking of Bulstrode's murderous attentions to Raffles represents a clear-cut police action on the part of the community; like the outlaw in a western, the banker is virtually ridden out of town. The melodramatic theatrics of the story seem to differentiate it, both in tone and method, from the more central stories of Dorothea and Lydgate. Yet these stories too end in the exile of their protagonists by the community, whose judgement is only more subtly delivered, dispersed among a number of pressure points. Typically, then, the nineteenth-century novel 'domesticates' a police apparatus – at a legal level, held in check on the periphery of the representation; at an extrajudicial level, diffused throughout it.

If such a pattern is not explained by literary history, it may make sense in a history of another kind. I have in mind Michel Foucault's 'history' of the new modalities of surveillance and punishment that begin to permeate Western societies around the end of the eighteenth century.[5] In place of the corporeal and spectacular forms of *punishment* that had previously been dominant, the nineteenth century substitutes an intangible and secluded *discipline*. Foucault locates the most obvious features of discipline in what is its most obvious institution, the modern prison. Legally, he reminds us, the modern prison pretends to a strictly ancillary relationship to the Law and its offices of detection and punishment. In fact, he shows, it extends these offices by inscribing its subjects in a minute and continuous surveillance that leaves nothing unencoded. The daily exercises, observances and routines that it imposes on its subjects recreate them as objects of a supervision prosecuted, above all, 'dans le détail'. The ideal site of this surveillance is embodied in Jeremy Bentham's Panopticon, a model plan for a circular prison disposed about a central watchtower. Bentham's model is 'ideal' in other ways as well. In addition to guaranteeing the permanent visibility of its inmates, it also secures the perfect *invisibility* of the power that watches over them. Moreover, it matters less in this arrangement that the prisoners are constantly watched than that they *can* be watched at any moment, and that they know this. The Panopticon diminishes the role of an actual supervisor by enlisting the consciousness of its inmates as a primary means of supervision. Optimally, the architecture would encourage a certain quietism, and the 'disappearance' of power could be doubly staged: first, as the concealment of the watch in the tower, and secondly, as the internalisation of the watch in the prisoners.

Yet the self-evident functions of the Panopticon are finally, in Poe's phrase, 'a little *too* self-evident' to make it fully exemplary of a discipline which is nothing if not subtle. Foucault's most interesting characterisation of modern discipline comes at the level of what he calls 'les panoptismes de tous les jours', those utterly ordinary institutions which traverse and control daily existence. Whether called the school, the factory, the hospital, or the barracks, an 'everyday panoptism' serves the deviousness of discipline far better than the prison. Its self-nominated function is never to '*surveiller et punir*', but rather to educate, to produce, to cure, to defend. Unlike the prison, which, despite its reformist pretensions, inescapably refers to a legal scenario of crime and punishment, everyday forms of discipline regulate areas of social life that have no felt connection with the law or the police. They operate on the surfaces of ordinary social practice from which the very idea of the police seems far removed. Paradoxically, their policing power is manifest only by remaining latent: carried in agencies that enjoy the alibi of nobler – or simply blander – intentionalities. In a sleight-of-hand that only increases its efficiency, disciplinary power shows up *where it can hardly be*.

Now the shift from a professional detective to lay detection in the story of *The Moonstone* is clearly a version of the move from punishment to discipline in Foucault's history of policing power. Indeed, we have claimed that the functions of a 'disciplinary apparatus' are taken over by the world of the novel in an even more diffuse form than Foucault recognises, carried in far more informal institutions than school or factory. Yet I shouldn't want to limit the relevance of Foucault's history by seeing discipline as simply the characteristic *content* of the nineteenth-century novel. For if the shift is a general one, then the texts we call nineteenth-century novels would not merely register it (as a feature of a referent in the real world), but relay it as well (within the literary institution of the Novel). According to Foucault, the disciplinary apparatus does not merely 'reflect' certain arrangements of power, but *enacts* them in the formal details of its set-up. Similarly, although I have argued that *The Moonstone* tells a story of modern power analogous to Foucault's, it would ultimately be more pertinent to show how this story is also the story of the novel's own telling. If Foucault is right, the text would do more than dramatise a certain ideology of power. It would produce this ideology as an effect – and in the mode – of its being read as a novel. Accordingly, our attention needs to turn from the 'discipline' that is represented in the novel to the 'discipline' that inheres in the machinery of representation itself.[6]

IV

Unlike the majority of Victorian novels, *The Moonstone* is not related by an 'omniscient narrator', whose unimpeachable authority imposes itself on the reader. Instead, the story is told in a succession of narratives written by some of the characters and organised through their limited points of view. The 'modernity' of such a procedure is seductively apparent, as are the implications that a post-Jamesian criticism might wish to draw from it. Thus, *The Moonstone* is currently thought to offer 'a narrative structure that is thoroughly subjective and unreliable' (A. D. Hutter) and 'to provide a continually shifting viewpoint on the action, offering not merely different but sometimes contradictory views of the same event or character' (Ian Ousby).[7] The text, it is implied in such claims, opens up the notion of truth to radically relativistic challenge – in the manner, say, of *Rashomon*. In Kurosawa's film (1950), one remembers, a crime is recounted four times, each time, by a different protagonist. Not only are the accounts incompatible, but there is no compelling standard of plausibility by which the contradictions might be adjudicated. The 'truth' is dissolved into four conflicting interpretations. Contrary to the example of *Rashomon*, however, the 'unreliable' and 'contradictory' narrative structure of *The Moonstone* works only as a ruse. To be sure, the text *claims* for itself all that Hutter and Ousby are ready to grant it. A reader is supposed to listen to the various witnesses, and to make up his mind about the validity of their reports as he will, 'like a Judge on the bench'. To all formal appearances, his reading is deprived of any grounding in an authoritative version. Yet the possibility of an authentic 'dialogism' in the text disappears once we recognise that, in every crucial case, all readers (including Hutter and Ousby) pass *the same judgement*. The different points of view, degrees of information, tendencies of suspicion are never allowed to tamper with more basic interpretative securities about character and language. Characters may be *known* because they are always equipped with stable, centred identities; and they may be known *in language* because it is incapable of ever escaping from its own veridicity.

For all its apparent 'subjectivity', for example, Betteredge's narrative can be counted on to give us a valid cognition of its 'subject': the faithful retainer himself, whose very naïveté is a guarantor of the truthfulness of his self-presentation. Moreover, to the degree that Betteredge's language unproblematically 'names' him, we know exactly what weight to give to its cognitive claims about other matters in the novel. To suspect this language, as a reader of *The Murder of Roger Ackroyd* might well try to do, is to play a more strenuous interpretative game against the text than it is ever willing to reward: Betteredge's normative-seeming perceptions are normative in fact, fully borne out in the rest of the novel. For all practical purposes of reading, the head servant's subjectivity shrinks down to a few idiosyncrasies which differentiate him as a 'character' and which we know to discount for. We don't, for instance, seriously expect *Robinson Crusoe* to figure in the solution to the mystery. Nor do we ever feel that Betteredge's misogyny interferes with the good sense of his intuitions about Rachel (high-tempered, but honourable) or Rosanna (fatally weak, perhaps, but no criminal). His narrative may not tell us 'the whole truth', but it can be relied on to tell us 'nothing but the truth'. The local uncertainties in his report never impair the possibility of his or our cognition, which is always able to designate them as such, and so to initiate a process of mastering them. Whatever Betteredge doesn't know, he knows he doesn't know, and so do we. In this sense, the actual cognitive problems posed by his language are infrequent and strictly minor. Thus, when he introduces Godfrey Ablewhite in the passage we cited earlier, it is unclear whether he means his language to be 'straight' or sarcastic. The undecidability of what Betteredge means, however, never carries over into what his language actually says. The reader inevitably recognises that, with or without Betteredge's knowledge, his text refuses to endorse Godfrey in any full way. That Betteredge's language is ambiguously motivated is irrelevant to a more fundamental readerly certainty about Godfrey's unique and suspicious hollowness.

The Moonstone, I am arguing, is more fundamentally about the securities of perception and language than about the problems they pose. To use Mikhail Bakhtin's term, the novel is thoroughly *monological* – always speaking a master-voice that corrects, overrides, subordinates, or sublates all other voices it allows to speak. This basic monologism shows up best, in fact, precisely where it seems threatened most: in the narrative of Miss Clack. In obvious ways,

Clack's perception differs radically from that of the rest of the community: she suspects Rachel, dislikes Franklin Blake, and adores Godfrey Ablewhite. Yet at least when it comes to representing the self-deceived spinster herself, Clack's language is incontestably truthful. At the start of her narrative, Blake appends a footnote telling us that

> 'the person chiefly concerned' in Miss Clack's narrative, is happy enough at the present moment, not only to brave the smartest exercise of Miss Clack's pen, but even to recognise its unquestionable value as an instrument for the exhibition of Miss Clack's character.
>
> (p. 236)

In addition to exculpating Rachel (who is, of course, 'the person chiefly concerned'), the note invites us to read Clack's narrative against its grain – to locate its truth in the blinds of its narrator's *inconscience*. Even without the invitation, Clack's perceptions are so blatantly self-betraying that a reader inevitably revises them to mean something very different from what Clack imagines. When she insists, for instance, that Rachel's haughtiness didn't anger her ('I only made a private memorandum to pray for her'), the piety is effectively 'de-sublimated' only a paragraph later:

> For my own part, knowing Rachel's spirit to have been essentially unregenerate from her childhood upwards, I was prepared for whatever my aunt could tell me on the subject of her daughter. It might have gone on from bad to worse till it ended in Murder; and I should still have said to myself, The natural result! oh, dear, dear, the natural result!
>
> (p. 244)

The ardent concern for Rachel's imperilled soul merely aggrandises the *ressentiment* of a poor relation, just as the hero-worship of Godfrey Ablewhite merely returns the sexual repression of a frustrated old maid. In the context of these transparent psychological aberrations, Clack's mistaken views of Rachel and Godfrey point to themselves as such, and thus they are neutralised even as they are presented. More than neutralised: they reinforce the dominant perceptions that a reader has already derived from Betteredge's narrative and will find confirmed in the narratives of Bruff and Blake. Although *The Moonstone* formally lacks a monological *narrator* who could refute Clack's words by direct comment ('Clack was lying to herself') or indirect insinuation ('Clack persuaded herself that Rachel's insolence roused no anger in her'), the text remains an essentially monological narration. Despite the intentions of its 'author', Clack's narrative is reduced to no more than a 'loyal opposition' within a single and coherent movement of disclosure.

There is a further point to be made. Not only is *The Moonstone* a monological text, but also its monologism quite literally *goes without saying*. Formally and linguistically, the master-discourse that organises the text is unwritten: carried only through the subjective narratives that are unwittingly but regularly obliged to postulate it. Collins's technique is a way to inscribe the *effects* of monologism in the text without ascribing them to the *agency* of an actual monologist. As a result, monologism doesn't strictly seem *in* the text (like the shifters and first-personal pronouns that identify the narrator in George Eliot or Trollope); nor does it seem fully *outside* the text (like an interpretative choice that one may, or may not, impose on it). Rather, it is staged like an 'invisible hand', programming the text without needing to be programmed into it. As such, of course, the monologism of the narration is exactly analogous to the work of detection in the representation. Just as a common detection transcends the single efforts of various detective-figures, a common narration subsumes the individual reports of various narrators. The world resolves its difficulties, and language finds its truth, according to the same principle of quasi-automatic self-regulation.

At both levels, *The Moonstone* promotes a single perception of power. In a consistent pattern, power in the novel is never gathered into an identifiable (and hence attackable) centre. Neither is it radically 'disseminated' so that the totality it claims to organise breaks down into discontinuities and incoherencies. Its paradoxical efficiency lies in the fact that an apparent lack of centre at the level of *agency* secures a total mastery at the level of *effect*. What finally justifies us in calling the novel's perception of power 'ideological' is that *The Moonstone* never really perceives power as such at all. The novel is itself blinded by the mystificatory strategy of power in the very act of tracing it. In practical terms, this means the novel must always 'say' power as though it were saying *something else*. As I've tried to suggest, the 'something else' is no less than the irresistible positivity of words and things 'as they are'. Just as detection surfaces only in the ordinary activities of amateurs, and monological narration only in subjective narratives, so too the discourse on power only comes to light in (as) a discourse on 'the way things are'. 'Revealing' the character of modern power only insofar as it 'masks' it as an ontology, *The Moonstone* is thus perfectly obedient to the imperatives of such power. Accordingly, the novel's discourse on power must finally be taken as a discourse of power – a discourse *spoken through* by a power that is simply extending its blinding strategy of displacement.

An argument might even be made that monologism forwards (is forwarded by) this 'discourse of power' in novels that make use of an omniscient narrator as well. For the omniscient narrator (say, as he appears in George Eliot or Trollope) is typically presented as one who merely *tells* a story that is assumed to have happened already. The staging of the text as the narration of an autonomous story thus advances both the reality-effect of the story and the reality-effect of its self-regulation. Power, on this showing, is not felt to lie in the hands of the teller (who in general appears to regret the adventures he recounts). Instead, power is seen to coincide with the 'reality' that is merely being re-presented: a reality whose authority may be lamented, but is never finally arguable. The 'case' of *The Moonstone* raises the possibility of a wider investigation to be pursued under the hypothesis that traditional novels – whatever stories they may choose to tell – always repeat and reimpose the same story of power.

From *Novel*, 13 (1979–80), 153–70.

NOTES

[D. A. Miller's reading of *The Moonstone* is based on the Foucauldian conception of a surveillance society in which every individual polices him or herself and everyone polices everyone else. The detective fever that breaks out in the novel is, thus, only a specific example of endemic and pervasive social practices. In this essay Miller argues that the narrative economy of the detective story is shaped by suspicion – the suspicion that every event or detail encountered and/or related might count as evidence. Ultimately, however, the economy of detection works to transform universal suspicion into a highly specific guilt by isolating those few signs which really do signify. Miller also takes issue with the widely shared view that Collins's use of multiple narration makes for subjectivity and relativism, arguing that Collins's narrative method is actually monological because the novel's many narrators all tell the same story (again the story of a highly specific guilt). Miller concludes that *The Moonstone* is ultimately a novel about securities rather than uncertainties of perception, and that in this respect it is no different from any other traditional novel, since all such novels – no matter what kinds of stories they tell – always reinscribe (and hence re-impose) the same story of power. Miller also develops this Foucauldian analysis of nineteenth-century literature as a form of social control in *The Novel and the Police* (Berkeley and Los Angeles, 1988). Ed.]

1. As Sherlock Holmes tells his client in 'The Naval Treaty', 'The principal difficulty of your case lay in the fact of there being too much evidence. What was vital was overlaid by what was irrelevant.'

2. Wilkie Collins, *The Moonstone* (Maryland and Harmondsworth, 1996), p. 136. Subsequent page references to this edition will be made in the text.

3. Charles Dickens, *The Mystery of Edwin Drood* (Maryland and Harmondsworth, 1974), p. 209.

4. Regis Messac's standard history – *Le Detective Novel et l'influence de la pensée scientifique* (Paris, 1929) – sets the standard here as well. Primo tempo: 'Collins était probablement celui qui êut été le mieux doué pour reprendre et continuer l'oeuvre de Poe … Collins, comme les autres, a entrevu ce que pouvait être le genre'; secundo tempo: 'mais il n'a jamais réalisé pleinement et de point en point le programme qu'il esquissait' (pp. 550–1).

5. Michel Foucault, *Surveiller et punir* (Paris, 1975). [*Discipline and Punish*, trans. Alan Sheridan (Harmondsworth, 1977). Ed.]

6. What follows is the identification of a single 'site' of discipline as it attaches to the form of the novel: monological narration. Though a fuller consideration of the novel form as a disciplinary apparatus would hardly stop here, it seemed wise in this preliminary account to concentrate on an aspect of form that was particularly foregrounded by the text under discussion.

7. A. D. Hutter, 'Dreams, Transformations, and Literature: The Implications of Detective Fiction', *Victorian Studies*, 19 (1975), 191 [see p. 175 above. Ed.]; and Ian Ousby, *Bloodhounds of Heaven* (Cambridge, MA, 1976), p. 117.

10

Family Secrets and the Mysteries of *The Moonstone*

ELISABETH ROSE GRUNER

> What brought good Wilkie's genius nigh perdition?
> Some demon whispered – 'Wilkie! have a mission.'
> (Swinburne, 'Wilkie Collins')

Swinburne's famous judgement on Wilkie Collins is not generally applied to *The Moonstone*, the work which T. S. Eliot called 'the first and greatest of English detective novels'.[1] While few readers today would go so far as to concur with William Marshall's opinion that the novel reveals a 'general absence of social criticism, overt or implied', still it is rarely considered one of Collins's 'message' novels – and probably for this reason it has received far more critical attention than those later works.[2] But *The Moonstone*, like those later novels with purpose which Swinburne found so unaesthetic, is a novel dominated by a social message – a message probably both riskier and more central to Collins's own life and those of his readers than some of those which pervade his later works, such as his diatribes against vivisection, prison life, the cult of athleticism, and Jesuits. Not easily reducible to 'beware opium', 'don't bring back sacred diamonds from India', or 'don't steal your cousin's jewels', the message of *The Moonstone* yet involves all three of these strictures. The novel calls into question what writers like Sarah Ellis had celebrated as 'one of [England's] noblest features ...

the home comforts, and fireside virtues' of the Victorian family, and it asks us not to trust in its appearance.[3] Drugs, imperialism, and theft are subsumed into the larger question of family relations (cousinly or closer) which is at the heart of *The Moonstone*. What is the Victorian family, and whose purposes does it serve? Collins asks, and the answer does not come back in the family's favour.[4]

Theorists of detective fiction usually discuss the genre's interest in the discovery and expulsion of a crime, perceived as a foreign element which has invaded a secure community or family.[5] While this tendency is apparent in *The Moonstone*, one of the genre's founding texts, a contradictory impulse runs equally strongly through the novel, one with profound implications for the security of the Victorian family. For *The Moonstone* is, to a great extent, motivated by an impulse to secrecy, not to tell, to cover up the family's complicity in crime. Franklin Blake's editorial strategy seems designed to this end: he has chosen witnesses loyal to the family, unreliable as observers (Gabriel Betteredge remarks, 'It is one of my rules in life, never to notice what I don't understand'), and often monomaniacal to the point of selective blindness.[6] They are, singly or together, almost incapable of telling 'the truth'. But the impulse to conceal is built as well into the very material of the novel, Collins's most important source for *The Moonstone*, the Road murder case of 1860, which remains unsolved today.

If we read *The Moonstone* in the context of the famous murder case on which it was in part based, we find a scathing commentary on the Victorian family in Collins's selective recapitulation of the details of the case. Far from remaining within the protected private space which Victorian ideology reserved for family, the Kent family in the Road case and the Verinder–Herncastle–Ablewhite clan of *The Moonstone* cross boundaries and break traditions, rules, and commandments. Yet, Collins implies, these transgressions are not anomalous; the reasons for them are deeply imbedded in the Victorian ideology of the domestic sphere, especially in the concept of domestic privacy. For Collins the Victorian family, far from protecting one from the increasingly complex and dangerous public world, is itself the source of many of its own complexities and dangers.

I

Early in the morning of 30 June 1860, the murdered body of four-year-old Francis Savile Kent was found in an outhouse close by his father's house.[7] (The house, known as Road House or the Road-Hill House, furnishes the popular name for the case.) The circumstances of the case soon made it clear that a member of the Kent household must be the murderer, and the case became a cause célèbre in both the local and the national press.

The case received national attention, as Richard Altick notes, primarily 'because it occurred in a substantial middle-class family'.[8] The murder and the arrests of two young female members of the household (first Savile's sixteen-year-old half-sister, Constance, then his twenty-one-year-old nursery governess Elizabeth Gough) raised the disturbing possibility that the security of the Victorian home was an illusion. Anthea Trodd writes:

> The whole Road case affronted the popular conception of the domestic sanctuary in the most violent manner imaginable ... A young lady had been dragged from under her father's roof into a police-court, and her reputation and prospects irretrievably blighted. ...[9]

She adds, 'All the features of the case recommended themselves to intense publicity', and Collins was certainly aware both of the case and of its publicity value (p. 441). As Collins and the rest of the newspaper-reading public must certainly have known, Francis Savile Kent (known as Savile) had been stabbed several times and his throat was cut, although he did not appear to have bled profusely. (This detail, as hardened readers of detective fiction now know, raises the possibility that the child was stabbed after death.) The child was the son of Samuel Kent and his second wife Mary (née Pratt) – who had been a nursemaid and governess in the Kent household before the death of the first Mrs Kent.

The appearance of the house and the testimony of the servants made it clear that the house had not been broken into, so the local police suspected those in the house: the family and the servants. It was suggested that Elizabeth Gough had admitted a lover into her room and that they had murdered the child when he awoke inopportunely. This was the most comforting suggestion possible, in an entirely uncomfortable affair, since it exonerated the immediate family and cast blame on a servant and – to some eyes – an outsider. When Jonathan Whicher, the celebrated Scotland Yard detective (and the model for Collins's Sergeant Cuff), entered the picture almost two weeks after the murder, he seized on one (missing) piece of evidence and arrested sixteen-year-old Constance Kent, Mr Kent's third daughter by his first marriage. The missing evidence was one of Constance's nightgowns, entered into the washing book but never received by the washerwoman. Since no bloodstained clothes were found in the house, Whicher surmised that Constance's missing nightgown was the bloodied evidence which could have incriminated her, and that she had destroyed it. Other examinations of the evidence, however, have turned up reports of no less than three nightgowns, one belonging to Constance's elder sister Mary Ann, stained by what witnesses euphemistically called 'natural causes'; Constance's, which some witnesses claimed to have seen – unstained – the morning after the murder; and a mysteriously bloodied 'night shift' which was discovered hidden in the boiler-stove and then lost by the bumbling police. By the time Whicher entered the case several days later, there was only the one – now missing – nightgown of Constance's to be reckoned with, and he arrested her. Her putative motive was jealousy of her stepmother and her father's second family.[10]

Local opinion was against Whicher, and soon after Constance was released on the grounds of insufficient evidence, Whicher resigned from the force in disgrace. Elizabeth Gough was arrested some months later after a second investigation and released when she was proved to know no one in town, thus disproving the 'outside lover' theory. Five years later, in 1865, Constance Kent confessed to the crime, and a weeping judge condemned her to death in a melodramatic courtroom scene. Constance's lawyer called no witnesses for her defence in the initial hearing and spoke in the second trial only to record her plea of guilty; Constance herself maintained a stony silence throughout the proceedings.

Like Rachel and Lady Verinder in Collins's transformation of the case, Constance, her stepmother, and Elizabeth Gough appear to have been hostile to or at least uncooperative with the police investigating the case. As Bridges remarks, this seems particularly strange on Mrs Kent's part, as she was by all accounts a fiercely devoted mother who could be expected to be zealous in her prosecution of her son's murderer. Like Rachel's belligerent silence after the theft of her diamond, Mrs Kent's refusal to cooperate seems to imply some special knowledge of the case which her personal concerns required her to hide; as the injured parties, both would seem to have had the most to gain by cooperating with the investigation. Constance's confession itself, which failed to account for many circumstances of the murder (including motive, and, especially, the lack of blood), appeared to many contemporary commentators to have been dictated, perhaps by her confessor in the Anglican convent where she had spent the last two years. In a letter written after her confession, Constance pointedly disavowed revenge or jealousy as a motive for the murder, although no other motives were ever suggested. Her confession and subsequent silence failed to convince many of her guilt, including, it seems, the judge who reluctantly sentenced her.[11]

Perhaps the most disturbing aspect of the whole disturbing Road case was the reluctance of the family to assist in the investigation of the crime. The suggestion that the family was not all it seemed, especially because its members would lie or at least remain silent even in the investigation of such a brutal murder, is inescapable. The Kent family's silence seems to imply that no one is innocent, least of all the young women whose innocence, in other circumstances, the family could have been expected most zealously to protect. Family secrets, the Kent case seems to say, are both disturbing and dangerous, and murder may not even be the worst of them.

II

The Moonstone, despite its narrative technique based on eyewitness testimony and a stated devotion to 'the interests of truth', is a novel characterised and perhaps even motivated by secrets.[12] The prologue's narrator has kept a secret which protects John Herncastle's theft of the moonstone, Mr Candy's secret trick keeps Franklin Blake's motivations mysterious, Godfrey Ablewhite's secret life must be uncovered to solve the crime, and Franklin Blake's secret from himself complicates both the mystery and his relationship with Rachel. Most obviously, perhaps, both Rachel Verinder and Rosanna Spearman keep secrets to hide Franklin's, and in some sense their own, guilt. Like the mystery of the Road case which inspired it, the plot of *The Moonstone* is complicated by the silence of women. Rachel, Rosanna, and even Miss Clack conceal their own motivations and what they know of others' in order to protect secrets of their own, thus complicating and ultimately doubling the plot: Franklin Blake's 'strange family story' becomes both a mystery and a courtship novel, a story of both theft and passion (p. 39). And the secrecy which creates this mystery is deeply implicated with the family's privacy.

The Victorian family depended on the privacy which earlier generations had carefully cultivated with innovations like corridors and
locks and had increased by rejecting earlier practices like fostering out
children and boarding in apprentices.[13] In *Sesame and Lilies*, John
Ruskin eulogised the family home in terms of its security and privacy:

> within [a man's] house ... need enter no danger, no temptation, no
> cause of error or offence. This is the true nature of home – it is the
> place of Peace; the shelter, not only from all injury, but from all
> terror, doubt, and division. In so far as it is not this, it is not home;
> so far as the anxieties of the outer life penetrate into it, and the in-
> consistently-minded, unknown, unloved, or hostile society of the
> outer world is allowed by either husband or wife to cross the thresh-
> old, it ceases to be home; it is then only a part of that outer world
> which you have roofed over, and lighted fire in.[14]

As Sissela Bok notes, domestic privacy and secrecy are closely related:

> The private constitutes, along with the sacred, that portion of human
> experience for which secrecy is regarded as most indispensable. In
> secularised Western societies, privacy has come to seem for some the
> only legitimate form of secrecy; consequently, the two are sometimes
> mistakenly seen as identical.[15]

In this context, the notion of 'family secrets' becomes almost re-
dundant: the family's privacy necessarily involves a certain amount
of secrecy, even if the two are not, as Bok notes, identical.

As Patrick Brantlinger has noted, sensation novels like *The
Moonstone* rely on secrecy for their appeal: 'the plot unwinds
through the gradual discovery – or, better, recovery – of knowledge, until at the end what detective and reader know coincides
with what the secretive or somehow remiss narrator-author has
presumably known all along'.[16] Even the supposed 'eyewitness'
character of *The Moonstone's* narration requires, because of its
retrospectivity, a certain suppression of evidence in the retelling.
Betteredge, for example, confesses that he is concealing his present
knowledge of the case in his reconstruction, leaving his readers 'in
the dark' (p. 233); and Miss Clack ('condemned to narrate', p. 241)
similarly includes in her narrative an exchange of letters which indicates her inability to 'avail ... herself of the light which later discoveries have thrown on the mystery' (pp. 241, 285).

The absence of testimony from several key witnesses, among
them Penelope Betteredge (whose diaries, we are told, provide many

of the important facts in Gabriel's narrative), Godfrey Ablewhite, and Rachel Verinder, is even more disturbing than possible omissions in the testimony we do have. Obviously their silence is a necessary element in the novel's mystery plot, but these characters are silenced for another reason as well: they are witnesses to the development of a counterplot involving a young woman's sexual passion and desire.[17] The counterplot of Rachel's passion for Blake is witnessed by Penelope and doubled in Godfrey's secret suburban life, but because this second story is told only or at least primarily through the voice of the demented Miss Clack it remains buried through most of the novel. Clack – like Franklin, keeping a secret from herself – provides a grotesque parody of Rachel in her determined suppression of her own and, by implication, of Rachel's desire.[18]

Rosanna Spearman provides another parallel to Rachel: her passion for Blake is an open secret, known at least to Penelope and Limping Lucy, and the narrative gives her, unlike Rachel, a voice – albeit a voice from beyond the grave. Her 'testimony' – the letter to Blake – is both a clue to the eventual solution of the theft mystery and a hint at the other, buried mystery; it is Rosanna who tells us, far more explicitly than Clack or Betteredge, of Rachel's desire for Franklin. It is Rosanna who unites the mystery and the marriage plots by her recognition that the paint on Franklin's nightgown is evidence against him, evidence of at least an illicit visit to Rachel's room, if not of his theft of the moonstone.

Female secrecy is, of course, not unique to *The Moonstone*. Elaine Showalter believes that 'secrecy was basic to the lives of *all* respectable women' of the mid-nineteenth century. She quotes Jane Vaughan Pinkney's *Tacita Tacit*, a novel of 1860: 'Women are greater dissemblers than men ... by habit, moral training, and modern education, they are obliged to ... repress their feelings, control their very thoughts.'[19] Margaret Oliphant went further than to note the tendency toward concealment; she endorsed it and regretted that young women in modern novels (particularly sensation novels, with which *The Moonstone* shares many generic characteristics) could not keep their feelings secret. She wrote in 1867, just one year before *The Moonstone* was published:

> That men and women should marry we had all of us acknowledged as one of the laws of humanity; but up to the present generation most young women had been brought up in the belief that their own feelings on this subject should be religiously kept to themselves.[20]

But the secrecy which Oliphant calls for in modern heroines becomes dangerous in *The Moonstone* when it becomes epidemic, as the women who in concealing their passions also conceal a crime and set off a chain of circumstances which includes theft, suicide, and murder. The family's reliance on secrecy for its normal maintenance quickly translates, in *The Moonstone*, into an almost pathological – and certainly criminal – secrecy. The secrecy of Collins's own family life seems benign by comparison to the secrecy which permeates both the Road case and *The Moonstone*.[21]

Collins makes it clear that the family is not, as Ruskin would have it, a place of peace; and the mysteries of *The Moonstone* do not arise from a foreign invasion which can be expelled, leaving the family complacently untouched – they are inherent in the very nature and structure of the family. The secrecy which, as Bok and Showalter agree, is part of family life, is primarily women's part. But the women of *The Moonstone's* extended family, like the women of the Road case, keep their secrets too well, covering up crime rather than expose their passionate secrets to a prying public (primarily the police, but also – especially in the Road case – the press). Like the mystery of the Road Murder of 1860, in which Collins found the original of Sergeant Cuff and the evidence of the missing nightgown, *The Moonstone's* mystery operates on at least two levels, only one of which – the fictional theft of the diamond or the actual murder of the child – can be publicly acknowledged. And, as the Road Murder seems to hinge on a familial conspiracy of silence, so *The Moonstone's* mysteries hinge on the silence and the secrecy of the Verinder–Herncastle clan, especially its women.

III

In its bare outlines, there seems to be little to connect the Road murder with *The Moonstone* beyond the ineptitude of the local police and the evidence of the missing nightgown. But Collins's focus on the social pathology of female silence seems also to derive from his understanding of the Road case. It is the silence which Constance and Rachel share which unites the cases and sets these women apart from many of their fictional counterparts, at least in the sensation novels Mrs Oliphant deplores; it is a silence which brings them under suspicion of one crime but may in fact have been designed to conceal another. In Rachel's case, and Collins probably believed in the Road case as well, the second 'crime' is illicit passion. In a letter to Collins on 24 October 1860 Dickens outlined his theory of the Road murder. As Dickens puts it:

> Mr Kent intriguing with the nursemaid, poor little child awakes in crib and sits up contemplating blissful proceedings. Nursemaid strangles him then and there. Mr Kent gashes body to mystify discoverers and disposes of same.[22]

Dickens's theory neatly domesticates the widespread – and more popular – theory of Elizabeth Gough's guilt, which involved a lover coming in from outside the house. Trodd cites other contemporary reports which did, however, in more guarded terms, express variations on the same theme.[23] Bridges proposes Constance's 1865 confession, then, as a form of self-sacrifice intended to protect her family, keep the secret, and lay the matter to rest. While Rachel keeps silent to protect her cousin-lover and to hide her own feelings for him, Bridges theorises that Constance's silence (and her step-mother's), and the odd way in which she broke it, were designed to protect her father and to hide his – and Elizabeth's – illicit passion.

Collins's two passionate and silent women – Rachel and Rosanna – recall aspects of Constance and Elizabeth without providing an easy parallel. Rosanna, a servant in love with her master, recalls Elizabeth Gough – but hides a criminal past rather than an (allegedly) adulterous present. And Collins conflates the two roles of Constance and Elizabeth (knower and lover) into the single character of Rachel, thus increasing the pressure on the family to solve or hide its own crimes and its own deviations from familial norms. Of course Rachel is neither murderer or fornicator, nor even an accomplice to any serious crime; yet her silence in the face of a police investigation suggests that Collins could expect her passion to be widely read as almost as guilty as the adulterous Elizabeth's. Any woman who would allow herself to be suspected of theft (or, in Elizabeth and Constance's case, murder) must, the reasoning goes, be hiding something far worse.

As Richard Altick notes, behind the shocking violence of the murder lay other shocking circumstances in the Kent family. The first Mrs Kent was widely believed to have gone mad after bearing her third child 'but her loss of mind did not deter her husband from begetting six more [children] on her body'.[24] Bridges hypothesises that the first Mrs Kent was not indeed mad but jealous of her husband's relationship with Mary Pratt the governess (and her successor), and she notes the striking similarities between the situations of the first Mrs Kent with Mary Pratt, and the second Mrs Kent (née Mary Pratt) with Elizabeth Gough. Whatever the particular circumstances, the Kent home clearly concealed a most unfamilial (or un-Ruskinian) reality.

So, of course, does the Herncastle–Verinder clan. Mr Ablewhite, Senior, acknowledges a seamy family history when he attributes Rachel's stubbornness to her Herncastle blood, implying that she is, unlike himself, 'descended from a set of cut-throat scoundrels who lived by robbery and murder' (p. 305). The moonstone, then, is not the only legacy Rachel has received from the wicked colonel; in some ways, however, it seems to be emblematic of them all. Perhaps we need to examine the moonstone itself more closely to determine just what these characters are protecting with their secrets.

IV

It is a commonplace of Collins criticism to see the moonstone as symbolic of Rachel's virginity – this bright jewel that 'seemed unfathomable as the heavens themselves', which Rachel displays proudly in the bosom of her dress (p. 97).[25] Hutter, building on this connection, notes the more important detail that the diamond is flawed, perhaps 'suggest[ing] some of the sexual prejudice so strongly attached to women in the nineteenth century'.[26] More threateningly, because the diamond would be more valuable cut into smaller stones, the flaw may suggest that a woman's value is not in her wholeness and self-sufficiency but in her multiplicity and her reproductive ability. In fact, as a symbol of woman's status as 'exchange value', one could hardly do better than the flawed diamond. For, as Luce Irigaray notes, only virgins are exchange value for men. Once violated (divided, cut up, married) they become use value, recognised only for their ability to reproduce themselves. Rachel and her (uncut) diamond are both more valued in a capitalist economy for their potential than for themselves.[27] Lady Verinder, recognising this, puts Rachel's inheritance in trust to protect her from a too-rapacious consumer such as Godrey Ablewhite. Only the Hindu priests, who are outside of English life and the capitalist economy, are able to value the diamond for itself; no one (with the possible exception of Franklin Blake) seems able to value Rachel for herself.

John Reed, in his interesting examination of *The Moonstone's* anti-imperialist implications, makes a similar claim for the symbolic value of the diamond but focuses on its status as sacred gem and stolen object:

> In itself ambiguous, its significance lies in its *misappropriation*. Because it is so desired by *men*, it signifies *man's greed*. ... More particularly, however, the Moonstone becomes the sign of England's imperial depredations – the symbol of a national rather than a personal crime.[28]

While I agree with Hutter that Reed 'oversimplifies the novel' in this symbolic reading, his insights are helpful. For, as he points out, Rachel Verinder has no more right to the diamond than Godfrey Ablewhite – it belongs, in fact, to the Indians from whom Franklin and Betteredge try so hard to protect it and to whom it is finally returned. Like a woman's virginity, its greatest value is a symbolic one: it is less valuable to the possessor (Rachel) than the desirer (whether Ablewhite or the Indians), it is most valuable in exchange, and the desirer is only and always male. The diamond thus points in (at least) two directions: outward, towards England's treatment of its colonies, and inward, to its treatment of women at home.[29] And Rachel's insistence on maintaining control of it challenges both of these (analogous) power structures: she refuses to treat the diamond as a prize, preferring to maintain it in its native setting (the Indian cabinet), and she refuses to give up her own independent judgement. Jenny Bourne Taylor claims that 'Rachel thus tacitly upsets the conventions of feminine propriety ... she is dark, positive, purposeful, independent – yet silent'.[30] Constance Kent, who once ran away from home to escape her stepmother's tyranny, was similarly accused (by her father) of a wish 'to be independent'.[31] Her habitual reserve and self-dependence are among the characteristics John Rhode – who believes in her guilt – notes when he claims that 'in a sense, the crime saved her character. Before it ... she was a wayward, passionate girl ... and she would probably have developed into a selfish, headstrong woman'.[32] The Verinder family lawyer, Bruff – more sympathetic to Rachel than Rhode is to Constance Kent – comments that Rachel's 'absolute self-dependence is a great virtue in a man ... [but] has the serious drawback of morally separating her from the mass of her sex' who are, presumably, more compliant (p. 319).

Bruff's comment points out a characteristic which all of Rachel's observers note. Rather than claiming that she has been changed by the theft of the diamond into a secretive person, Gabriel, Clack, Lady Verinder, and Bruff agree that she has always been 'secret and self-willed' (p. 262; see also pp. 87, 205). Bruff's correlation of secrecy with self-will corresponds with Bok's observation that 'secrecy guards against unwanted access by others – against their coming too near, learning too much, observing too closely. Secrecy guards, then, the central aspects of identity.'[33] Rachel's secrecy, both after the theft of the diamond and after her broken engagement with Ablewhite, signifies her insistence on maintaining herself as a separate identity and her refusal to be known and thereby possessed.

Why does Rachel's secrecy so annoy her family, when she seems simply to be complying with the Oliphantian code of self-suppression? I believe it is because she, and Constance Kent, and Elizabeth Gough, are forced into the ironic position of defending their identities through the very means Oliphant would use to urge their suppression. Silence for Oliphant signifies a lack of desire – for these women, it signifies an excess.[34]

When Franklin steals the diamond and Rachel refuses to condemn him, we can see that she is tacitly accepting his right to her sexuality, even to her virginity – but not her identity.[35] Her silence, however, cuts two ways: while protecting Franklin, it puts Rachel herself under suspicion, as well as endangering Rosanna Spearman. While Rachel keeps silent, the truth will remain hidden. Thus the plot of the mystery – the discovery of the diamond – is inextricable from woman's passion, and her identity.

If the mystery plot is inextricably linked with passion, perhaps marriage, the courtship plot is similarly mysterious. Not only must Rachel conceal her passion for Franklin until he becomes a 'suitable' suitor, but the moonstone itself becomes a pawn in the marriage negotiations. Money and marriage are often related, both in novels and in life; in *The Moonstone* Gabriel Betteredge first hints at the connection which will later loom large by giving us his own history.

> Selina, being a single woman, made me pay so much a week for her board and services. Selina, being my wife, couldn't charge for her board, and would have to give me her services for nothing. That was the point of view I looked at it from. Economy – with a dash of love. I put it to my mistress, as in duty bound, just as I had put it to myself.
>
> 'I have been turning Selina Goby over in my mind', I said, 'and I think, my lady, it will be cheaper to marry her than to keep her.'
>
> (p. 43)

Betteredge's euphemistic 'services' implies an illicit relationship with Selina not unlike the one Rachel and Franklin metaphorically begin when he enters her boudoir. And, as Betteredge's account implies, money enters into both relationships. Rachel seizes on Franklin's implied debts to explain his 'theft' of the diamond: 'I had reason to know you were in debt, and ... that you were not very discreet, or very scrupulous about how you got money when you wanted it' (p. 400). When Franklin comes to Rachel for an explanation of her actions, she immediately assumes that as he has inherited his father's wealth, perhaps he has come to 'compensate [her] for the loss of [her] Diamond' (p. 392). The compensation for the symbolic loss (of virginity) will of course be marriage, but here Rachel's concern is with literal, monetary compensation.

Jean E. Kennard argues that the conventional marriage plot of the Victorian novel most often involves a choice between suitable and unsuitable suitors and that each of the suitors 'represents one pole of value in the novel in which he appears'.[36] Rachel's suitors take on roles which mask their suitability, however: Godfrey appears as 'the Christian Hero' and Franklin as a philandering debtor and suspected thief (p. 239). According to Kennard, when these roles are sorted out – a sorting out which here requires the solution to the mystery – the marriage plot can be satisfactorily, conventionally, concluded. In *The Moonstone*, however, the sorting out muddles the 'poles of value': we establish that Godfrey is both a philandering debtor and a thief, but we never really establish that Franklin is neither. In fact he is certainly, according to Betteredge's testimony, at least a philanderer and a debtor. Twice constrained from returning to England by 'some unmentionable woman', on his return he borrows money from Lady Verinder to repay an earlier debt (p. 48). The conclusion of the courtship plot does, however, literalise the 'poles of value': Franklin, who has inherited his father's wealth, is simply worth more than Godfrey.

But Franklin is Rachel's choice even before his father's death makes him wealthy; so while convention demands a fortune for the novel's heroine, Collins also provides her with passion. Rachel's love for Franklin survives her conviction that he is a philanderer, a debtor, and even a thief – it is only his seeming hypocrisy in calling the police which threatens to destroy her love. For the reader, her passion is an ill-kept secret, but among the characters of the novel only the voiceless Penelope seems to be privy to Rachel's passionate secret – as to so many other secrets of the novel.

Penelope, one of *The Moonstone's* silent women, only comes to us filtered through her father Gabriel. Her narrative silence helps conceal Rachel's love, since her correct observations are always followed by her father's contradictory opinions. Her silence does more than conceal Rachel from us, however; it also conceals herself. Since her diaries supply dates and times for Gabriel, he suggests that 'she should tell the story instead of me, out of her own diary, [but] Penelope observes, with a fierce look and a red face, that her journal is for her own private eye, and that no living creature shall ever know what is in it but herself' (p. 46). Her insistence on her own privacy, which mystifies her father, is a more benign version of another important silence in the novel: Rosanna Spearman's. Both women are, of course, servants, and as such are barely even named by the other narrators of the novel – Miss Clack remembers Penelope only as 'the person with the cap-ribbons' (p. 259). But servants are part of the extended family, at least in Gabriel's view, and as such privy to and part of family secrets. Resented for 'her silent tongue and her solitary ways', Rosanna, as Gabriel informs us, is hiding a criminal past; and, as we later discover, she is also hiding an unsuitable and uncontrollable passion (p. 55). In this, she not only doubles Rachel but provides another connection to the Road case: like Elizabeth Gough, she is a servant in love with a master, although her passion is not, like Gough's, adulterous. By comparison, Penelope's 'Sweethearts' seem insignificant – and they are, except as evidence of the need for concealment in even the most complacent and commonplace of families (p. 46).

The women of *The Moonstone*, from Penelope to her mistress and including Rosanna and Clack, are forced to conceal their passions, forced to conform to Oliphant's rules. But this conventional concealment has fatal consequences; Collins seems to suggest that these rules are not, in fact, designed so much to protect female modesty or propriety as to conceal the criminal underpinnings of the Victorian family. While the secret of Penelope's sweethearts seems to have no effect on her household, the 'necessary' concealments practised by the other three women create the mystery, complicate relationships, and prevent simple solutions. Again, the line between benign and fatal secrets is not easy to draw.

Because she is complying with Oliphantian strictures against self-revelation, Rachel must not speak until Franklin proposes. But Franklin is not in a position to propose through most of the novel – he is poor, and his chosen lover suspects him of a crime. The situation is a stalemate: only Rachel can solve the crime, but because Franklin is the suspect, she cannot solve it without revealing her passion (and her acceptance of his presence in her bedroom at night). Despite its mysterious underpinnings, however, Rachel's dilemma is not unlike that of any other courtship heroine; any such heroine, of course, must not speak of love until she is spoken to. According to Kennard, she must also learn to read her suitor correctly and must 'adjust ... to society's values'.[37] Ruth Bernard Yeazell similarly argues that marriage in the Victorian novel is usually a metaphor recognising the heroine's internal growth and an enactment of the 'union of Self and Other ... [resolving] the tensions between the individual and the larger human community'.[38] Although she already finds him desirable, Rachel must learn to see Franklin as acceptable. Her 'growth', then, may look to us like regression, as it involves both a rejection of her former status as self-dependent and a recognition of society's commercially-derived values; she must relinquish her 'unnatural', unwomanly, anti-social silence and allow herself to be mastered by the now-wealthy Blake. After Franklin has inherited his father's money, he confronts Rachel about her silence; only then can he claim that 'while her hand lay in mine I was her master still!' (p. 393).

Of course, Godfrey Ablewhite's mercenary machinations also make him an unsuitable suitor. Again, it is Betteredge who first makes Ablewhite's character clear: 'Female benevolence and female destitution could do nothing without him' – for he uses female benevolence to create female destitution (p. 89). Ablewhite's aborted engagement to Rachel and his secondary theft of the diamond are both evidence of his deviance from acceptable behaviour. As Barickman, and others, point out:

> Godfrey Ablewhite's secret ... involves Victorian sexual roles at their worst; he hypocritically becomes a champion of charitable ladies while he is keeping a mistress, embezzling another man's money, and preying upon Rachel in order to gain control of her money.[39]

It is not so much Ablewhite's preoccupation with wealth as his hypocrisy which condemns him; ironically, he is really guilty of just the kind of hypocrisy of which Rachel suspects Blake.

So Franklin becomes the right suitor when Rachel learns to read him 'correctly', when Ezra's hypothesis about his behaviour proves a more satisfying one than her own; she must believe that he came to protect, not steal, her virginity. And Collins, having upset convention by valorising his passionate, secret, self-willed heroine and exposing the hypocrisy and criminality of the Victorian family, quietly reinscribes her into the system with her marriage to Franklin.

V

The Moonstone is, then, a detective story, but it is also a family story. Indeed, it is perhaps not even the '*strange* family story' Franklin believes it to be, but simply a story about the necessary concealments families practise (p. 89; my emphasis). Gabriel even comments on the text's reliance on secrets, insisting in the 'Eighth Narrative' that his 'purpose, in this place, is to state a fact in the history of the family, which has been passed over by everybody, and which [he] won't allow to be disrespectfully smothered up in that way' (p. 518). Godfrey Ablewhite – himself a member of the family – *has* been rather disrespectfully smothered up, but not so Gabriel's news.

Yet even in this triumphant conclusion, Gabriel himself contributes to the pervasive silence of the novel by cutting Franklin off with 'You needn't say a word more, sir', and leaving the news of Rachel's pregnancy – which may stand both as visible evidence of female passion and as final proof of her capitulation to her status as 'use value' – unspoken (p. 519). The family, even in its triumphant return, is still relying on secrecy, is still, perhaps, not entirely innocent. The 'scattered and disunited household', disrupted by the theft and Rachel's cover-up, is never wholly restored (p. 225). Although Rachel and Franklin are married, Rosanna, Lady Verinder, and Godfrey are dead, Gabriel is retired, and Clack is exiled.

Cuff's failure to solve the crime on his own, like Whicher's failure in the Road Murder, clearly implies that there are family secrets which the police cannot penetrate – secrets not, perhaps, worse than murder or theft, but more difficult to reveal. Cuff's low interpretation of Rachel's behaviour considers the possibility of 'family scandal', but this version of the family scandal, involving as it does debts and pawnbrokers, is entirely *outside* what Ruskin and even Gabriel Betteredge would recognise as the sphere of family, in the more common and public realm of the police. And, in fact, when this realm becomes central to the case in Ablewhite's unmasking,

Cuff acquits himself brilliantly. As D. A. Miller shows in his discussion of *The Eustace Diamonds*, fictional police are notoriously inept when forced to act within the sphere of family; thus 'the plot of the novel "passes on", as it were, the initial offence until it reaches a place within the law's jurisdiction'.[40] But it is not really the family's inviolability which the police cannot penetrate; it is precisely its inseparability from the public sphere which confounds them. For the police, like the family, still believed in the family's privacy in the mid-1860s; remember that the police in the Road case waited to be invited in, preserving a boundary which had presumably already been broken. While we may want to read Godfrey's crime as a crime outside the sphere of family, involving as it does pawnbrokers and Indians and London and its suburbs, we cannot separate the spheres so easily. Like Rachel's implied crime, Godfrey's is both a family scandal and a police matter; the two spheres are inextricably linked, and no amount of artistic pleasure in neat solutions can separate the two. 'The complexity and even incomprehensibility of the truth' are not, as Kalikoff would have it, 'related to the invasion of the respectable', so much as they are related to the instability of the respectable.[41] No family is secure, Collins's novel implies, from the dangers of its necessary concealments.

The lesson of *The Moonstone*, like the lesson of the Road Murder, is that the family is complicit in the failings of the larger society; murder and robbery are not invasions from without but manifestations of societal tensions – involving especially the dangerous desires of greed and sexuality – within. The fabled privacy of the domestic sphere protects it not from the public world but from discovery. If we are to understand the Victorian family at all, we must examine its pathological need for secrecy and understand, as does Collins, the kinds of secrets it protected.

From *Victorian Literature and Culture*, 21 (1991), 127–45.

NOTES

[Elizabeth Gruner situates the diamond and its various thefts in the context of *The Moonstone's* critique of nineteenth-century class, gender and imperial ideologies. She argues that *The Moonstone* interrogates the social, sexual, and psychological organisation of the Victorian family, and asks

ELISABETH ROSE GRUNER

fundamental questions about whose interests it serves. Noting the similarities of the details of Collins's plot to those of the Road murder case of 1860, Gruner suggests that the mysteries of both are based on the concepts of secrecy and privacy around which the Victorian middle-class family is constructed, and which serve to protect it from the discovery of its own dangerous forces. In a reading which calls into question the conventional view that in the detective story a stable conservative society is invaded by dangerous alien elements, Gruner argues that in *The Moonstone* the family is the site and source of danger, rather than the means of protection from it, and robbery and murder are not invasions from without, but are produced within the family by its tensions, dissensions and desires. Ed.]

1. T. S. Eliot, 'Wilkie Collins and Dickens', *Selected Essays, 1917–1932* (New York, 1932), pp. 373–82.

2. William H. Marshall, *Wilkie Collins* (New York, 1970), pp. 77–8. John R. Reed and D. A. Miller are two notable exceptions to this trend, although they find different (and, in Miller's case, deeply buried) messages in the novel. (John R. Reed, 'English Imperialism and the Unacknowledged Crime of *The Moonstone*', *Clio*, 2 [1973], 281–90, and D. A. Miller, *The Novel and the Police* [Berkeley, CA, 1988].) Even Philip O'Neill, however, in his recent attempt to unify the Collins Oeuvre in terms of social criticism, finds little to say about *The Moonstone*, reading it primarily as an allegory of literary criticism. (Philip O'Neill, *Wilkie Collins: Women, Property and Propriety* [Towota, NJ and London, 1988].) But see Sue Lonoff, who writes of *The Moonstone* that 'none of [Collins's] novels is as profoundly critical of Victorian values ... and none is more subtle in linking its political, social and religious censure to its central messages and symbols'. Lonoff finally sees Collins's social criticism as less conflicted than I do, but her reading is nonetheless perceptive and interesting. (Sue Lonoff, *Wilkie Collins and His Victorian Readers: A Study in the Rhetoric of Authorship* [New York, 1982], p. 211.)

3. Sarah Stickney Ellis, *The Women of England: Their Social Duties, and Domestic Habits* (New York, 1839), p. 2.

4. I take the term 'family' in its broadest possible sense here, meaning both 'blood kin' and 'members of a household'. As we will see in my discussion of the Road case and Collins's novel, the 'traditional' nuclear family is something of a chimera. The Kent household comprised parents, children of two mothers, and servants; the Verinder household consists of only one parent, a daughter, and servants – as well as frequent visitors, most of them cousins. Most of the primary characters in *The Moonstone* – Rachel, her mother, Godfrey Ablewhite, Franklin Blake, Drusilla Clack, Rosanna Spearman, and Gabriel Betteredge – are members of the same 'family', either by blood or service. See Steven Mintz, *A Prison of Expectations: The Family in*

Victorian Culture (New York, 1983) for a review of recent work in family history (esp. pp. 11–20).

5. See, for example, W. H. Auden 'The Guilty Vicarage', in *The Dyer's Hand and Other Essays* (New York, 1948). George Grella also claims that 'the fabric of society will be repaired after the temporary disruption' of crime ('Murder and Manners: The Formal Detective Novel', *Novel*, 4 [1970], 30–48, p. 38). Many readings of *The Moonstone* depend on seeing the criminal Godfrey Ablewhite as an outsider; Beth Kalikoff, for example, claims that the crime in *The Moonstone* represents an 'invasion of the respectable' (*Murder and Moral Decay in Victorian Popular Literature* [Ann Arbor, MI, 1986], p. 125); see also Miller (*The Novel and the Police*, pp. 4–46). Yet Ablewhite and Blake stand in exactly the same relation to Rachel; both are her cousins, and both are clearly established and accepted as family members – thus Ablewhite's father, Rachel's nearest male relative, becomes her guardian on her mother's death.

6. Wilkie Collins, *The Moonstone*, ed. J. I. M. Stewart (Harmondsworth, 1969). All further page references are to this edition and are given in the text.

7. The case is detailed by Yseult Bridges, *The Tragedy of the Road Hill Case* (New York, 1955); John Rhode, 'Constance Kent', in *The Anatomy of Murder*, ed. Helen Simpson, John Rhode and others (New York, 1937), pp. 43–86; Richard Altick, *Victorian Studies in Scarlet* (New York, 1970), and Mary S. Hartman, *Victorian Murderesses: A True History of Thirteen Respectable French and English Women Accused of Unspeakable Crimes* (New York, 1977). As Bridges's is the most detailed account, my summary of the case relies most heavily on her reconstruction of it (as verified by Hartman).

8. Richard Altick, *Victorian Studies in Scarlet*, p. 130.

9. Anthea Trodd, 'The Policeman and the Lady: Significant Encounters in Mid-Victorian Fiction', *Victorian Studies*, 27 (1984), 435–60, pp. 442–3.

10. Bridges here relies on the testimony of the police and an account of the crime written by Mr Kent's doctor and friend, J. W. Stapleton (pp. 72–3, 77–84).

11. Contemporary accounts of the trial reveal that Constance was asked three times to enter a plea before she would say the word 'guilty', and that the judge was forced to pause twice while pronouncing the sentence to choke back sobs (Bridges, *Tragedy*, pp. 237–9).

12. In my use of the concept of secrecy I am relying on Sissela Bok's discussion of the topic. Her definition makes it clear that while not all secrets involve deception or are necessarily wrong, our conceptions of secrecy almost always involve 'prohibition, furtiveness, and deception' as well as 'sacredness, intimacy, privacy, [and] silence' (Sissela Bok,

Secrets: On the Ethics of Concealment and Revelation [New York, 1984], p. 6). 'The defining trait of secrecy', she says, is 'intentional concealment' (p. 9) – although she later discusses the possibility of keeping a secret from oneself – also an issue for Franklin Blake (See Bok, *Secrets*, pp. 59–72).

13. Ian Watt discusses the rise of domestic privacy in relation to the novel in chapter 6 of his *The Rise of the Novel* (Berkeley, CA, 1957), see esp. p. 188. See also Michel Perrot's claim that 'the nineteenth-century family tended to subsume all the functions of private life' (Michel Perrot [ed.], *From the Fires of Revolution to the Great War. A History of Private Life*. Vol. IV, trans. Arthur Goldhammer [Cambridge, MA, 1990], p. 97). Lawrence Stone's evidence concurs with Watt's and Perrot's; he characterises the intense privacy of the mid-Victorian family as an 'explosive intimacy' (Lawrence Stone, *The Family, Sex and Marriage in England 1500–1800* [New York, 1979], p. 423; see also p. 169). Hartman, writing specifically of the Kent case, claims that 'new middle-class privacy provided relative isolation from outside pressures', especially with regard to the treatment of children and Mr Kent's alleged adultery (Hartman, *Victorian Murderesses*, p. 117).

14. John Ruskin, 'Of Queen's Gardens' (1871), *Sesame and Lilies; The Two Paths; The King of the Golden River* (London, 1970), pp. 48–79. p. 39.

15. Sissela Bok, *Secrets*, p. 7.

16. Patrick Brantlinger, 'What is "Sensational" about the "Sensation Novel"?', *Nineteenth-Century Fiction*, 37 (1982), 1–28. [see pp. 30–57 above – Ed.]

17. Jenny Bourne Taylor writes, 'Rachel's silence is the essential secret that generates the Story; but in its very structural indispensability this suppression turns the conventions of moral management into hysterical suppression on the one hand, and on the other suggests that the ascription of hysteria is the uncomprehending response to female autonomy.' (Jenny Bourne Taylor, *In the Secret Theatre of Home: Wilkie Collins, sensation narrative and nineteenth-century psychology* [London, 1988], p. 201.)

18. Beth Kalikoff argues that 'Clack is a comic distortion of the other passionate women in the novel. Cloaking all her prejudices and greed beneath excessive religiosity, she seeks attention, love, and money' (*Murder and Moral Decay in Victorian Popular Literature*, p. 201).

19. Elaine Showalter, 'Desperate Remedies: Sensation Novels of the 1860s', *Victorian Newsletter*, 49 (1976), 1–5, p. 2.

20. Margaret Oliphant, 'Novels', *Blackwood's*, 102 (1867), 257–80, p. 259.

21. The irregularities of Collins's family life are now well known, although they were perforce 'secrets', at least from the novel-reading public, during his lifetime and have been obscured rather than clarified by his

biographers. He lived for most of his adult life with a mistress, Caroline Graves, and her daughter Harriet; and he kept for some years a 'second family' consisting of Martha Rudd and her three children by Collins. Martha Rudd and Caroline Graves were equally provided for in Collins's will. Nuel Pharr Davis's highly imaginative biography makes the most of these irregularities, to the extent of using Collins's fiction to 'comment' on the still sketchy picture of his domestic life (see, for example, pp. 164, 166 of Nuel Pharr Davis, *The Life of Wilkie Collins* [Urbana, IL, 1956]). Robert Ashley's biography refers to Caroline Graves as an 'alleged "intimacy"' and while reporting speculation that she was his mistress, suggests as well that Collins's bequest to her may simply have been a reward to 'an affectionately respected housekeeper' – a hypothesis which is by now largely rejected (Robert Ashley, *Wilkie Collins* [New York, 1952], pp. 72, 73). The two relationships are also discussed by Kenneth Robinson in *Wilkie Collins: A Biography* (New York, 1952). [The details of Collins's domestic life have recently been discussed very fully and authoritatively by William M. Clark, who has had access to the private papers of Collins's family. See William M. Clark, *The Secret Life of Wilkie Collins* (London, 1988 – Ed.]

22. Quoted in Yseult Bridges, *The Tragedy of the Road Hill Case*, p. 187. It seems more likely that the child was – like Godfrey Ablewhite – smothered, not strangled. In the outline of means and motive, however, both Bridges and Hartman substantially agree with Dickens.

23. Anthea Trodd, 'The Policeman and the Lady', p. 443. Lonoff puts forth the more traditional view that 'the [Road] murder itself has nothing in common with the crime or the plot of *The Moonstone*' (*Wilkie Collins and His Victorian Readers*, p. 179).

24. Richard Altick, *Victorian Studies in Scarlet*, p. 131.

25. Psychoanalytic critics such as Charles Rycroft and Lewis Lawson have made the most of this symbolism. Rycroft's perceptive and often amusing reading also notes that Franklin Blake gives up cigar smoking during his courtship; Collins provides both hero and heroine with symbolic representations of their sexuality. (Rycroft, 'A Detective Story: Psychoanalytic Observations', *Psychoanalytic Quarterly*, 26 [1957], 229–45, p. 235; see also Lewis A. Lawson, 'Wilkie Collins and *The Moonstone*', *American Imago*, 20 [1963], 61–79, p. 66.)

26. Albert D. Hutter, 'Dreams, Transformations, and Literature: The Implications of Detective Fiction', *Victorian Studies*, 19 (1975), 181–209, pp. 200–1. [See p. 184 above – Ed.]

27. Irigaray writes:

> *The virginal woman ... is pure exchange value*. She is nothing but the possibility, the place, the sign of relations among men. In and of herself, she does not exist: she is a simple envelope veiling what is

really at stake in social exchange ... The ritualised passage from woman to mother is accomplished by *the violation of an envelope*: the hymen, which has taken on the value of *taboo*, the taboo of virginity. Once deflowered, woman is relegated to the status of use value, to her entrapment in private property; she is removed from exchange among men. (Luce Irigaray, *This Sex Which Is Not One*, 1977, trans. Catherine Porter with Carolyn Burke [Ithaca, NY, 1985], p. 186.)

28. John R. Reed, 'English Imperialism and the Unacknowledged Crime of *The Moonstone*', p. 286; emphasis added.

29. See Mark M. Hennelly Jr, for a discussion of Collins's research into gemology. Hennelly sees the diamond itself as uniting the major themes of the novel, which he characterises as both detective and domestic. (Mark M. Hennelly Jr, 'Detecting Collins' Diamond: From Serpentstone to Moonstone', *Nineteenth-Century Fiction*, 39 [1984], 25–47.)

30. Jenny Bourne Taylor, *In the Secret Theatre of Home*, p. 200.

31. Yseult Bridges, *The Tragedy of the Road Hill Case*, p. 39.

32. Apparently Constance's most unforgivable behaviour was cutting off her hair and running away from home – at age thirteen – with her younger brother William (see Hartman, *Victorian Murderesses*, p. 110).

33. Sissela Bok, *Secrets*, p. 13.

34. Hartman writes of Constance's confession, 'Ironically, this act of confession was finely "female", just the sort of submissive, sacrificial, and self-destructive act which, in lesser forms, was explicitly demanded of all respectable creatures of her sex' (*Victorian Murderesses*, p. 127). Anita Levy discusses the way in which what in one context is good and 'feminine' becomes in other contexts destructive and 'masculine', especially in her discussion of the 'Venus Hottentot' and the 'Bushwoman' dissection (Anita Levy, *Other Women: The Writing of Class, Race and Gender, 1832–1898* [Princeton, NJ, 1991], pp. 69–72). She writes:

> When anthropological writing contrasted the 'bad' female, disruptive of the familial and sexual order, with the 'good' female, the upholder of that order, it pinpointed female choice as the decisive factor in the transition from nature to culture ... Most important, anthropological writing helped middle-class women to understand their gender as a contradictory phenomenon precisely because it was both crucial to woman's identity and the gravest threat to it. Being female meant (as it does today) constant self-regulation; neither too little nor too much femininity would do (p. 74).

35. A. D. Hutter, 'Dreams, Transformations, and Literature', pp. 202–3 [see p. 185 above – Ed.]; Lewis A. Lawson, 'Wilkie Collins and *The Moonstone*', p. 69. I seem to be arriving, by somewhat different

methods, at John Kuchich's thesis that 'Victorian repression produced a self that was actually more responsive libidinally, more self-sufficient, and oddly enough – more antisocial than we have yet understood.' (John Kucich, *Repression in Victorian Fictions: Charlotte Brontë, George Eliot and Charles Dickens* [Berkeley, CA, 1987], p. 3.) While I would not claim that Rachel's secrecy is typical of Victorian repression – certainly Bruff and Betteredge find it unusual enough to remark on it – it seems to be operating as Kucich defines the term here.

36. Jean E. Kennard, *Victims of Convention* (Hamden, CT, 1978), p. 13.

37. Ibid., p. 18.

38. Ruth Bernard Yeazell, 'Fictional Heroines and Feminist Critics', *Novel*, 8 (1974), 29–38, pp. 34–5, 37.

39. Richard Barickman, Susan MacDonald, and Myra Stark, *Corrupt Relations: Dickens, Thackeray, Trollope, Collins and the Victorian Sexual System* (New York, 1982), p. 143.

40. D. A. Miller, *The Novel and the Police*, p. 13; see also pp. 33–57.

41. Beth Kalikoff, *Murder and Moral Decay in Victorian Popular Literature*, p. 125.

11

Blank Spaces: Ideological Tensions and the Detective Work of *The Moonstone*

TAMAR HELLER

In Collins's *The Moonstone* (1868), which T. S. Eliot called 'the first and greatest of English detective novels',[1] the major feat of ratiocination is performed not by Sergeant Cuff, the inspector from Scotland Yard, but by a freakish-looking outcast and doctor's assistant, Ezra Jennings. Jennings proves what others already know – that Franklin Blake stole the Moonstone. More important, though, Jennings figures out that Blake did this to protect his cousin Rachel and that he acted in a trance caused by a dose of opium administered without his knowledge. Jennings's method for arriving at this conclusion vindicates not only Blake but the process of detection itself. Piecing together the 'broken phrases'[2] spoken in a delirium by the doctor, Mr Candy, who slipped Blake the dose of laudanum, Jennings demonstrates the power of reason and of reading. He shows both that in delirium the 'superior faculty of thinking' continues despite the apparent 'incapacity and confusion' of language (p. 415), and that the person who tries to interpret this confusion can extract intelligibility and coherence from what is fragmentary and unintelligible.

Ezra Jennings's version of detection, however, is riddled with gaps and silences. Since the only clues he has are broken words surrounded by empty spaces, the narrative he reconstructs, as Ross Murfin argues, may not be the truth of what happened so much as a fictional account arrived at by guesswork.[3] Moreover, the zeal with which Jennings fills in gaps in equalled only by his determination that his own story remain 'a blank' (p. 511). Such paradoxes show how in *The Moonstone* detection defers rather than fixes meaning, uncovering mysteries only to suggest that others stay covered up.

This chapter argues that Jennings's ambiguous act of detection emblematises how *The Moonstone* is Collins's great cover-up. With greater subtlety and complexity than the works that preceded it, this novel written at the end of the decade of his greatest achievement simultaneously expresses and suppresses the ideological and generic tensions that had animated his fiction from the beginning of his career. Critics have praised *The Moonstone* as Collins's most seamless transformation of the Gothic into the detective novel, a genre that brings to light and banishes the buried secrets so prominent in the Gothic. This genealogy, in which feminine genres are the matrix for the male-dominated detective novel, locates *The Moonstone* as the triumphant finale to Collins's revision of his female predecessors. Yet this critical tradition tends to ignore how the novel that 'fathered' detective fiction[4] resembles the female Gothic in the thematics of blankness and silence that puncture its narrative of revelation and rational interpretation.

The tension between Gothic and detective fiction in the novel is symptomatic of Collins's continued and heightened ambivalence about his literary project. *The Moonstone*, written near the close of the decade that began with *The Woman in White*, followed two novels that critics considered particularly shocking and sensational (*No Name* and *Armadale*), mainly because they place at centre stage fallen women who embody a bold critique of Victorian conventions and gender roles. In both novels, however, these women are chastened by being married off (*No Name*) or killed off (*Armadale*). By the time he wrote *The Moonstone*, then, Collins, whose enormous popularity relied on his being a kind of literary outlaw, had apparently strained to the limit the expression of radical impulses in his fiction. Setting most of *The Moonstone* in the same revolutionary period of 1848–49 that he had chosen as the backdrop for *The Woman in White*, he creates a narrative that self-reflexively focuses on the fate of subversive fictions.

The central image in this narrative, the theft of the Moonstone, represents an exposé of Victorian culture that recognises the links between types of domination – of the colonisers over the colonised, of men over women, and of the upper over the lower classes. Yet the novel also papers over the traces of its own exposé, an erasure attested to by its obsession with images of buried writing. Rosanna Spearman, the servant who sinks her love letter to Franklin Blake in the quicksand that is the site of her suicide, spectacularly introduces this theme, which culminates when Ezra Jennings requests that his writing – letters, journals, and his daring unfinished book on the 'intricate and delicate subject of the brain and the nervous system' (p. 414) – be buried with him. The buried writing of these outcasts – particularly that of Jennings, who becomes Collins's figure for his own project – is a synecdoche for the novel's tendency at once to diffuse its social criticism and to draw attention to its own self-censorship.

ANATOMIES OF EMPIRE: READING THE THEFT OF THE MOONSTONE

Readings of the mystery plot of *The Moonstone* have tended to focus on the psychosexual symbolism of Franklin Blake's stealing Rachel's jewel from her boudoir at night.[5] This Freudian reading of the theft as a 'symbolic defloration'[6] associates detection with the analyst's work of interpreting a psychological and familial narrative, since Blake's unconscious motivations are bound up in his role as his cousin's suitor. Another influential reading, however, argues that the novel's criticism of imperialism makes its emphasis more political than domestic: John Reed claims that Britain's exploitation of its 'jewel', India, symbolised by Colonel Herncastle's greedy plunder of the diamond, is the central target in Collins's indictment of an 'oppressive society'.[7]

The psychosexual and historical readings of the novel have yet to be fully integrated. The novel itself, however, is structured around a comparison between the private world of English families and the public dimension of imperialism. The parallels Collins draws between the two thefts of the diamond – the first in India, the second in England – demonstrate the interpenetration of the realms of empire and domesticity by showing how the hierarchies of gender and class that undergird British culture replicate the politics of colonialism.

Imperialism is, then, both an important subject in *The Moonstone* and a thematic bridge between the foreign and English worlds in its narrative. The novel is framed by its references to imperialism, tracing a history of British rule in India that begins with the storming of Seringapatam in 1799, a crucial moment in consolidating the sway of the East India Company, and ends with the restoration of the jewel to its temple by the Indians. Although this final act of native resistance recalls the Indian Mutiny of 1857, Collins's response to such rebellion differs from that of most of his contemporaries by locating the source of violence in imperialism itself. This is not to say that the novel is unmarked by British paranoia in the wake of the Mutiny and other colonial uprisings; unabashedly Orientalist, *The Moonstone* portrays the conspiratorial Indians as shady and sinister Others, a colonial version of the terrorist Brotherhood in *The Woman in White*.[8]

Yet the novel also breaks down the terms of the imperialist ideology represented by Gabriel Betteredge's comment 'here was our quiet English house suddenly invaded by a devilish Indian Diamond' (p. 36). Betteredge, whose Bible is that classic imperialist text *Robinson Crusoe*, voices the naïve Orientalism that opposes inside to outside, English to foreign, and good to evil. *The Moonstone*, however, blurs these polarities, an effect Dickens noticed when he described its narrative as 'wild, and yet domestic'.[9] Dickens's comment suggests how the seemingly opposed realms of exotic (wild) and English (domestic) permeate each other: what is wild is still domestic, yet what is domestic may also be wild. Whereas the Indians are motivated by an apparently 'English' sense of justice, Englishmen like Blake appear, to the horrified eyes of Betteredge, to have turned foreign. Indeed, the distinction between English and Indian, orderly interiors and disorderly exteriors, is most radically disrupted by the revelation that Blake stole the Moonstone.

Although making the decadently foreign Blake the thief reinforces the novel's Orientalism (particularly since he takes the gem under the influence of the Eastern drug opium), Collins's decision to have a second Englishman steal the Moonstone becomes the linchpin for his radical reading of British culture. Just as the history of imperialism becomes a family story – the revelation of Herncastle's guilt is 'extracted from a family paper' (p. 1) – so the 'strange family story' (p. 7) of Blake's theft mirrors the larger narrative of imperialism. By juxtaposing the plots of courtship and colonialism, Collins suggests an analogy between sexual and imperial domination.

Both thefts resemble a symbolic violation: Rachel's loss of her jewel, read by many critics as her virginity, echoes the plunder of the Moonstone, which had originally graced the statue of an 'inviolate deity' (p. 2). That Rachel is dark underscores her likeness to the

Indians: 'Her hair was the blackest I ever saw. Her eyes matched her hair' (p. 58). These repeated parallels imply that, like colonial possessions, femininity is a Dark Continent to be explored and ultimately controlled; Blake's searching the drawer in Rachel's Indian cabinet echoes the eroticised language of empire that Mr Bruff uses when he claims that Murthwaite, the authority on India, is intent on returning there and 'penetrating into regions left still unexplored' (p. 313). Moreover, just as a colonised territory loses its sovereignty when it is subordinated to an imperial power, so Blake's theft of the jewel anticipates Rachel's loss of autonomy within Victorian marriage. Indeed, the theft symbolically corrects Rachel's desire for independence. As male characters in the novel are all too happy to point out, her main 'defect' (p. 58) is her tendency 'to shut herself up in her own mind' to think (p. 303) – an image that suggests that the jewel (which also has a single flaw) signifies not merely her virginity but what Bruff calls her 'self-dependence' as well (p. 303).

Even the way that Blake's act is finally defended reinforces the analogy between Victorian ideologies of gender and imperialism. Ezra Jennings's experiment clears Blake, not of the act of the theft, but of a bad motive for the act: he is free of moral responsibility not simply because he stole the jewel in an unconscious state, but because even while unconscious he wished to protect Rachel from the threat of the Indians lurking outside the house. Blake's fears, reminiscent of the paranoia about female chastity whipped into hysterical fury by the Mutiny, also reveal how his 'innocence' is a social and rhetorical construction. Blake's reason for stealing the jewel mirrors the rationalisation of imperialism as 'the white man's burden', protecting people who presumably cannot take care of themselves. That Blake appropriates the jewel Rachel had insisted on placing in an unlocked drawer is a sign of how marriage 'locks up' women's independence and desire, transferring their possessions to their husbands with the blessings of an ideology that assumes wives need such protection.

The character of Rosanna Spearman adds another level to this analysis of types of domination by introducing the issue of class. If the question of Blake's moral responsibility is raised most insistently concerning the theft, it is suggested also by Rosanna's suicide, since what comes between her and Blake is not so much a literal as a metaphorical 'plainness', her working-class status. The lack of communication between Rosanna and Blake shows how members of the working class are invisible to those they serve. In the letter she leaves for him, Rosanna describes Blake's indifference – 'I tried – oh, dear, how I tried – to get you to look at me' (p. 349) – and notes how he ignored her labour when she straightened his room: 'You never noticed it, any more than you noticed me' (p. 352). Blake himself unwittingly supports Rosanna's claim when, responding to her accusation that he deliberately snubbed her, he says, 'The writer is entirely mistaken, poor creature. I never noticed her' (p. 362).

Because she is a woman as well as a servant, however, Rosanna's story also links the issue of class to that of gender. Just as Rachel's story demonstrates the analogy between Victorian ideologies of gender and imperialism, Rosanna's narrative shows how gender and class are mutually reinforcing categories. That her domestic labour in cleaning Blake's room is also a labour of love suggests how Victorian wife and Victorian servant were both, in Leonore Davidoff's words, 'mastered for life'.[10] (Rosanna signs her letter to Blake 'your true lover and humble servant' [p. 368].) Although Rosanna and Rachel appear to be rivals for Blake's affections, these women from vastly different class backgrounds thus are also doubles, linked by a desire to serve the man they love that ensures their silence about his role in the theft.

RESISTANCE ON THE MARGINS: THE SYMBOLISM OF THE SHIVERING SAND

Sergeant Cuff also sees a bond between Rachel and Rosanna, but he believes this to be partnership in crime. Even though he is mistaken in his belief that the two women sold the jewel to pay Rachel's debts, his theory reveals that the novel is not just about types of domination but also about types of resistance, of which female insubordination is the most important. The novel that recalls the Indian Mutiny also alludes to a notorious criminal case that was read by contemporaries as an example of female mutiny against male law. Sergeant Cuff, who tries to track down criminal women, is modelled on an Inspector Whicher, who investigated the Road Murder of 1860, in which a nightgown stained with blood linked a young girl, Constance Kent, to the murder of her stepbrother. Cuff's suspicions about Rachel reflect the paranoia about female rebellion expressed in accounts of the Road Murder; Constance Kent's father claimed that his daughter's criminality stemmed from her wish 'to be independent', a claim paralleling men's uneasiness about Rachel's 'defect' of 'self-dependence' in *The Moonstone*.[11]

The imagery of defect or disfigurement to describe women's 'self-dependence', or resistance to conventional roles, links Rachel to other rebellious female characters. Rosanna's deformity – one shoulder higher than the other – images her desire to 'get above herself' through her love for an upper-class man.[12] And Rosanna's closest friend, Limping Lucy, another female character associated with both rebellion and disfigurement, expresses the independence she shares with her friend in her denunciation of Blake as Rosanna's 'murderer' (p. 205) and in her rejection of heterosexuality ('if she had only thought of the men as I think, she might have been living now' [p. 206]). Like Marian Halcombe's passion for Laura in *The Woman in White*, the erotic intensity of Lucy's love for Rosanna represents an alternative to the novel's heterosexual plot. But the shattering of Lucy's dream of living in London with Rosanna 'like sisters' (p. 206) evokes from her a protest, not just against men, but against class privilege: 'Ha, Mr Betteredge, the day is not far off when the poor will rise against the rich. I pray Heaven they may begin with *him*' (p. 207).

Lucy's cry, the novel's clearest allusion to the revolutionary period of 1848 that is its setting, shows how women's rebellion also can symbolise other types of resistance; like women, Indians and the working class are not just subdued victims but possible trouble-makers and instigators of revolt. That Limping Lucy voices this cry, however, also demonstrates how the thematics of revolution that are so important to *The Woman in White*, set in the same period, here have been moved from centre stage. Not only is Lucy a more minor figure than Anne Catherick, the character in the earlier novel she most resembles in her resentment of the wrongs of women and of the lower classes, but this diminished status mirrors the marginality of other images of resistance. The Indians are voiceless presences lurking on the margins of the text, and even the letter that finally gives Rosanna a narrative voice must first be rescued from burial in the Shivering Sand.

The Shivering Sand, which hides both Rosanna's body and her letter, becomes Collins's central image for a resistance that is reduced to a trembling beneath the surface of the text:

> The sand-hills here run down to the sea, and end in two spits of rock jutting out opposite each other, till you lose sight of them in the

water. ... Between the two, shifting backwards and forwards at certain seasons of the year, lies the most horrible quicksand on the shores of Yorkshire. At the turn of the tide, something goes on in the unknown deeps below, which sets the whole face of the quicksand shivering and trembling in a manner most remarkable to see, and which has given to it, among the people in our parts, the name of the Shivering Sand.

(p. 24)

A Gothic site of what is 'most horrible', the Shivering Sand represents everything that the novel has identified as being 'below' in the body politic. It is an image for the female body, with a 'face' that at the turn of the tide 'dimple[s] and quiver[s]' (p. 136) like, as Albert Hutter says, 'some grotesque coquette'.[13] Since it hides the secret of Rosanna's transgressive desire, it is also appropriate that it is a female sexual symbol, lying between 'two spits of rock' and deriving its name from its parody of female orgasm, its 'shivering and trembling in a manner most remarkable to see'. But the face of the Sand is specifically described as a 'broad brown face' (p. 28), thus linking it not only to women but also to the Indians. Moreover, Rosanna Spearman's comment to Betteredge that the Sand reminds her of 'hundreds of suffocating people ... all struggling to get to the surface' (p. 28) suggests the lower classes struggling (as she does) to rise above their 'place'. Unlike Lucy, however, who insists that the poor will successfully rise up, Rosanna identifies this struggle as a failed one: those who seem to rise only sink 'lower and lower in the dreadful deeps' (p. 28).

The burial of resistance in the Shivering Sand only emphasises its resemblance to the female Gothic text, where women's rebellion is similarly submerged and hidden. The tension in the novel between the genres of detection and the Gothic is coded by the scenes where male detectives try to penetrate the secrets of the marginal and feminine space of the Sand. Sergeant Cuff, who dogs Rosanna's footsteps as she goes back and forth between her 'hiding-place' on the Sand (p. 174), is a major figure for this male project, as well as being, with his love of roses and eye for trifling clues, a déclassé version of William Collins, the Romantic artist who had been portrayed in the *Memoirs* as an inveterate detective of Nature ('his power of observation ... thus regulated, it was seldom that the smallest object worthy of remark escaped its vigilance' [*Memoirs*, II, 310]). Although Collins's father had successfully interpreted Nature, however, Sergeant Cuff's efforts to track down Rosanna (his 'rose') are frustrated; in one of the most wildly Gothic scenes in the novel he traces her footprints to the Sand to discover that, by committing suicide, she is beyond his grasp.

The more crucial clash between female Gothic and male detection, however, occurs in the scene where Blake confronts the quicksand face to face to retrieve from it Rosanna's letter and the stained nightgown:

> In this position, my face was within a few feet of the surface of the quicksand. The sight of it so near me, still disturbed at intervals by its hideous shivering fit, shook my nerves for the moment. A horrible fancy that the dead woman might appear on the scene of her suicide, to assist my search – an unutterable dread of seeing her rise through the heaving surface of the sand, and point to the place – forced itself into my mind, and turned me cold in the warm sunlight. I own I closed my eyes at the moment when the point of the stick first entered the quicksand.
>
> (p. 343)

The eroticised terms in which detection is described here – the phallic stick penetrating the Sand's *vagina dentata* – represents interpretation as male virility that controls the mystery of femininity. Having 'penetrated the secret which the quicksand had kept from every other living creature' (p. 345), Blake makes two erotic discoveries: the stained nightgown, which is evidence for his symbolic violation of Rachel, and the letter, which contains the secret of Rosanna's desire. This mysterious feminine desire recalls related types of mysterious Otherness in the novel; the Sand's 'fathomless deeps' and its 'false brown face' (p. 342) resemble the 'unfathomable' and 'yellow deep' of the Indian diamond (p. 68) and, synecdochically, of the East. Like Mr Murthwaite's travels 'penetrating into regions left still unexplored', detective work maps and colonises these Dark Continents.

Although critics have read this scene in psychoanalytic terms as Blake's confrontation with the id, or 'a threatening second self',[14] he in fact discovers not so much the Other within himself as the Other outside it. As in earlier descriptions of the Sand, female sexuality figures the unruly rebellion that is potentially beyond the control of the Englishman. At the site of Rosanna's buried desire Blake witnesses the return of the repressed, the reawakening of feminine sexuality signified by the 'hideous shivering fit' of the quicksand. A sense of the threat (already vividly conveyed by the name

Spearman) that this female sexuality poses to his masculine identity pervades the language he uses to describe his reaction to the Sand. Not only are his nerves shaken, as if he were a neurasthenic woman, but he confesses to overpowering fear at the moment he penetrates the quicksand: 'I own I closed my eyes.' Blake's triumph as a detective – when he finds the box he is 'throbbing with excitement from head to foot' (p. 343) – dispels both this sexual fear and the Gothic narrative represented by his fantasy that he is haunted by Rosanna's ghost.

MALE DETECTIVES AND SILENT WOMEN: THE DOUBLE VOICE OF *THE MOONSTONE*

Although Blake's detective work appears to overpower the Gothic, the discovery there of his apparent guilt leads him to confront the woman who embodies both the repression and the potential unruliness of the Gothic text. The stillness of the Shivering Sand, that site of all that is hidden and buried, is a mirror for the novel's central Gothic silence – Rachel's silence, around which its mystery plot is structured. The scene on the Sand is a prelude for the climactic scene where a male detective penetrates female secrets; hoping she can prove his innocence, Blake arranges a surprise meeting with Rachel in order to induce her to tell him what she knows.

Collins's staging of this scene makes it clear that the battle to break women's silence is, like the scene on the Shivering Sand, a battle over the control of knowledge. In Foucauldian terms, this knowledge is understandable as a form of power; Blake's role as a detective, his search to repossess Rachel's knowledge, reinforces the control over women that Victorian gender ideology gave to men within courtship and marriage. In an exchange that reads as both a love scene and an interrogation, Blake gets answers to his insistent questions by assuming once more the role of Rachel's suitor: 'while her hand lay in mine I was her master still' (p. 383). When he boasts that after more of this persuasion 'she willingly opened her whole mind to me' (p. 384), he implies that Rachel's willingness to open her mind obligingly reverses her previous unwillingness to have the drawer opened and her jewel stolen ... [when he] (p. 382) provokes the revelation most damaging to his case – that she saw him take the diamond – his reproach of her silence ('if you had spoken when you ought to have spoken') causes him decisively to lose his 'influence' over her: 'the few words I had said seemed to have lashed her on the instant into a frenzy of rage' (p. 388). So powerful are Rachel's angry words ('The hysterical passion swelled in her bosom – her quickened convulsive breathing almost beat on my face' [p. 393]) that they provoke a reaction in Blake similar to the near-hysteria he had felt on the Shivering Sand. He had said earlier, 'I roused my manhood' (p. 379) before going in to see Rachel, but by the end of the scene he is reduced to tears (p. 393).

Rachel's hysteria not only unmans her lover but subverts the language of Victorian courtship and marriage. Castigating Blake with a 'cry of fury' (p. 388), she accuses him of duplicity: 'he wonders I didn't charge him with his disgrace the first time we met: "My heart's darling, you are a Thief! My hero whom I love and honour, you have crept into my room under cover of the night, and stolen my Diamond!"' (p. 389). In this passage, a woman's 'heart's darling' is in fact a thief; her 'hero', who like a husband receives 'love and honour', practises deception and sexual violation. In this sense, Rachel's words express the critique of marriage implicit in Collins's figuration of the theft as the domination of women.

The introduction of the thematics of hysteria, however, causes the scene to convey an increasingly reductive message about gender. Although Rachel's 'hysterical passion' at first blurs gender roles by making the manly detective cry, the references to hysteria work more strongly to reinscribe the notion of sexual difference. As in *The Woman in White*, to label woman's speech a symptom of hysteria defines it as defective and normalises male speech.[15] In *The Moonstone*, medicine provides the greatest help of all professional languages in charting, and controlling, the Dark Continent of femininity (it is no accident that at the birthday dinner Rachel is seated between the explorer Mr Murthwaite and the doctor Mr Candy).[16] Rachel's power to voice the novel's hidden critique of bourgeois marriage is weakened as she is transformed into the object of diagnostic scrutiny. The hysterical symptoms written on her body (her angry words, her 'convulsive breathing' [p. 393]) invite an interpretation that undercuts the authority of her subversive reading of the events surrounding the theft.

In the nineteenth-century medical discourses of which Freud's is the culminating example, hysteria is a sign of women's fruitless rebellion against the things they secretly desire but will not acknowledge: heterosexuality and the subordination to men that its institutionalisation represents. As Hélène Cixous explains, the hysteric's initial resistance to male law is transformed into acquiescence: 'She asks the master "What do I want?" and "What do you want me to want, so that I might want it?"'[17] In *The Moonstone*, the narrative that consists of an interrupted and then resumed courtship is the 'master' text that teaches Rachel to want the man she accused of symbolically violating her; indeed, her learning to acknowledge this need is as important a revelation as any other in the mystery plot. Just as Cixous says that 'silence is the mark of hysteria',[18] so Rachel's silence is not just her way of protecting her lover but a sign of pathology, of her difficulty in voicing her need. During the period of her estrangement from Blake, both her silence and her hysterical outbursts suggest her sexual frustration at the separation, as she herself admits when she reveals her thwarted love to Godfrey Ablewhite and then asks, 'Is there a form of hysterics that bursts into words instead of tears?' (p. 262). The exchange with Blake is the climactic scene where her anger against him may in fact be read as the mark of her hidden desire for him. That her protests signify the opposite of what they supposedly mean is demonstrated not only by her starting to return Blake's kisses when he first enters the room, but also by the way she lets him hold her 'powerless and trembling' hand while saying, with obvious lack of conviction, 'Let go of it' (p. 383).

The symptomatology of hysteria thus neutralises the power of what had seemed most threatening about women: their words and their sexuality. The deviant and defiant women of the novel are explained by a single aetiology that assigns them the status of various hysterical types: in her letter Rosanna 'bursts into words' to reveal her unrequited love for Blake, and even Limping Lucy's hysterical cries of ressentiment signal the defectiveness of her desiring a woman rather than a man. The centrality to the novel of this reading of femininity is embodied in the figure of the only woman assigned a narrative, the evangelical spinster Miss Clack, whose hysteria is coded by her failure to acknowledge her desire for Godfrey Ablewhite. After watching from behind a curtain as Godfrey proposes to Rachel, Miss Clack attributes her voyeurism to 'suppressed hysterics' (p. 263). The very inaccuracy of her diagnosis points, ironically, to the underlying hysteria of her text; the reader must become the analyst who perceives how her hypocrisy in cloaking her feelings renders her narrative inauthentic, a meaningless 'clacking' that emblematises the fate of female language in the novel.[19]

The Moonstone's use of the discourse of hysteria to invalidate women's voices supports D. A. Miller's Foucauldian reading of the text. For Miller, the detective work in Collins's novel is another example of how Victorian novels in general are implicated in the operations of surveillance and social policing that secure bourgeois hegemony. He argues that the tendency of the multiple narratives in *The Moonstone* to endorse Blake's version of what happened – some, like Miss Clack's, by being transparently 'wrong' – demonstrates how the novel stifles dissent and establishes instead a 'master-voice that corrects, overrides, subordinates, or sublates all other voices it allows to speak'.[20] Yet despite the way *The Moonstone* silences women's voices, the model of a master voice is finally not as useful for understanding the text as is the theory of the double voice that feminist critics have used to describe the subversive undercurrent, conveyed by irony and indirection, that underlies the conventional plot in nineteenth-century women's writing.

It may seem in itself ironic to locate such a feminine strategy in a novel that deauthorises female language. Yet since women's voices (Rachel's, Rosanna's, and Limping Lucy's) convey the novel's social criticism, for Collins to silence their dissent is also to silence his own. Although this containment of radical tendencies is not new in Collins's fiction, it is even more pronounced than it is in *The Woman in White*, where ideological conflict is also reflected in the conflict between men's and women's voices. Unlike Marian Halcombe, though, Rachel has no narrative of her own, so Blake's narration in the scene of their meeting can more effectively rewrite her protest as acquiescence. Yet this type of voice-over attests, finally, not to the 'monological' nature of the text, as Miller claims,[21] but to the continued ideological doubleness that causes the novel to speak in two voices, one of which, according to the double voice theory, is a palimpsest. Paradoxically, even as Collins's art becomes more masculine in *The Moonstone* – more allied with the male science of detection – it becomes increasingly more feminine, fissuring the official version of what happened with ironies and indirections. In this way, the feminine and Gothic space of the Shivering Sand, where resistance trembles beneath the surface, becomes a symbol for the novel itself.

One scene where this double voice of irony and indirection is particularly apparent is that where Franklin Blake reads Rosanna's letter after discovering the evidence of his guilt in the Sand. Blake's narration portrays this scene as one more painful step in his detective safari from 'the darkness to the light' (p. 369). Rosanna's text is stranded in 'darkness' because she (like Rachel and Miss Clack) does not correctly interpret what she sees; all these women either suspect or know that Blake took the diamond, but they turn out to be wrong about why he took it. Although this devaluation of female knowledge is typical of detective work, Rosanna's letter, by representing one of the novel's more subversive analyses of gender and class, shows that in this regard she is more knowing than Blake. When he refuses to finish reading Rosanna's letter, handing it to Betteredge half-read, the novel draws attention to how Blake continues not to 'notice' Rosanna or her narrative, which is a criticism of class privilege.

As an allegory of reading, this scene comments on the fate of Collins's own art. That Blake puts aside the letter he finds offensive demonstrates the fate of texts that offend the middle-class reader, even when the text's author is trying (like Rosanna, the faithful servant) to please. As the detective plot of *The Moonstone* unfolds, Collins does not so much offend as he does what Rosanna does with her letter before Blake reads it: buries his social criticism so deep that the reader can only with difficulty dig it out again. This transformation of the radical elements in the text into a subtext explains why, as detection works to disclose all, the novel becomes obsessed with images of alienated writers who censor themselves. Whereas Rosanna's jumping into the quicksand that buries her letter is *The Moonstone*'s most dramatic image of self-erasure, Ezra Jennings, the detective who solves the mystery yet obstinately refuses to tell his story, becomes the novel's main figure for authorial self-censorship.

BURIED TEXTS AND THE VICTORIAN ROMANTIC: THE ROLE OF EZRA JENNINGS

As a figure for the double impulse of the text toward revelation and self-censorship, Ezra Jennings embodies the ideological and generic contradictions in *The Moonstone*. Entering the novel by interrupting the reading of Rosanna's letter, he signals simultaneously the outcast status he shares with her and the way he will become the male detective who leads Blake 'from the darkness to the light'. This doubleness is inscribed on his body, making him a walking set of contrasts:

> Judging him by his figure and his movements, he was still young.
> Judging him by his face, and comparing him with Betteredge, he
> looked the elder of the two. His complexion was of a gipsy dark-
> ness; his fleshless cheeks had fallen into deep hollows, over which
> the bone projected like a penthouse. His nose presented the fine
> shape and modelling so often found among the ancient people of the
> East, so seldom visible among the newer races of the West. His fore-
> head rose high and straight from the brow. His marks and wrinkles
> were innumerable. From this strange face, eyes, stranger still, of the
> softest brown – eyes dreamy and mournful, and deeply sunk in their
> orbits – looked out at you, and (in my case, at least) took your atten-
> tion captive at their will. Add to this a quantity of thick closely-
> curling hair, which, by some freak of Nature, had lost its colour in
> the most startlingly partial and capricious manner. Over the top of
> his head it was still of the deep black which was its natural colour.
> Round the sides of his head – without the slightest gradation of grey
> to break the force of the extraordinary contrast – it had turned com-
> pletely white. The line between the two colours preserved no sort of
> regularity. At one place, the white hair ran up into the black; at
> another, the black hair ran down into the white.
>
> (pp. 358–9)

With the most obvious contradiction in Jennings's appearance, the
colonial plot of the novel resurfaces. In this passage the disjunction
between youth and age is not as riveting as the mingling of black
and white in Jennings's piebald hair, which signals, as Blake puts it,
'the mixture of some foreign race in his English blood' (p. 411).
The references to Jennings's 'gipsy complexion' and the 'fine shape
and modelling' of his nose are signifiers leading to this final image
of miscegenation ('The line between the two colours preserved no
sort of regularity').[22]

This physical 'freak of Nature' symbolises the transgression of
the boundary between coloniser and colonised that permitted
Jennings's birth: 'I was born, and partly brought up, in one of our
colonies. My father was an Englishman, but my mother – We are
straying away from our subject, Mr Blake ... (p. 411). This passage
shows how Jennings, who blends the identities of English 'gentleman' (p. 410) and colonial Other, nonetheless feels a tension
between these origins. The man whose detective work in the novel
consists of filling in blanks resolutely leaves a blank after 'my
mother' because of his desire to cloak the racial background that
would account in part for why he is distrusted. (Betteredge, for
example, refers contemptuously to him by the signs of racial differ-

ence, 'the man with the piebald hair, and the gipsy complexion' [p. 359].) That Jennings prefixes 'colonies' with 'our' attests to his desire to identify not with his native mother but with white men – his father and Blake, to whom he is speaking. When Jennings does note his affinity with women, he emphasises that this is an undesirable attribute. Confessing that he burst into tears after saving Mr Candy's life, he offers Blake a 'bitterly professional apology': 'An hysterical relief, Mr. Blake – nothing more! Physiology says, and says truly, that some men are born with female constitutions – and I am one of them!' (p. 414).

Jennings's diagnosis of hysteria draws attention to what Jenny Taylor calls his 'double role'.[23] The novel's most able practitioner of the male science of detective work, he appropriately is a doctor. Yet, paradoxically, Jennings speaks with the voice of male professionalism to diagnose his own powerless and feminised position (at one point he even claims that it is 'useless to appeal to my honour as a man' [p. 420]). This confusion in gender roles also manifests itself as a generic confusion: the novel's most scientific detective, Jennings is also its most Gothic figure, not just in his flamboyantly weird appearance but in his embodiment of the Gothic plot of silence and potential subversion. In the same conversation with Blake where he diagnoses himself as female, he becomes an image for a potentially dangerous radicalism. When Blake tries to gain access to Jennings's notes, he commands him to stop:

> I looked at him in astonishment. The grip of some terrible emotion seemed to have seized him, and shaken him to the soul. His gipsy complexion had altered to a livid greyish paleness; his eyes had suddenly become wild and glittering; his voice had dropped to a tone – low, stern, and resolute – which I now heard for the first time. The latent resources in the man, for good or for evil – it was hard, at that moment, to say which – leapt up in him and showed themselves to me, with the suddenness of a flash of light.
>
> (p. 419)

The flash of light illuminates Jennings's resemblance to other Gothic images of ressentiment – Mary Shelley's monster, whom he resembles in his freakish appearance and outcast state, and also Collins's version of that monster in *Basil's* Mannion, whose history of being blacklisted because of his scandalous past anticipates that of Jennings. Jennings's threatening expression, in fact, recalls the scene in the earlier novel where Basil sees Mannion's look change from deference to maniacal hatred as a flash of lightning reveals his face.[24]

Unlike these Gothic predecessors, however, Jennings almost immediately contains his subversive energy. He not only attributes his extraordinary reaction to self-hatred rather than to hatred of Blake (whom he does not wish to expose to someone whose 'character is gone'), but he also admits he wants to help the more privileged man in order to stifle his bitterness about social inequality: 'A man who has lived as I have lived has his bitter moments when he ponders over human destiny. You have youth, health, riches, a place in the world, a prospect before you. You, and such as you, show me the sunny side of human life, and reconcile me with the world that I am leaving, before I go' (p. 422). As Jennings becomes (appropriately enough in this novel that alludes to *Robinson Crusoe*) a kind of Friday who serves the upper-class Blake, he also becomes an image of the writer who reconciles himself to the social order instead of challenging it.

In this context, Jennings's wish for amnesia – 'Perhaps we should all be happier ... if we could but completely forget' (p. 410) – expresses the novel's own impulse to erase its origins in the Gothic and in radical Romanticism. The script that Jennings writes for the 'experiment' that exonerates Blake is the novel's climactic example of how it erases both its subversiveness and its generic antecedents. Jennings's re-enactment of the theft begins as a Gothic narrative, casting him in the role not only of Frankenstein's monster but also of Frankenstein himself, the daring scientist whose theories provoke, as Jennings puts it, 'the protest of the world ... against anything that is new' (p. 463). Jennings convinces hostile witnesses like Bruff and Betteredge that he is right, and he persuades Rachel's exceedingly proper chaperone Mrs Merridew that he is not so disruptive a force as she had feared, causing Blake to comment that 'there is a great deal of undeveloped liberal feeling in the world, after all' (p. 480). Yet Mrs Merridew's fears about Jennings are revealing: she is sure that his experiment will set off an explosion that, presumably, would literalise his association with a revolutionary 'flash of light'. She is mollified, however, because, as she explains after the experiment, 'Explosions ... are infinitely milder than they were' (p. 480).

What makes this comment so funny, of course, is the reader's knowledge that there was no explosion. This absence of disruption implies that the writing of the Victorian Romantic is not 'explosive', like that of his predecessors, but instead serves domestic ideology. Jennings is not the Frankenstein, or Frankenstein monster, who attacks families but the physician who cures their ills. In this role he resembles Dickens, Collins's great model for this kind of literary activity, whose domestic fiction diagnoses social disease by stabilising the family and normalising gender roles. By reuniting Rachel with Blake, the experiment replaces the hysteria that 'bursts into words instead of tears' with conventionally feminine language. Jennings describes her response to his letter explaining the circumstances of the theft as 'A charming letter! ... She tells me, in the prettiest manner, that my letter has satisfied her of Mr Blake's innocence' (p. 442). This charming and pretty female text is a paean to romantic love: 'the rapture of discovering that he has deserved to be loved, breaks its way innocently through the stoutest formalities of pen and ink' (p. 442).

This channelling of female writing into the expression of heterosexual desire precedes the re-enactment of the theft in which Rachel reprises her role as silent witness of Blake's theft: 'She kept back, in the dark: not a word, a movement escaped her' (p. 473). Whereas Blake's theft had represented men's domination of women, this repeat performance stages the ritual with the woman's consent to her own invisibility. Unlike her horrified silence during the original theft, Rachel's silence during the experiment expresses her happy anticipation of her impending marriage. Watching Blake sleep off the effects of the opium, she reverses the effects of her hysteria by bursting into tears instead of words: 'She looked at him in a silent ecstasy of happiness, till the tears rose in her eyes' (p. 477).

Yet Jennings, who engineers this happy ending, never makes it to the wedding of Franklin Blake and Rachel, when for the duration of the festivities he was to have been a 'guest in the house' (p. 479). Even though he has been a figure for the writer of domestic fiction who pleases his readers with scenes of married bliss, Jennings dies before he himself can enter the 'house', or the terms of the domestic ideology he has served so well. If in life the Romantic he evoked was Thomas De Quincy, whose *Confessions of an English Opium Eater* he lends to Blake, in death he resembles the Romantic figure most closely associated with buried writing. The language in Mr Candy's letter, which describes Jennings's death, echoes the account of the death of John Keats written by his friend Joseph Severn.[25] In particular, Severn's line 'the letters I put into the coffin with my own hand'[26] is echoed by Mr Candy's account of how, at his friend's request, he buried his letters and other writing with him ("Promise," he said, "that you will put this into my coffin with your own hand; and that you see that no other hand touches it afterwards"' [p. 512]). All that was buried with Keats were other people's letters, but Jennings requests that the 'locked volumes' (p. 511) of his journal and his unfinished book be buried with him as well. As if to mimic this total erasure of his writing, Jennings begs that no tombstone mark his grave – a namelessness even more profound than that of Keats, who requested as an epitaph 'here lies one whose name was writ in water'.[27]

That the Victorian version of Keats buries his writing in an even more hyperbolic fashion than his predecessor had comments on the fate of Romanticism in the Victorian period. Writing about Charlotte Brontë's *Villette*, Mary Jacobus claims that the image of the buried letter symbolises for the Victorians the 'divorce of the Romantic imagination from its revolutionary impulse'.[28] Similarly, Jennings's buried writing records a grim fable about the suppression of radical Romanticism, which becomes, like his journal, a locked volume. All that remains of Jennings's writing is the conventional domestic narrative of the experiment, not his projected daring book on psychology. This narrative about the suppression of Romanticism is based on the recognition that the radical writer will meet with critical disapproval. The Victorian mythologies of Keats's death attributed it to the harsh attacks of critics, an account echoed by Jennings's history of being hounded, until his death, by mysterious slanders. In making Jennings a Keats-like figure, Collins represents his anxieties about the critical hostility that greeted his own Romantic and unconventional impulses.[29]

In this way, Ezra Jennings becomes the novel's most important mirror of its author. Collins and his creation have obvious similarities: both are opium addicts who live on the margins of respectability, and both respond satirically to convention (hence Jennings's scathing remark that there is a 'wonderful sameness in the solid expression of the English face' [p. 464]). Like Collins, Jennings becomes a figure for the non-canonical writer, dismissing the classics of 'Standard Literature' in Blake's bedroom as boring (p. 464). Both Collins and Jennings, however, try to muffle their unconventional tendencies in order to write domestic fictions that will win the approval of their audience. In the preface for the revised edition of 1871, Collins describes his struggle to complete the novel, despite severe attacks of gout and grief over the death of his mother, in terms that echo Jennings's. Like his character, who struggled despite his illness to bring the experiment to its happy conclusion, Collins claims that he overcame 'merciless pains' and 'useless tears' in order not to disappoint his 'good readers' (p. xxxiii). For Collins, the result of these efforts, which recall the stereotypical sufferings of the Romantic artist, is triumph in the Victorian marketplace: 'Everywhere my characters made friends, and my story roused interest' (p. xxxiv). Yet the fate of Jennings, who finally makes some friends but never publishes his writing, provides an ironic counterpoint to Collins's tale by implying that the price of this popularity is self-suppression. Whereas Jennings figures the aspect of Collins that prevented him from being considered sufficiently respectable by the critics, the burial of Jennings's writing and his death represent Collins's attempts to achieve this respectability.

In light of Collins's erasure of Romanticism in *The Moonstone*, it is only fitting that he later claimed to have been so dazed by the influence of opium that he did not remember writing the end of the novel! Although this self-mythologising narrative is Coleridgean in its plot of drug-induced inspiration, it suggests the suppression of Romantic artistry. By claiming that he wrote the end of the novel unknowingly, Collins writes himself into the role of Blake, who stole the Moonstone in a drugged trance. But, unlike the erstwhile bohemian Blake, whose dark secret is his most unrespectable moment, Collins suppresses the secret of the self-suppression he undertook in the interest of respectability. Forgetting that he created Jennings, he achieves in parodic fashion Jennings's goal of forgetting everything. In the stage version of *The Moonstone*, Collins takes this wilful amnesia to an even more remarkable extreme, excising Ezra Jennings, Rosanna Spearman, the Indians, and even opium, and attributing Blake's sleep-walking to a fit of indigestion.[30]

The novel, however, does not forget its ideological doubleness but rather underscores it; like Jennings and Collins – the author within the text and the author outside it – *The Moonstone* never manages to be respectable enough. The narrative ends twice, once in England, the second time in India. The relation between these two endings reflects the tensions within the novel's double voice. The English ending is the finale to the novel's suppression of all that is outcast and Other. The death of Godfrey Ablewhite, killed by the Indians while he is in blackface, represents the novel's most horrifying image of what happens when white men go native (as Miss

Clack says, 'How soon may our own evil passions prove to be Oriental noblemen who pounce on us unawares!' [p. 222]). That this character with a double life is punished only emphasises how Blake, who has led a similarly bohemian bachelor existence, is now a family man. The novel, however, moves from the warm contentment of English domesticity (with Rachel expecting a child, her new jewel) to the foreign, dark, and impersonal realm of the colonial Other, where the Moonstone is finally restored to its temple. Although described by a Westerner, the explorer Murthwaite, the Indian ending opens up possibilities closed down when Gabriel Betteredge says he is going to 'shut up' the English part of the story (p. 515). Even though, in Murthwaite's narrative, the Indians who have recaptured the gem disperse amid 'dead silence' (p. 521) to become outcasts, the end of the novel promises a repetition of the historical cycle in which repression is followed by resistance. In choosing to conclude on the margins of resistance, Collins thus resists the falsely comfortable closure of the English narrative to end instead with the riddling ambiguity of a question mark: 'So the years pass, and repeat each other; so the same events revolve in the cycles of time. What will be the next adventures of the Moonstone? Who can tell?' (p. 522).

From Tamar Heller, *Dead Secrets: Wilkie Collins and the Female Gothic* (New Haven, CT, 1992), pp. 142–95.

NOTES

[This extract is a chapter from Tamar Heller's book *Dead Secrets*, which explores Collins's revision of 'Female Gothic', and the complexities of his relationship to 'Literature' and the professional organisation of writing at a time when the novel was becoming increasingly defined and dominated by male writers. Heller takes her title from Collins's *The Dead Secret* (1857), a novel whose plot focuses on buried writing. Heller's thesis is that the recurrent image of buried writing in Collins's fiction 'represents social and textual marginality, as well as a subversiveness lurking beneath the surface of convention' (*Dead Secrets*, p. 1). Ed.]

1. T. S. Eliot 'Wilkie Collins and Charles Dickens' (1927), in *Selected Essays: New Edition* (New York, 1950), p. 413.

2. Wilkie Collins, *The Moonstone*, ed. Anthea Trodd (Oxford, 1982), p. 214. All subsequent references will be to this edition which follows Collins's revisions of 1871, and are cited by page in the text.

3. See Ross Murfin, 'The Art of Representation: Collins' *The Moonstone* and Dickens' example', *ELH*, 49 (1982), 653–4, for another discussion of Jennings's detective work.

4. Anthea Trodd uses the word 'fathered' in her introduction to *The Moonstone*, p. xv. In the tradition of Eliot, many studies have located *The Moonstone* as an important influence on English and American mystery and detective fiction. See, for example, Julian Symons, *Mortal Consequences: A History – From the Detective Story to the Crime Novel* (New York, 1972); Ian Ousby, *Bloodhounds of Heaven: The Detective in English Fiction from Godwin to Doyle* (Cambridge, MA, 1976); and Dennis Porter, *The Pursuit of Crime: Art and Ideology in Detective Fiction* (New Haven, CT, 1981).

5. As Albert D. Hutter says, 'What is stolen from Rachel is both the actual gem and her symbolic virginity'; see 'Dreams, Transformations, and Literature', in *The Poetics of Murder: Detective Fiction and Literary Theory*, ed. Glenn W. Most and William W. Stowe (New York, 1983), p. 242. [See p. 184 above – Ed.] Hutter's is the most recent and sophisticated of the psychoanalytic readings of the novel; earlier examples include Charles Rycroft, 'The Analysis of a Detective Story', in *Imagination and Reality: Psychoanalytical Essays, 1951–1961* (London, 1968), pp. 114–28, and Lewis A. Lawson, 'Wilkie Collins and *The Moonstone, American Imago*, 20 (1963), 61–79.

6. The phrase is Sue Lonoff's; see *Wilkie Collins and His Victorian Readers: A Study in the Rhetoric of Authorship* (New York, 1982), p. 210.

7. John R. Reed, 'English Imperialism and the Unacknowledged Crime of *The Moonstone*', *Clio*, 2 (1973), 287, 281.

8. For Orientalist discourse, I draw on Edward Said's classic study, *Orientalism* (New York, 1978). Collins's relation to Orientalism, and to imperialism in general is complicated. In the aftermath of the Indian Mutiny he co-authored with Dickens for *Household Words* the series *The Perils of Certain English Prisoners*, which, as its title implies, focuses on attacks against the colonists during the rebellion. The tone of this work is consonant with Dickens's virulent response to the Mutiny and his strongly pro-imperialist position; for more on this subject, see William Oddie, 'Dickens and the Indian Mutiny', *Dickensian*, 68 (1972), 3–15; for the British reaction to the Mutiny more generally, see Patrick Brantlinger, *Rule of Darkness: British Literature and Imperialism, 1830–1914* (Ithaca, NY, 1988), pp. 199–224. Yet, as Anthea Trodd points out, Collins's own response to the Mutiny, 'A Sermon for Sepoys' (*Household Words*, 27 [February 1858], 244–7), is 'pointedly unexcited' (introduction to *The Moonstone*, p. xviii); it is, in fact, pointedly enigmatic, a fable that warns against cruelty but praises the Moslem faith. Given Dickens's violent response to the Mutiny (he wished to 'exterminate the Race

upon whom the stain of the late cruelties rested'), it might have been difficult for Collins to voice any more explicit reservations about imperialism. One wonders if, after an initial enthusiasm, Dickens disliked *The Moonstone* – whose construction he labelled 'wearisome beyond endurance' – because he disapproved of its portrayal of race and imperialism (for Dickens's response to *The Moonstone*, see Norman Page, (ed.), *Wilkie Collins: The Critical Heritage* [London, 1974], p. 169). Sue Lonoff sees the critical picture of imperialist greed in *The Moonstone* as Collins's response not only to the Mutiny but also to another controversy in which Dickens adopted a strongly pro-imperialist stand – the debate during the late 1860s about Governor Edward Eyre's brutal repression of a Jamaican rebellion (*Wilkie Collins and His Victorian Readers*, pp. 178–9). Soon after *The Moonstone*, in fact, Collins wrote and staged with Charles Fechter a play called *Black and White* (1869) set in the West Indies before emancipation. Despite stereotyped portraits of blacks, the play, which supports an anti-slavery position, ends with the mulatto hero marrying a white heiress.

There may be, moreover, an intriguing, though studiously buried, allusion to anti-imperialist discourse in a scene late in *The Moonstone*. Among the books in Franklin Blake's room that Ezra Jennings dismisses as soporific 'Standard Literature' (p. 464) is Henry Mackenzie's *The Man of Feeling* (1771), which contains a critique of the spread of British imperialism in India that is both scathing and unusual (for Collins's day as well as Mackenzie's): 'You tell me of immense territories subject to the English: I cannot think of their possessions, without being led to enquire, by what right they possess them' (Henry Mackenzie, *The Man of Feeling*, ed. Brian Vickers [Oxford, 1987], p. 102; see also p. 103).

9. Charles Dickens to W. H. Wills, 30 June 1867, *Charles Dickens as Editor; Being Letters Written by Him to William Henry Wills, His Sub-editor*, ed. R. C. Lehmann (London, 1912), p. 360.

10. Leonore Davidoff, 'Mastered for Life: Servant and Wife in Victorian and Edwardian England', *Journal of Social History*, 7 (1774), 406–28. Rosanna's love for a man who is socially 'above' her is interestingly reminiscent of the relationship between Arthur Munby, a middle-class writer, and Hannah Culliwick, a Victorian maidservant, which Davidoff analyses in her essay 'Class and Gender in Victorian England', in *Sex and Class in Women's History*, ed. Judith L. Newton, Mary P. Ryan, and Judith R. Walkowitz (London, 1983), pp. 17–71. Although Munby and Culliwick, unlike Blake and Rosanna, were mutually attracted and lived together for many years, the dynamics of power in the relationship – Munby's manipulation of Hannah and the masochistic overtones of her devotion to the man she called 'massa' – shed light on the kind of gender and class issues to which Collins is drawing attention in *The Moonstone*. Like Franklin Blake, for example, Munby was the reader and editor of Hannah's journal and

other autobiographical sketches she wrote at his instigation; like Rosanna's letter, however, these texts represent more than a woman's obedience to a male imperative and constitute a powerful testimony to Hannah's voice. See *The Diaries of Hannah Culliwick, Victorian Maidservant*, ed. Liz Stanley (New Brunswick, N, 1984). Like the relationship between Culliwick and Munby, Collins's relationship with his mistress, Martha Rudd, whom he met in the 1860s, was also a cross-class one.

11. In her discussion of the Road Murder, Mary Hartman theorises that Constance's father was the murderer and that his daughter covered up for him with her confession to the crime in 1865. Hartman's account is useful for its analysis of the contemporary reading of crime as a moral fable about female rebellion and depravity. See her *Victorian Murderesses: A True History of Thirteen Respectable French and English Women Accused of Unspeakable Crimes* (New York, 1977), pp. 85–129. To see how Collins drew on details of the case, compare the statement by Constance's father that his daughter's 'wish to be independent' was a quality laudable in a boy, but not a virtue for a girl (Hartman, *Victorian Murderesses*, p. 109) with Mr Bruff's opinion that Rachel's 'absolute self-dependence is a great virtue in a man. In a woman it has the serious drawback of morally separating her from the mass of her sex' (*The Moonstone*, p. 303).

12. I am indebted to Charles Hatten for drawing my attention to this point.

13. Hutter, 'Dreams, Transformations, and Literature', p. 246. [See p. 188 above – Ed.]

14. The phrase is Lonoff's, in *Wilkie Collins and His Victorian Readers*, p. 198.

15. Among the relevant discussions of nineteenth-century medical discourses about femininity, hysteria, and the language of the hysteric are the volume of essays entitled *In Dora's Case: Freud–Hysteria–Feminism*, ed. Charles Bernheimer and Claire Kahane (New York, 1985); Nina Auerbach, *Woman and the Demon: The Life of a Victorian Myth* (Cambridge, MA, 1982), pp. 7–34; and Mary Jacobus, *Reading Woman: Essays in Feminist Criticism* (New York, 1986), pp. 197–274. For a discussion of hysteria in *The Moonstone*, see Jenny Bourne Taylor, *In the Secret Theatre of Home: Wilkie Collins, Sensation Narrative, and Nineteenth-Century Psychology* (London, 1988), pp. 200–1.

16. I am indebted to Navin Girishankar for pointing out to me the significance of Rachel's position at the birthday dinner.

17. Hélène Cixous, 'Castration or Decapitation?', trans. Annette Kuhn, *Signs*, 7 (1981), 49.

18. Ibid.

19. It is significant that Miss Clack, the female narrator and poor relation, is also a ressentiment-ridden version of the artist in the marketplace, since Franklin Blake pays her to write a section of the text (an arrangement she refers to with much, presumably hypocritical, grumbling). Miss Clack is also a member of women's clubs and reform groups – female communities that pose an implicit challenge to the world of men; as Gabriel Betteredge paraphrases her conversation with Godfrey Ablewhite at the birthday dinner, 'all the women in heaven would be members of a prodigious committee that never quarrelled, with all the men in attendance on them as ministering angels' (p. 76). Miss Clack is thus associated, as was Anne Catherick in *The Woman in White*, with a kind of feminist millenarianism, a vision that here – even more so than in the earlier novel – is mercilessly satirised and devalued.

One target of this satire is women's writing; Miss Clack's favourite author is the tract writer Miss Jane Ann Stamper, whom no one wants to read. As in *The Woman in White*, however, the novel's devaluation of female community is more important as a function of the story it tells about heterosexuality. Mothers die and potential female communities are disbanded so that women can 'grow up' and get married. The spinster Miss Clack is associated with Rachel's mother, who has befriended her and whose place she tries to take after Lady Verinder dies. Yet Miss Clack is rebuffed as a mother surrogate by Rachel, who goes away with Mr Bruff and later marries Franklin Blake. In this context it is ironic that, since Collins's own mother died while *The Moonstone* was being written, the dedication is 'In Memoriam Matris'.

20. D. A. Miller, 'From *roman-policier* to *roman-police*: Wilkie Collins's *The Moonstone*', *Novel*, 13 (1980), 168. [See p. 216 above – Ed.]

21. Ibid.

22. Collins's use of piebald hair as a symbol for miscegenation is striking, but not original. In his *An Account of the Regular Gradation in Man, And in Different Animals and Vegetables; And From the Former to the Latter* (London, 1799), Charles White, a gynaecologist who propounded a theory of Anglo-Saxon racial superiority, relates stories of 'pyebald, blotched, or party-coloured, black-and-white people' like the following one about the child of an interracial union: 'In 1759, a girl was born in Somersetshire, with the hair of her head of two remarkably distinct colours. After she was grown up a little, the hair on the right side appeared of a jet black, resembling the father's; whilst that on the left side was of a carroty red, resembling the mother's; each occupying one half of the head, from a vertical section of the front' (p. 123). I am indebted to Susan Meyer for introducing me to White's book.

23. Taylor, *In the Secret Theatre of Home*, p. 189. For Taylor's discussion of Ezra Jennings, see pp. 189–92. Although I agree with Taylor that Jennings is a 'cross-category figure', I would not say as she does that he thus breaks down 'all the systems of difference in the novel'

(p. 189). Rather, I would argue that Jennings's role is to underscore the unresolved tensions between the dualities he embodies. Another reading of Ezra Jennings as a figure for the writer is Murfin, 'Art of Representation'; a useful reading of Jennings's relation to Victorian medicine is Ira Bruce Nadel, 'Science and *The Moonstone'*, *Dickens Studies Annual*, 11 (1983), 239–59.

24. As this discussion of Jennings indicates, he is a character with a past in Collins's novels. He recalls not only Mannion but also (in his association with a thematics of blankness) his fellow scientist Louis Trudaine in 'Sister rose', whose chemistry can erase writing (Jennings, of course, restores other people's erased words while erasing his own). I believe that this type of hunted outcast with a buried past, a figure most evocatively realised in Ezra Jennings, is of all his fictional creations the one in which Collins had the greatest emotional and artistic investment. Certainly, versions of this character haunt Collins's works, which resurrect him (or sometimes, as in *The Dead Secret's* Sarah Leeson, her) again and again. Although one could say he appears in some form in almost everything Collins ever wrote, Ezra Jennings's most immediate antecedents are the figure of Mr Lorn in the short story 'The Dead Hand' (which appears in *The Queen of Hearts* and was inspired by Collins's meeting with a strange-looking medical assistant while on a walking trip with Dickens), and Ozias Midwinter in *Armadale*. Midwinter, from the novel written just before *The Moonstone*, strikingly anticipates Jennings in his association with feminine hysteria and racial difference (Midwinter's mother is of black West Indian origin).

25. Compare Mr Candy's letter to Franklin Blake (pp. 511–13) with Severn's letter to Charles Brown of 27 February 1821. Keats's request to Severn to lift him before his death ('be firm, and thank God it has come') is echoed by Jennings's similar request to Mr Candy to lift him as he is dying ('It's coming'). In addition to echoes in the accounts of their deaths, there are other connections between Keats and Jennings. Keats had medical training, and Jennings was his mother's maiden name. One source in which Collins could have encountered these details and Severn's letter is *The Life and Letters of John Keats* by Richard Monckton Milnes, Lord Houghton, originally published in 1848 but reissued in 1867, the year before *The Moonstone's* publication (the edition I refer to in subsequent notes). Collins not only knew Lord Houghton, whose biography was the important early one of Keats, but had even met Joseph Severn while on a trip to Italy with his family during his adolescence; see William M. Clark, *The Secret Life of Wilkie Collins* (London, 1988), p. 31.

26. Milnes, *The Life and Letters of John Keats* (London, 1867), p. 323.

27. Compare Keats's request (recorded in a letter by Severn dated 14 February 1821 and reproduced in Milnes, *The Life and Letters of John Keats*, p. 320) with Jennings's request of Mr Candy (p. 512).

28. Mary Jacobus, 'The Buried Letter: Feminism and Romanticism in *Villette*', in *Women Writing and Writing About Women*, ed. Mary Jacobus (London, 1979), p. 57.

29. It is significant in this regard that the critical attacks on Keats were motivated by his connections to radical circles; as Milnes says, 'it was ... at once assumed by the critics that Keats was not only a bad poet, but a bad citizen'. *The Life and Letters of John Keats*, p. 165.

30. Kenneth Robinson discusses the stage version of the novel in *Wilkie Collins: A Biography* (New York, 1952), pp. 286–7.

Further Reading

EDITIONS

The four novels discussed in this volume are available in several reprinted editions. The following have useful introductions and notes:

The Woman in White, ed. and intro., John Sutherland (Oxford: Oxford University Press, 1996). [This is the first edition to make use of Collins's manuscript.]

The Woman in White, ed. and intro., Julian Symons (Harmondsworth: Penguin, 1974).

No Name, ed. and intro., Virginia Blain (Oxford: Oxford University Press, 1986).

No Name, ed. and intro., Mark Ford (Harmondsworth: Penguin, 1994).

Armadale, ed. and intro., Catherine Peters (Oxford: Oxford University Press, 1989).

Armadale, ed. and intro., John Sutherland (Harmondsworth: Penguin, 1995).

The Moonstone, ed. and intro., Anthea Trodd (Oxford: Oxford University Press, 1992).

The Moonstone, ed. and intro., J. I. M. Stewart (Harmondsworth: Penguin, 1966).

BIBLIOGRAPHIES

There is no definitive bibliography of Collins's work, but the following are very useful:

Robert P. Ashley, 'Wilkie Collins', in *Victorian Fiction: A Second Guide to Research*, ed. Lionel Stevenson (New York: MLA, 1978).

Kirk H. Beetz, *Wilkie Collins: An Annotated Bibliography, 1889–1976* (Metuchen, NJ: Scarecrow Press, 1976).

Kirk H. Beetz, 'Wilkie Collins Studies, 1972–83', *Dickens Studies Annual*, 13 (1983), 333–5.

Robert Lee Wolff, *Nineteenth-Century Fiction: A Bibliographical Catalogue*, Vol. I [A–D] (New York: Garland, 1981).

BIOGRAPHICAL STUDIES

There are several twentieth-century biographies. The two most recent are fuller and more accurate than their predecessors. Clarke focuses mainly on the complex details of Collins's private life, Peters looks at Collins the man of letters.

William M. Clarke, *The Secret Life of Wilkie Collins* (London: Allison & Busby, 1988).
Catherine Peters, *The King of Inventors: A Life of Wilkie Collins* (London: Secker & Warburg, 1991).

OTHER COLLECTIONS OF ESSAYS

Two recent volumes contain a range of essays on Collins, many of which had their origin as papers at the Wilkie Collins Centennial Conference at the University of British Columbia.

Dickens Studies Annual, 20 (1991).
Nelson Smith and R. C. Terry (eds), *Wilkie Collins to the Forefront* (New York: AMS Press, 1995).

RECENT BOOKS

Tamar Heller, *Dead Secrets: Wilkie Collins and the Female Gothic* (New Haven, CT: Yale University Press, 1992).
Sue Lonoff, *Wilkie Collins and his Victorian Readers: A Study in the Rhetoric of Authorship* (New York: AMS Press, 1982).
William H. Marshall, *Wilkie Collins* (New York: Twayne, 1970).
Lilian Nayder, *Wilkie Collins Revisited* (New York: Twayne, 1997).
Philip O'Neill, *Wilkie Collins: Women, Property, Propriety* (London: Macmillan, 1988).
Jenny Taylor, *In the Secret Theatre of Home: Wilkie Collins, Sensation Narrative and Nineteenth-Century Psychology* (London: Routledge, 1988).
Peter Thoms, *The Windings of the Labyrinth: Quest and Structure in the Major Novels of Wilkie Collins* (Ohio: Ohio University Press, 1992).

RECENT ESSAYS AND ARTICLES

The Woman in White

Diane Elam, 'White Narratology: Gender and Reference in *The Woman in White*', in Lloyd Davis (ed.), *Virginal Sexuality and Textuality in Victorian Literature* (Albany, NY: State University of New York Press, 1993), pp. 49–63.
Barbara Fass, 'Wilkie Collins' Cinderella: The History of Psychology and *The Woman in White*', *Dickens Studies Annual*, 10 (1982), 91–141.
Laurie Langbauer, 'Women in White, Men in Feminism', *The Yale Journal of Criticism*, 2 (1989), 219–43.
Pamela Perkins and Mary Donaghy, 'A Man's Resolution: Narrative Strategies in Wilkie Collins' *The Woman in White*', *Studies in the Novel*, 22 (1990), 392–402.

No Name

Lewis Horne, 'Magdalen's Peril', *Dickens Studies Annual*, 20 (1991), 259–80.

G. Robert Stange, 'Wilkie Collins's *No Name*', *Nineteenth-Century Fiction*, 34 (1979), 96–100.

Armadale

David Blair, 'Wilkie Collins and the Crisis of Suspense', in *Reading the Victorian Novel: Detail into Form*, ed. Ian Gregor (London: Vision Press, 1980), pp. 32–50.

Philip O'Neill, 'Illusion and Reality in Wilkie Collins's *Armadale*,' *Essays in Poetics*, 7 (1982), 42–61.

The Moonstone

Patricia Frick, 'Wilkie Collins's "Little Jewel": The Meaning of *The Moonstone*', *Philological Quarterly*, 63 (1984), 313–21.

Ross C. Murfin, 'The Art of Representation: Collins's The Moonstone and Dickens's example', *ELH: A Journal of English Literary History*, 49 (1982), 653–72.

Ira Bruce Nadel, 'Science and *The Moonstone*', *Dickens Studies Annual*, 11 (1983), 239–59.

John R. Reed, 'English Imperialism and the Unacknowledged Crime of *The Moonstone*', *Clio*, 2 (1973), 281–90.

John R. Reed, 'The Stories of *The Moonstone*', in Nelson Smith and R.C. Terry (eds), *Wilkie Collins to the Forefront* (New York: AMS Press, 1995), pp. 91–100.

Collins's representation of women

Patricia Frick, 'The Fallen Angels of Wilkie Collins', *International Journal of Women's Studies*, 7 (1984), 342–51.

Kathleen O'Fallon, 'Breaking the Laws About Ladies: Wilkie Collins's Questioning of Gender Roles', in Nelson Smith and R. C. Terry (eds), *Wilkie Collins to the Forefront* (New York: AMS Press, 1995), pp. 227–39.

Keith Reierstad, 'Innocent Indecency: The Questionable Heroines of Wilkie Collins's Sensation Novels', *Victorians Institute Journal*, 9 (1980), 57–69.

OTHER USEFUL MATERIAL ON COLLINS AND HIS LITERARY HISTORICAL CONTEXTS

Richard Barickman, Susan MacDonald, and Myra Stark, *Corrupt Relations: Dickens, Thackeray, Trollope, Collins and the Victorian Sexual System* (New York: Columbia University Press, 1982).

Winifred Hughes, *The Maniac in the Cellar: Sensation Novels of the 1860s* (Princeton, NJ: Princeton University Press, 1980).

Ann Cvetkovich, *Mixed Feelings: Feminism, Mass Culture and Victorian Sensationalism* (New Brunswick, NJ: Rutgers University Press, 1992).

John Kucich, *The Power of Lies: Transgression in Victorian Fiction* (Ithaca, NY: Cornell University Press, 1994).

D. A. Miller, *The Novel and the Police* (Berkeley, CA: University of California Press, 1988).

Lyn Pykett, *The Sensation Novel: From 'The Woman in White' to 'The Moonstone'* (Plymouth: Northcote House, 1994).

Nicholas Rance, *Wilkie Collins and Other Sensation Novelists* (London: Macmillan, 1991).

Anthea Trodd, *Domestic Crime and the Victorian Novel* (London: Macmillan, 1989).

Notes on Contributors

Patrick Brantlinger is Professor of English and Cultural Studies at Indiana University. He is the author of *Bread and Circuses: Theories of Mass Culture as Social Decay* (Cornell University Press, 1983), *Rule of Darkness: British Literature and Imperialism, 1830–1914* (Cornell University Press, 1988), and *Fictions of State: Culture and Credit in Britain, 1694–1994* (Cornell University Press, 1996).

Ann Cvetkovich is Associate Professor of English at the University of Texas at Austin. She is the author of *Mixed Feelings: Feminism, Mass Culture, and Victorian Sensationalism* (Rutgers University Press, 1992).

Deirdre David is Professor of English at Temple University. Her most recent book *Rule Britannia: Women, Empire, and Victorian Writing* (Cornell University Press, 1995) reveals how Victorian women, as writers and symbols of colonisation, served as critics of empire. She is also the author of *Fictions of Resolution in Three Victorian Novels* (1981), and *Intellectual Women and Victorian Patriarchy* (1987). She is currently working on a study of the construction of America in Victorian culture.

Elisabeth Gruner is assistant professor of English at the University of Richmond, where she also coordinates the Women's Studies Programme. She received her PhD from UCLA in 1992. In addition to her work on Wilkie Collins, she has published on Fanny Burney and is currently working on a project about the sibling relationship in Victorian novels, especially novels by women.

Tamar Heller received her PhD from Yale University in 1988 and currently teaches at the University of Louisville. The author of *Dead Secrets: Wilkie Collins and the Female Gothic* (Yale University Press, 1992), she has also published essays on Charlotte Brontë, Sheridan Le Fanu, and Margaret Oliphant, and is co-editing a collection of essays with Patricia Moran entitled *Scenes of the Apple: Food and the Female Body in Nineteenth- and Twentieth-Century Women's Writing.*

Mark M. Hennelly, Jr, teaches at California State University, Sacramento. He is the author of numerous articles on nineteenth-century fiction.

A. D. Hutter is Associate Professor of English and Comparative Literature at UCLA. He is also a board-certified psychoanalyst with a part-time practice, specialising in work with writers and other creative artists. He has published work on Dickens, Collins, Shakespeare, critical theory and the novel, in addition to short fiction and a novel of his own, and is currently working on a book entitled *The Frozen Sea: The Myths of Writer's Block*. His second novel, *The Other Side of Silence*, is due to be published next year.

Walter Kendrick, Professor of English at Fordham University, New York City, is the author of *The Novel-Machine: The Theory and Fiction of Anthony Trollope* (Johns Hopkins University Press, 1980), *The Secret Museum: Pornography in Modern Culture* (Viking, 1987; Penguin, 1988), and *The Thrill of Fear: 250 Years of Scary Entertainment* (Grove Weidenfeld, 1991; shortly to be reissued by the University of California Press). He is also co-editor, with Perry Meisel, of *Bloomsbury/Freud: The Letters of James and Alix Strachey, 1924–1925* (Basic Books, 1985; Chatto & Windus, 1986, and Norton paperback, 1990).

U. C. Knoepflmacher is Paton Foundation Professor of Ancient and Modern Literature at Princeton University. He has published four books and numerous essays on Victorian Literature, and has co-edited three collections of essays. His latest book, *Ventures into Childland: Victorians, Fairy Tales, and Femininity*, will appear in 1997.

D. A. Miller teaches at Columbia University. His books include *Narrative and its Discontents: Problems of Closure in the Traditional Novel* (Princeton University Press, 1981), and *The Novel and the Police* (University of California Press, 1988).

Jenny Bourne Taylor, Senior Lecturer in English at the University of Sussex, is the author of *In the Secret Theatre of Home: Wilkie Collins, Sensation Narrative and Nineteenth-Century Psychology* (Routledge, 1988), and editor of *Wilkie Collins, The Law and the Lady* (Oxford: The World's Classics, 1992). Other recent publications include *Embodied Selves: An Anthology of Psychological Texts, 1830–1890*, ed. with Sally Shuttleworth (Oxford University Press, 1997), and 'Obscure Recesses: Locating the Unconscious in Victorian Culture', in *Writing and Victorianism*, ed. J. B. Bullen (Longmans, 1997). She is currently completing *Illegitimate Fictions: Narratives of Bastardy in English Culture, 1750–1900* for Cambridge University Press.

Index